MW01628196

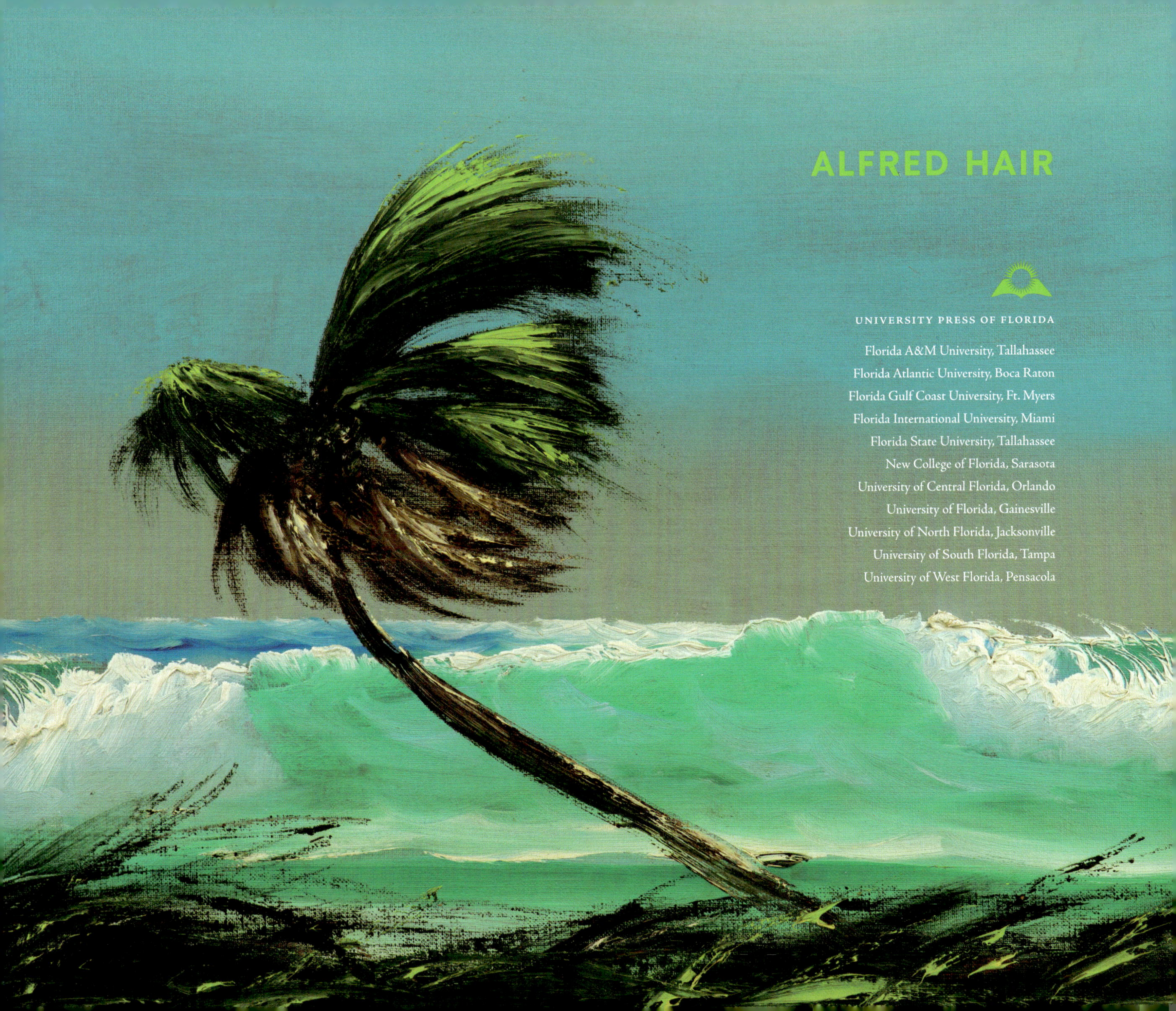

ALFRED HAIR

UNIVERSITY PRESS OF FLORIDA

Florida A&M University, Tallahassee
Florida Atlantic University, Boca Raton
Florida Gulf Coast University, Ft. Myers
Florida International University, Miami
Florida State University, Tallahassee
New College of Florida, Sarasota
University of Central Florida, Orlando
University of Florida, Gainesville
University of North Florida, Jacksonville
University of South Florida, Tampa
University of West Florida, Pensacola

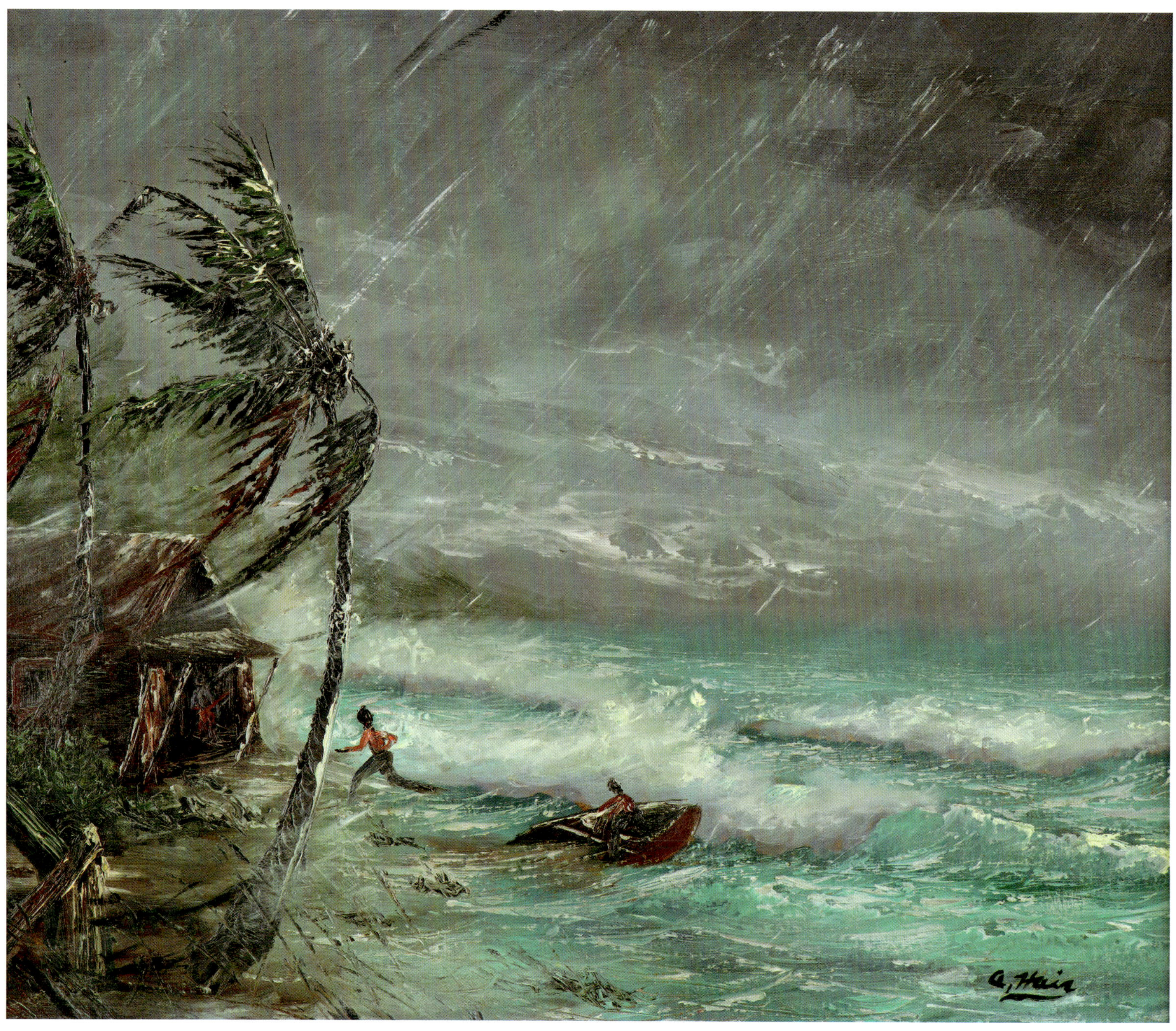
A. Hair

ALFRED HAIR

Heart of the Highwaymen

GARY MONROE

University Press of Florida

Gainesville · Tallahassee · Tampa · Boca Raton

Pensacola · Orlando · Miami · Jacksonville · Ft. Myers · Sarasota

Published in the United States of America. Printed in Canada on acid-free paper.

25 24 23 22 21 20 6 5 4 3 2 1

ISBN 978-0-8130-6670-7
Library of Congress Control Number: 2020938186

The University Press of Florida is the scholarly publishing agency for the State University System of Florida, comprising Florida A&M University, Florida Atlantic University, Florida Gulf Coast University, Florida International University, Florida State University, New College of Florida, University of Central Florida, University of Florida, University of North Florida, University of South Florida, and University of West Florida.

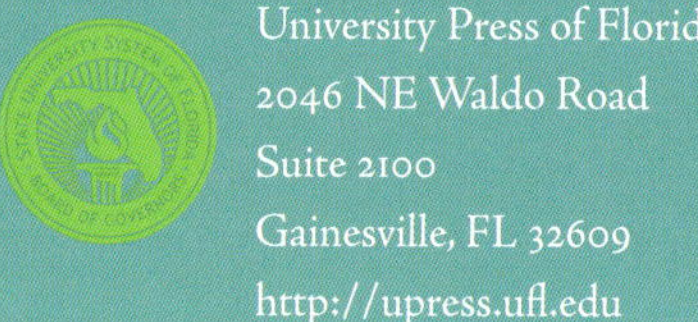

University Press of Florida
2046 NE Waldo Road
Suite 2100
Gainesville, FL 32609
http://upress.ufl.edu

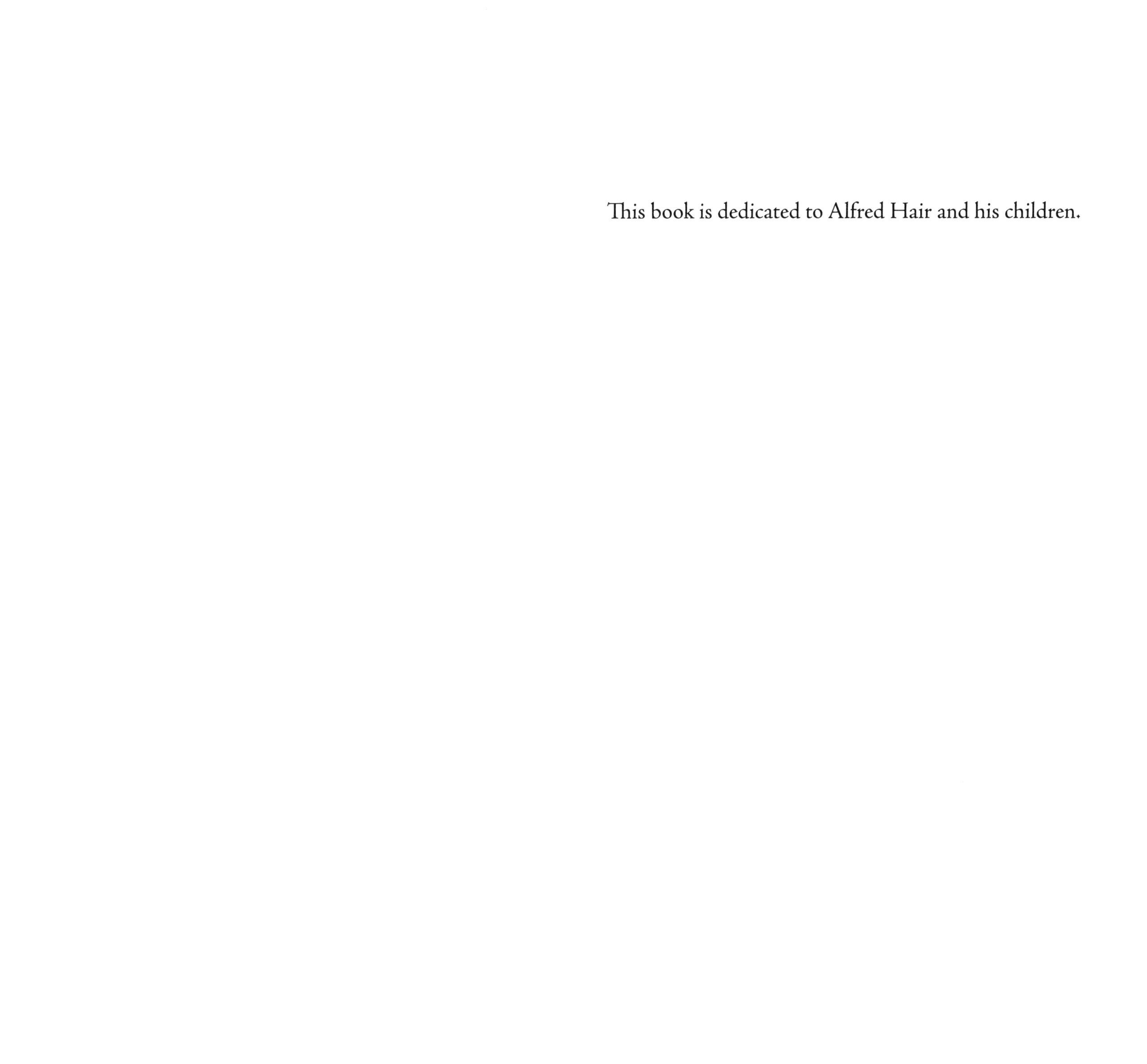

This book is dedicated to Alfred Hair and his children.

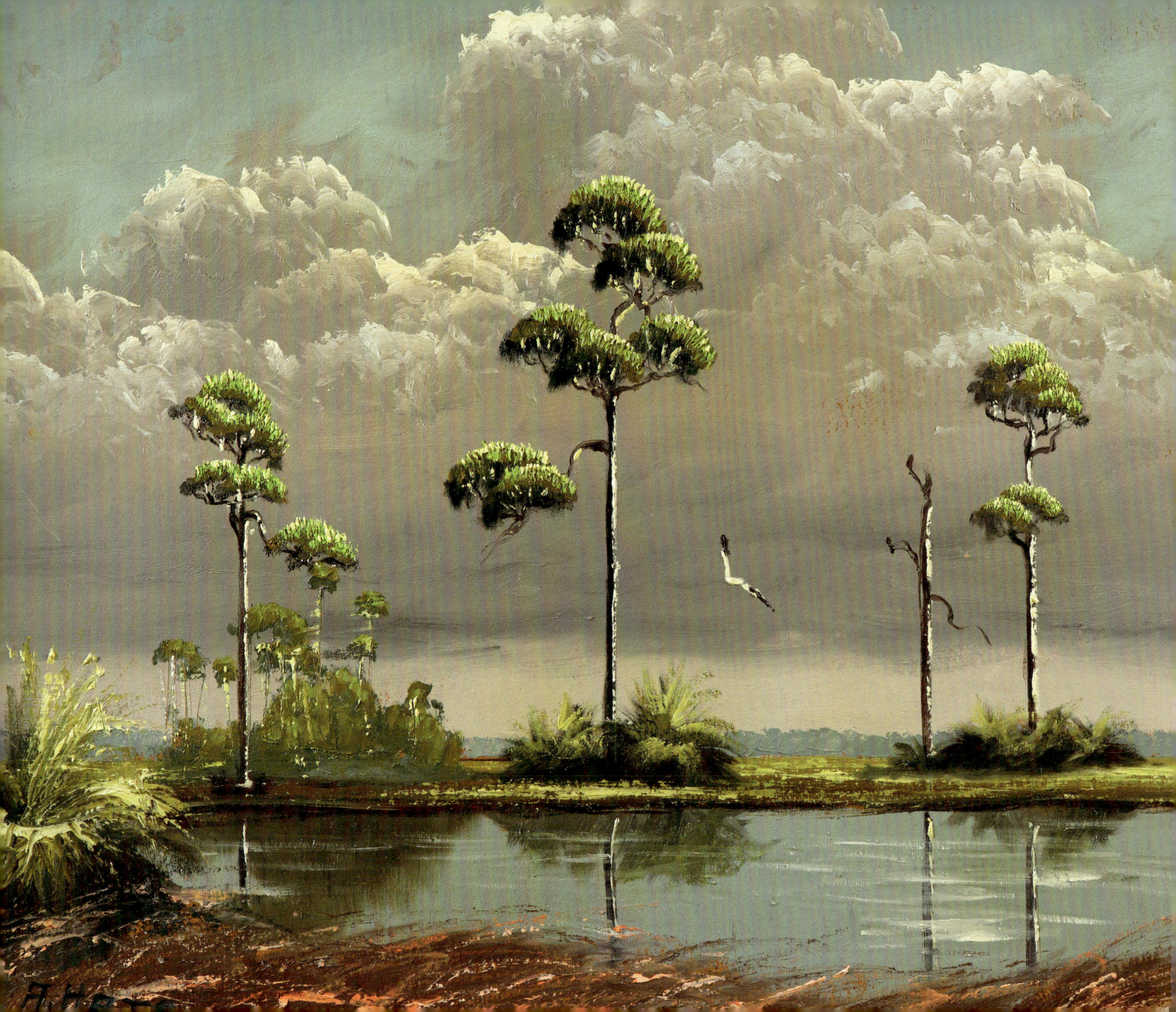

ACKNOWLEDGMENTS

I am indebted to Lisa Stone, of Lisa Stone Arts, who accompanied me on all of the meetings I had with the many people whose ideas and recollections formed the book's essay. Lisa's clarity of thought and insights into human nature informed my understandings and brought depth to my thinking and writing.

Jean Ellen Wilson, folk historian and fine writer, is the unsung hero whose knowledge about Fort Pierce was indispensable. A folk historian is someone who, besides possessing academic skill, loves her subject and can decipher its history with deep empathy and an insider's understandings, generally without remuneration. Jean Ellen is also a superb editor who humbled me with her every read at the varying stages of this essay's development. She shared her research with me unconditionally to better my writing. She is a treasure to her city and our state.

Of course I am grateful to all the people with whom I spoke during the three years of research and writing. Samuel Gaines and Don Brown were especially forthcoming and knowledgeable and a pleasure to spend time with. Because I investigate areas in which there is negligible source material, these people are primary. Jean Ellen Wilson deserves special recognition for her original research about Estes Wright.

I am especially grateful to Doretha Hair Truesdell for sharing with me unconditionally and trusting me to tell this story as many voices informed it.

Always, I thank my longtime editor, friend, and conscience Margie Miller. Margie keeps me on my toes and keeps me going. I might throw in the towel if ever she's not in my corner.

The University Press of Florida has for two decades published my books. The people there have always done well by my books and me, giving good advice and being supportive; this is especially true of Meredith Babb. Meredith refined the essay well beyond my own abilities. The press has also been good for those who have an interest in Florida by publishing a spectrum of books about our wild, crazy, and fascinating state.

Teresa Gurucharri and our children, Mathew and Jessica, now adults with engaging lives and families of their own, have watched and supported me during the long periods of tedium and loneliness that come with photographing endlessly and writing books. They are my muses, and I am forever grateful.

Soon after beginning the research for the first Highwaymen book, I quickly realized that what happened in the early 1960s in Fort Pierce revolved around a young, handsome, and gracious man, Alfred Hair. This is his story and my tribute. He seeded the tens of thousands of paintings that the group of painters made and sold. The Highwaymen's artwork spread across the state, contributing to a shared consciousness about what Florida means and to a collective unconscious about how we dream about the essence of Florida.

This is not a book solely about art. It is not a book about a black man's life in Florida in the 1960s, when Jim Crow was the law of the land. It is a book about somebody who managed to achieve the unimaginable during times that were not conducive to creative thinking, much less creative living. It is a book about how one person, in twenty-nine short years, managed to encourage at least two dozen other people to live better lives. This is a book about a legend who has influenced even the generations that have followed his.

This is a book about a man who gained recognition through art but whose life story defies ramifications and restrictions. It is a book about a man who lived during some very defining, explosive years in the United States of America. It is really a history book, one filled with lessons to be learned and social implications to be heeded. It is a book about Alfred Hair, who truly was the heart of the Highwaymen, the cohort of black landscape painters. It is a sociological study of a distant time. It is a book that reflects upon the triumph of the human spirit.

* * *

The following people lent their paintings for reproduction in this book, which Tariq Gibran expertly photographed:

Lance and Patricia Walker
Tim and Eileen Jacobs
The Doretha Hair Collection, Widow of Alfred Hair
The Collection of Scott Schlesinger
The Monroe Family Collection
The Asselstine Collection
The Lightle Collection

A MALLEABLE LAND

Alfred was easy to love!

DORETHA HAIR TRUESDELL

THE ARTWORK OF ALFRED HAIR and those he inspired who eventually became known as the Highwaymen marked the end of one kind of image codification associated with new frontiers and the beginning of another kind of imagery. The glorification of nature was part and parcel of the Hudson River School of art in the mid-nineteenth century, and the idea accompanied that of Manifest Destiny. Some artists who were influenced by the Hudson River School came to Florida when Henry Flagler's railroad made the peninsula accessible in the early twentieth century. Artists' studios in Flagler's grand Ponce de Leon Hotel in St. Augustine made for pleasant monthly exhibits where the well-heeled could acquire Florida art. The paintings maintained Hudson River School artistic norms as artists experienced this new land, a largely inhospitable subtropical tangle. The school's painterly conventions would reign through the art of A. E. "Bean" Backus of Fort Pierce, Florida's premier regionalist in the mid-twentieth century.

In the early 1950s Harold Newton came to Backus for advice about his own painting. Alfred Hair, while a high school student, took painting lessons from Backus in the late 1950s. Both Newton and Hair found inspiration and subject matter from Backus, but each man would follow his own course and develop his own painterly approach, which became the parameters of the Highwaymen aesthetic.

Alfred Hair's multiple life trajectories outdo one another, but in the end, beyond life's foibles, is an accomplishment that is still garnering thought and attention, as his paintings are finding their place in the realm of contemporary aesthetics. As the 1960s dawned, Hair and Newton, the bookends of the Highwaymen story, enhanced the idea of Florida through their art. Unknowingly, they established a legacy, the art of the Highwaymen. Newton has long been seen as the champion among the Highwaymen; his art addresses time and place most elegantly. Newton's lovely paintings exist in another realm from Hair's extemporaneous paintings. Perhaps Newton's paintings are timeless while Hair's are temporal. Alfred Hair's paintings offer a fresh way to think about landscape painting, one that would place the viewer in the land remembered.

The romantic notion of finding God in the wilds and oneself in the process harkens back to the origins of the sublime in landscape painting. At the very least, people often long to connect to the essential self in an otherwise chaotic world, to find communion with the divine in nature. It seems apparent that Alfred Hair shared these ambitions as he expressed himself, however unconsciously, through painting. Al Black, a friend and fellow painter, has commented, "Alfred could paint as fast as he wanted and as good as he wanted," but he wanted to paint fast because that enabled him to make more money. For Alfred, accumulating wealth was as much sport as it was business. Fast painting also liberated any inhibitions that staunched the free flow of intuition and paint, and the resulting freshly informed images beckoned viewers to become patrons or at least consumers as they took stock of what they saw.

Alfred Hair made countless Florida landscape paintings, as did the other artists who took their cues from him. Harold Newton's paintings, in a class of their own, belonged more to the tradition of American landscapists than to the aesthetic emerging from Hair's informal atelier. Newton's aesthetic was akin to that of A. E. Backus, to whom the fledgling artists looked for inspiration, and that of the legion of professionally trained painters, all of whom carried on the conventions to preserve the charm of place through pictorial representation. While Hair and most of the other Highwaymen worked away during those fevered halcyon days of the 1960s and 1970s, sacrificing trained technique to trademark rapidity, their paintings did not cause the awe of recognition of the divine. Theirs were snapshots of sorts, not knee-weakening compositions, in comparison. However, there is something to be said for the spontaneity and unpretentiousness of snapshots.

Alfred Hair's paintings are easily distinguishable from other Highwaymen paintings. Of course, each artist had a style, but Hair's style set him apart. His work was especially loose and gestural with a noticeably carefree flair that guided him across the boards' surfaces as he painted. Samuel Gaines, the owner of the Stone Brothers Funeral Home in Fort Pierce, and his family are entrenched in that city's African American neighborhood Lincoln Park and the lives of its residents, including Alfred Hair and his family. Gaines said of Hair, "It was something to see him when he was painting. He strapped boards to the wall and go down one to the next. It was the speed in which he would do it." Gaines pointed out that people came to the family house on Dundas Court where Hair painted to watch, mesmerized, as he brought life to his images. Few, at that time, appreciated what he was doing artistically.

When Al Black commented about Alfred's ability to paint "as fast as he wanted," he was referring to those boards he knocked out without a care in the world, paintings he produced for the next morning's run up and down the seaboard. Hair also created works "as good as he wanted," in Black's observation, with an ineffable oneness with the world. These paintings seem, to this biased viewer, to have been realized with introspection. Hair's high school art teacher, Zanobia Jefferson, summed up the transcendent nature of Alfred's best paintings: "You become part of the paintings."

Hair's images are infused with the same abandon with which he painted. His own sense of liberation while engaged in wielding his palette knife not only comes through on the surfaces of his boards but becomes the substance of his paintings. This ineffable quality distinguishes him and his art; it sets his creations apart from others' of the group and in the broader art world. And this quality comes not out of being part of academic art making or traditional thinking about art. It was rather ambition, zest, and identity that set him on an original course that would redefine what a landscape painting can be and more tangibly lead to the creation of the visual legacy of modern Florida, and this by what might at first blush seem to be the unlikeliest of artists. But on further consideration, the painters who decades later would be so recognized were nearly anointed to be these artists. The stars aligned, and it couldn't be any others.

Alfred Hair was a young African American artist who wanted to be wealthy at a time when black people had little opportunity to rise above the economic and social limitations of the times. His is a unique story in which art and commerce were complementary, even synergistic. He did not need a moral compass; morality came naturally to him, and during his short life his conscience guided some and affected many, most of whom were unconscious of his influence. As soon as Hair graduated from Lincoln Park Academy high school in 1961, he began painting luminous South Florida landscapes and selling the paintings door to door. Though racial tensions were rising all around him, he focused on his goal. In the aftermath of the Civil Rights Act of 1964, the pushback against integration by southerners, and the resulting outbreaks of regional strife, Hair, in a peaceful zone of concentrated effort, painted and sold landscapes to consumers of all degrees of racial prejudice.

He empowered others to explore their own potential, and he never allowed himself to be bound by Jim Crow shackles; he did not buy into the prejudices of others but rather simply and naturally rose above such matters. He was driven to succeed, and the fellow strivers who came together around him were to realize more than they dared to dream. Within two decades the painters created a trove of artwork that would reside in modest living rooms or fall from favor and be discarded, only to be rediscovered. Their revival even surprised the aging artists who had dismissed those early fecund years as youthful escapade. Their talent buried in local familiarity, the cohort went nameless and forgotten in the 1960s and 1970s. Only in retrospect, when dormant appreciation of the group's works was awakened decades later, would they be dubbed the Highwaymen.

When the Highwaymen began painting their loose-knit association and improvisational style substituted for product design and marketing strategy. Their accidental scheme worked wondrously. These young, eager, naive artists had somehow retained a postwar optimism in an otherwise cynical and difficult era.

During World War II an estimated two million recruits trained at military camps in the state, and many of them returned to Florida after the war to raise their families where summer reigned over winter. Those who flocked to Florida after the war, veterans and others during the boom time, were prime customers, as were established residents. The artists' timing was excellent. They produced an estimated 200,000 paintings. Their artwork seemed to be everywhere, yet the unsung individual painters were seemingly inconsequential. The creations were so ever-present that they became part of the collective imagination of the state's residents and visitors, and like the makers of the gladiola vase in the picture window and the plastic flamingo in the yard, the artist was anonymous. The art works became emblems of Florida. The landscape paintings by these uninhibited artists represented the values of a place that the citizens held dear in their unique state; owning one was a testimony of their affection for their surroundings.

ABOUT HAIR AND BACKUS

Don Brown, manager of the Fort Pierce art studio of A. E. Backus, would tell you that Alfred Hair, whom he got to know at the studio, was friendly and funny, always building himself up in an endearing way. For instance, Alfred Hair would say, "I'm going to be a millionaire," about which Brown observed, "He had the skill. He probably would have." As Brown pondered that prospect, though, he doubted Alfred would have actually become wealthy.

This judgment has nothing to do with Alfred's personality or character but rather with his ambition and ultimately his art. Although one might assume that ambition would be a prerequisite for success, in Alfred's case Brown thought otherwise: "He was too ambitious to make money. You got to mold yourself into what you do to make it marketable. Alfred was not developing a marketable style because he painted too fast." Backus, who was affectionately called "Bean" or "Beanie," and others, felt Alfred should slow down. But that wasn't going to happen; Alfred was just too driven. He could not paint with restraint. In fact, sitting idle wasn't an option. A lust for life fueled his energy and informed his art.

Brown's observation sprang from a reaction to an unconventional approach that was something fresh and outside his own experience as a fellow landscape painter. Fast painting would yield Alfred's style, albeit one that might be referred to as styleless, as in an artless art that he was unconsciously developing. Lost to a process boosted by rapidity, the art and artist seem to dissolve into one and the same. Because making money was more important to him than making art, Alfred was further freed from creative pressures. His was a fine environment to paint unselfconsciously, in an immediate and unmediated way, and perhaps in tune with the world.

Humanity was the central lesson in Backus's studio where Don Brown was a student from 1960 to 1969, during which time he became studio manager. He spent "three months shy of thirty years" with the revered artist. When Don arrived, Alfred had already been part of the studio's life. Being human was at least as important as the painting lessons there. Backus was a bohemian in a conservative town.

Zanobia Jefferson took a high school group including Hair to see Backus on a field trip to his studio, and she later escorted him there alone too. Anne Wilder, then bureau chief for the *Miami Herald* in St. Lucie County, reported in a December 1962 article that Backus's framer Willie Pelt encouraged Alfred to show Backus one of his paintings, which led to learning art techniques there; he needed guidance in mixing oils.

Sol Knighton, Alfred's high school chum, said it was in about 1960 that Alfred came to the studio through Pelt. Through the vocational education program that Ms. Jefferson would have facilitated, Alfred was able to receive school credit for working and studying at Backus's studio. He began by making frames for Backus's canvases. Alfred would soon be the artist's special protégé, twice accompanying his mentor to his studio in Jamaica. He would soon paint Jamaican scenes, as had Backus; others in Hair's circle would also try their hands at this. To be sure, it was an anomaly. Another blip was that Alfred signed some of the paintings as "Freddy." It is believed they are a result of his having been contracted by a South Florida businessman to create a hundred paintings. Hair's colleague James Gibson said the businessman gave Alfred and him one hundred canvases each. Since Alfred painted more quickly, he gave Alfred twenty more canvases to paint, half the amount Gibson had left when Alfred completed his hundred. So perhaps there are a hundred and twenty paintings signed "Freddy." Alfred Hair's widow, Doretha Hair Truesdell, offered that Alfred signed "Freddy" to paintings because he had been flooding the market with those signed "A. Hair."

Legions of young people who came to be affectionately known as "Backus Brats" learned to paint effectively with Backus's instruction, and some became professional artists. "Everyone paints similar to him," Brown asserted about those who learned at the studio and others who aspired to paint Florida intimately. But no one of the era matched the sublime imagery that flowed from Backus's hand.

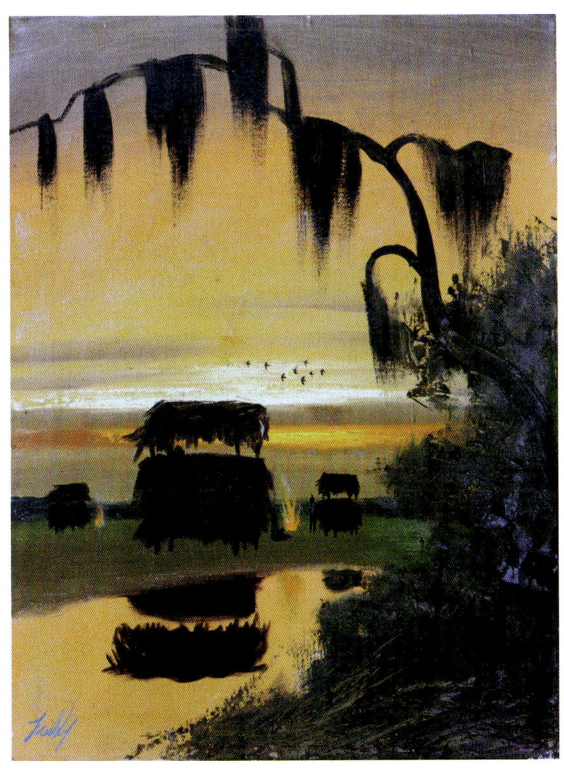

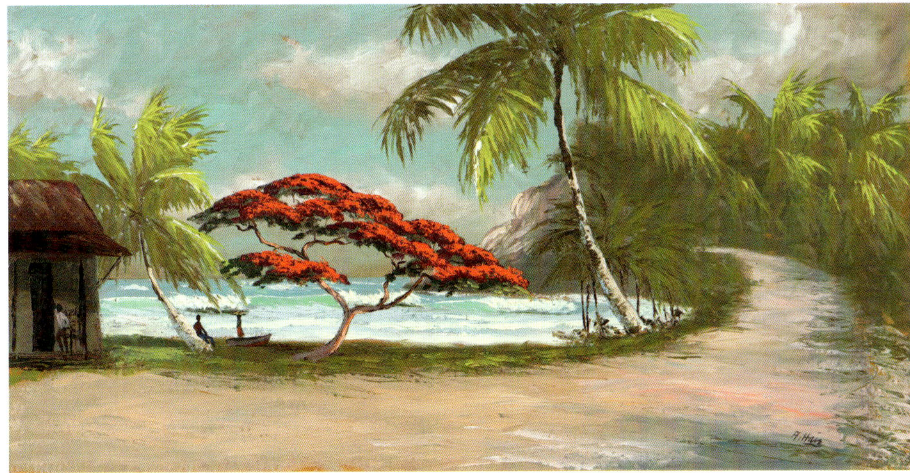

Alfred Hair also had the benefit of nurturing community. And away from home, he had Backus, an affable and progressive man whose moral social character outpaced the times. His studio was a refuge. Don Brown put it this way: "At the studio the world stood still. You didn't worry about outside things. The atmosphere, the jazz, people coming and going. It was a safe haven, a place to become your own person." Everyone was visible and mattered at the Backus home studio. Along with jazz music, rum was ever present and freely flowing. Backus was a bohemian in a town as unlikely as any to welcome such a person and his requisite lifestyle, yet the native son of Fort Pierce was a cherished presence and driving force.

BEING IN THE SHADOWS

African Americans had been living a bad dream for a long time, but the US Supreme Court's *Brown v. Board of Education of Topeka* decision of 1954 trumpeted change. The ruling gave rise to the civil rights movement and would eventually end Jim Crow segregation. Although southern black youths grew up in a climate of hostility and alienation, the community in which Alfred Hair was reared was a nurturing enclave surrounded by uncertainty. Lincoln Park, as his Fort Pierce black neighborhood was named, encouraged good education, family values, and faith in God, all of which added to Alfred Hair's odds of success. Beyond that village that looked after its children, Alfred's generation walked a color line. They could not eat with white people, drink from whites' water fountains, ride in buses beside whites, or sit alongside them in movie theaters. African Americans tried to be as invisible as possible in the presence of white folk, even averting eye contact and crossing the street so not to cross their paths.

The Civil Rights Act of 1964 prohibited segregation on the basis of race, sex, age, national origin, or religion; it was timed to take maximum advantage of the 1960s era of unprecedented social progress and resulted in a rising consciousness of opportunity. President Lyndon Johnson was elected to his own term of office promoting a Great Society that "demands an end to poverty and racial injustice, to which we are totally committed in our time."

Florida played a role in the rise of the civil rights movement. Amazingly, though hostile reaction to the push for equality in the Sunshine State was widespread and harassment of people of color increased amid the unrest, a self-assured Alfred Hair and the other artists sold their paintings unmolested, with poise and purpose.

Incendiary incidents continued to cause new crises. During the banner year of 1964, Jimmy Brock got caught up in the racial maelstrom. Nervous about his fledgling motel in St. Augustine, he played right into the hands of civil rights organizers. On June 18, he poured muriatic acid into the swimming pool of his Monson Motor Lodge to ward off a group of protesters, black and white, who had jumped into its whites-only pool. A photographer's pictures of his pouring the gallon bottle's contents into the pool as frightened swimmers huddled hit the wire services and became headline news. People heard "acid," not "muriatic acid," a pool masonry cleaner that is caustic but not life-threatening, which certainly did not matter as one looked at the still images. The protest was staged in retaliation for refusing service to Martin Luther King Jr. and his guests at the motel restaurant a week prior. The embarrassing pictures became instrumental in focusing the movement by removing any doubt as to the need to pass the Civil Rights Act.

Before the St. Augustine protests, the first assassination of a black civil rights leader occurred in Florida with the murders of Harry and Harriet Moore. The Moores lived in Mims, a citrus-growing community north of Cape Canaveral. In 1934 Harry Moore started the Brevard County NAACP, and a few years later, with the backing of Thurgood Marshall, he filed the first lawsuit in the Deep South seeking to equalize black and white teachers' salaries. Although the case was unsuccessful, it spawned a dozen other federal lawsuits in the state that eventually led to equal pay. Moore's political activism led him to register black voters en masse through the Florida Voters' League, which he founded. As a full-time organizer Moore was increasingly vocal, ignoring the prevailing go-along-to-get-along Jim Crow attitude.

On July 16, 1949, African Americans Ernest Thomas, Charles Greenlee, Samuel Shepard, and Walter Irvin from Groveland, near Orlando, were falsely accused of raping a seventeen-year-old white woman and assaulting her husband in Lake County. The allegations were sufficient cause for a sheriff's posse to put at least one hundred bullets into Thomas. Confessions were beaten out of Greenlee and Shepard but not Irvin. An all-white jury convicted them. Greenlee was sentenced to life in prison because he was a minor. Shepard and Irvin were sentenced to death.

Harry Moore, then executive director of the Florida NAACP, campaigned against the convictions. Greenlee did not appeal, but two years later the court overturned the convictions of Shepard and Irvin. In November 1951, notorious segregationist Sheriff Willis McCall shot both men while transporting them from Raiford State Prison back to the county seat of Tavares for retrial, claiming they tried to escape. Shepard died, but Irvin feigned being dead. After surviving gunshots from the sheriff and his deputy, Irvin told the FBI that the shooting was cold-blooded.

Moore called for the suspension of Sheriff McCall. On Christmas night 1951, a bomb placed beneath the floorboards of the Moore's bedroom exploded, killing the sleeping couple. Their murders were never solved, but their deaths were not at all in vain. *Ebony* magazine in April 1952 titled a short article "The Bomb Heard around the World."

Through Harry Moore's efforts, Thurgood Marshall, who in 1967 became the first African American justice to serve on the US Supreme Court, reopened the case of the men who came to be known as the Groveland Four. Although the four accused men received the brunt of racially motivated brutality and injustice, Irvin, standing alone, was again found guilty by an all-white jury and again sentenced to death. But with the FBI discovery of suppressed evidence, Florida Governor LeRoy Collins commuted Irvin's death sentence in 1955 to life in prison; he was paroled in 1968 but died the next year. It took seventy years until on January 11, 2019, under the direction of newly inaugurated Governor Ron DeSantis, full pardons were issued posthumously for the Groveland Four.

Florida was the scene of other acts of defiance and determination that factored into the rising consciousness of social inequality. Just a year after Rosa Parks famously refused to give up her seat to a white woman on a Montgomery bus as the law required, a relatively unheralded action gave rise to the Tallahassee Bus Boycott. In 1956, two Florida Agricultural and Mechanical University students sat in a whites-only section of a city bus instead of in the back-of-the-bus "colored" section. They were arrested for "placing themselves in a position to incite a riot." Although the charges were dropped, FAMU students mounted a bus boycott after a cross was burned in front of the two women students' apartment building. Soon people throughout the city joined the boycott, causing a loss in the bus company's revenue that forced the city to rescind the segregation mandate and thereby integrate seating on the buses.

Then in 1960 Jacksonville students staged sit-ins at various downtown department stores, starting with a centrally located, well-established Woolworth's, in opposition to lunch-counter segregation. After purchasing items throughout the store, the student protesters assembled and filled the stools, where they were denied counter service because the seats were reserved for white patrons only. In other words, they showed the hypocrisy in that they could buy merchandise along with white customers but could not dine alongside them. Counter service was suspended when the protesters refused to leave. Sit-ins continued during the following days throughout downtown Jacksonville. Harassment and insults escalated to white-on-black violence, culminating in "Ax-Handle Saturday," August 27, when club-wielding whites attacked African Americans attempting to order lunch and escalated the melee to the streets. Police and local media turned a blind eye to the day's atrocities. Eventually negotiations resulted in the desegregation of lunch counters and restaurants there and elsewhere.

In the southernmost state, the winds of change against entrenched segregation and prejudice were slow, almost stagnant, and blacks did not receive anything close to immediate acceptance into mainstream society. Florida Governor Claude Kirk, who held office from 1967 to 1971, was an ardent segregationist whose stance hindered the dissolution of Jim Crow policies in the state. A common fear then was that tourism would suffer if hoteliers registered black guests. In Daytona Beach, at the northern end of the Highwaymen's primary sales route, police and white bathers at the World's Most Famous Beach intimidated black citizens to deter them from enjoying the surf. At the end of the Highwaymen's southern route, Miami hoteliers hired recently arrived Cuban refugees, educated professionals who had fled Castro's rule, instead of African Americans who had customarily held these positions. This shift was seen as discrimination against the black service workers and caused further dissatisfaction among those affected.

Amid this widely reported strife, the young black artists traversed the region with little if any opposition. Perhaps their paintings took people's minds off skin color, or perhaps to the legions of northern transplants, racial prejudice was not the driving force that it was to native southerners. After all, by then the wartime boom had brought people to Florida whose attitudes were more liberal. It has long been said that Florida is not part of the South, meaning that its ethos differed from the old plantation mentality. But there is no doubt that pockets of good-old-boy mentality existed in the Sunshine State, as in the Highwaymen's hometown of Fort Pierce, on the Atlantic coast.

ART AND LIFE

From the start Alfred preferred traveling south from his home to take advantage of the wealth that the cities of Palm Beach, Fort Lauderdale, and Miami offered. Traveling north from his home to the laid-back beach towns like Cocoa, Melbourne, and Daytona was less tempting. He followed the money, and he took his paintings to the clientele he targeted, people who were not customarily art buyers. He turned them into connoisseurs of a sort, believers in themselves and in what they saw. Alfred Hair's paintings were not just about the landscape; they were about the viewers' aspirations. Because the images complemented people's sense of self, they sold like hotcakes, and like hotcakes Alfred priced them affordably. He and fellow artists sometimes delivered their paintings to the consumers' doorsteps, even hanging the artwork on a wall for a proud new owner. Since the paintings were typically sold before the oils had time to dry, the images appeared to glow from within. The damp images, more times than not, had the scent of paint still emanating from them. Everything about the paintings implied deliverance.

Alfred Hair was not cut out to practice the European art of easel painting, nor was he a plein air artist painting on location. Rather, he painted landscapes that he knew, images he gleaned from the environment where he grew up and tempered by his own nature. His paintings seemed to be more about experiencing the land than merely recording it. Stripping artifice to its barest by fast painting left archetypal imagery that was visceral in its effect. The paintings might not have been site-specific, but they functioned to well represent the locales to which they alluded. Alfred was meant to be a fine artist, free from extraneous influences and free to express himself. He knew he was not to become a commercial artist. Studying commercial art was not for him. He said, "I don't want to draw straight lines."

Alfred was raised in the church, served as an usher, sang in the choir, and was imbued with the church's moral values. He was an early practitioner of nonviolence. During the rise of the civil rights protests, he would not join when others took to the streets. Alfred was nonviolent by both nature and nurture. Alfred's mom was one of the "church mothers" at the family's Friendship Missionary Baptist Church in Fort Pierce's Lincoln Park. In accord with African American oral tradition, her beliefs and values were passed on to her children. Self-reliance was a primary theme, a lesson her son learned well.

Alfred was talented and driven to excel. He was an excellent football player, a guard and at times a tight end. Lincoln Park Academy's championship Greyhounds won the tri-county playoffs, beating the competition in Stuart, Vero Beach, and Fort Pierce. He was set on his future and turned down a sports scholarship to Bethune-Cookman College, the revered all-black school in Daytona Beach. Perhaps it was to his brother that Alfred first voiced the ambition that would drive him so relentlessly, to become a millionaire while still a young man. Alfred's brother Donald Hair recalled hearing Alfred make that vow. Ambition was supported by persistence. "Anywhere he can lay his paintbrush he would lay his paintbrush," Donald said. "He was ahead of his time."

After graduating from high school, Alfred faced the military option. Many graduates in St. Lucie County, in which Fort Pierce is the county seat, viewed enlistment in the service as the only alternative to manual labor in the fields and groves, but Alfred had another choice—his art. And he led a corps of painters down that track. "People wanted to be like him," Donald said, "to get tips from him." The painters' camaraderie was infectious then. Once a stack of landscapes was produced, the selling phase began. There was little money to be had in their hometown for African Americans, with few expectations beyond labor. As the sun rose, the artists and salesmen would pack their cars with paintings and set out on their day trips up and down the coast as well as inland to the towns around Lake Okeechobee. They would return later in the day with wads of money and sans paintings.

In addition to his high school art classes with Ms. Jefferson, Alfred studied art with Backus and observed Harold Newton's beginnings as a professional artist. He took his cue from both men. Alfred had seen Newton, who was also African American, sell his paintings of Florida's tropical landscape by going on the road, making one-on-one sales. Backus had persuaded Newton to paint marketable images like he was doing. Newton easily made the change from his religious-oriented pictures and quickly found his voice in the landscape genre. Although schooled by Backus to paint the region's picturesque beauty, Alfred's fast-painting process altered the studied images and hence their meanings. His paintings appealed to a different audience than those paintings made by Backus and even by Newton.

Backus and Hair "were very close," Don Brown recalled. After graduating from high school and leaving painting lessons to a new crop of students, Alfred would visit his friend and mentor Backus once or twice weekly. On his own, Alfred attracted aspiring painters, and with the goodwill that he engendered, they too would visit Backus. "His door was always open," Brown said of Backus. Harold Newton came by Backus's studio most often, Brown said, "especially when he ran out of money and needed supplies."

But none of the other young painters who aspired to learn from the master, even if by osmosis, came by the studio on a regular basis. They would "get supplies and a drink." Backus gave both graciously. He also facilitated their painting, Brown said, with "just a critique here and there." He said, "Their paintings were so abstract compared to Beanie's." It did not matter to Backus that the artists didn't fit the prominent aesthetic model that was being practiced at the studio. What did matter to him was righteous living, particularly when it came to race relations. "He had no eye for skin color," Brown said, adding that Backus served as an advisory board member for Fort Pierce's Biracial Council.

Alfred and the others were making a living with their versions of the tropical paradise. Backus was not threatened by the growing legion of African Americans whose success was largely based on his own art. "He never felt they encroached," Brown attested, in opposition to rumors about Backus having his fill of the painters invading his space.

Backus deserves credit for the way Alfred painted. Although Alfred's strategy was a radical departure from conventional representation, Backus had encouraged Alfred to "follow your heritage." By this he meant that his pupil need not subscribe to established modes of representation but rather be free of old-school, European artistic conventions. Alfred and the others did this with free-flowing color palettes. They managed to maintain vivid hues with their quickly applied wet-on-wet oils. They were well aware of the intensity of light and depth of colors of the environment they depicted, but the temper of their paintings differed meaningfully from that of trained artists who seemed, in comparison, to settle the wilds a bit prematurely.

ROOTS AND ROUTES

For a few years after graduating from high school, Alfred enticed friends, acquaintances, and even family members to learn to paint. He invited others who had been painting to join him, too. Harold Newton and Roy McLendon, both older than he, were working artists, but Alfred gave them all greater opportunity and the spur of vigor. Alfred was unknowingly building a cottage industry of sorts in which there were no rules or dues or restraints. Each artist did his or her own thing. They often painted together; it was social for them. They were going out drinking along the way to the jai alai fronton or the dog track as the money came in. Some members of the group slowed down as they began to have families or to accept other employment. Some had full-time jobs and painted in their leisure time. Fewer than half of the twenty-six Highwaymen were devoted to their art practice full time.

Alfred's energy and optimism spurred them on as they traversed South and Central Florida in search of the white clientele who would buy their oil paintings. The tense social times seemed to work in favor of these young entrepreneurs as they drove through the region and the state vending their artwork. The tenor of the era in the United States and abroad was marked by social unrest and political protest, especially over the war in Vietnam. The news was broadcast on national television, and dramatic confrontations and violent demonstrations erupted across the land.

Unlike so many other black people whose lives were kept in check some hundred years after the Emancipation Proclamation, Alfred Hair dreamed big as he entered the adult world that was marked by Jim Crow racism. But racial divisiveness didn't appear to mar his work or life any more than had failure. His American dream seemed to be more than owning a nice home with a well-maintained lawn. "You really had to know Alfred. He was all-inclusive, with everybody, the more the merrier. He was one of a kind," said Doretha Hair Truesdell, Alfred's wife.

Doretha Smith was born on October 15, 1942, in Lynchburg, South Carolina. She was one of twelve children born to Alison and Fannie Smith; three of the siblings died at birth. The family settled in Glen White, West Virginia, where Alison worked in the coal mines. Doretha, in June 1959, graduated from Beckley Springs High School near her hometown. There were no high schools in Glen White, black or white, so all schoolchildren were bused separately, about twelve miles, to Beckley Springs, where they attended segregated high schools.

A few days after Doretha graduated, her father murdered Doretha's mother. In Fort Pierce, Doretha's oldest sister, Christine Reeves, was working at a fish market when she received the tragic news of the death of their thirty-six-year-old mother. Christine hitchhiked to Glen White to care for her brothers and sisters.

The older brother, Tony Johnson, was in Fort Pierce working in the orange groves. So, after the funeral, it was Christine who managed moving seven youngsters south.

Doretha and her sister JoAnn arrived in Fort Pierce and stayed with cousins who, she recalled, "had lots of kids." Perhaps her mother's death and its surreal aftermath intensified her perception that "it was different here. They [the people] seemed a little poorer, even coming from West Virginia." Fort Pierce would prove to be different indeed.

Doretha was not familiar with Florida's landscape.

> I was used to mountains. Florida was so flat. I remember thinking to myself on the bus, "God, the Bible said everything You made was beautiful, but I got to tell you Florida is not beautiful." Fort Pierce was not beautiful in the summertime. They said the town looked bleak because everyone went up the road. I later found out the contractors would follow the crops and take the workers with them. I was sorry I said the car was too small because the others were not with us. I had lost my world. I felt alone in the world. My mom was gone. I was in an unknown place with my sister. My cousin picked us up at the bus station. My brother came to see us the next day. I was lost. Everything seemed so unreal when you lose both parents at the same time; my

father was lost along with my mother because I never did nor did I want to see him again. I did attend his funeral.

Doretha met Alfred at a drive-in theater within days of arriving in Fort Pierce, and it was love at first sight—sort of. She met him in the evening and dreamed about him that night. He had piercing brown eyes, the kind that make a woman feel as if she's the only girl in the world. "I was in love. It was love at first sight. It really exists," she exclaimed.

Her cousin Dot Wilder had taken her to the drive-in; it was where young people hung out. Doretha asked her about Alfred. She told Doretha that he had completed military service and built a house for his mother, her home on 709 North 13th Street. Doretha was shocked to learn soon afterward that Alfred was, in fact, in the eleventh grade. Needless to say, he was not a veteran, nor had he built the family's house. Alfred Hair was born in Fort Pierce on May 20, 1941. He was seventeen months older than Doretha. "He and all the other boys looked so much older," Doretha said. "They all had mustaches and muscles."

Doretha and Alfred's next encounter was at Gollett's, a local bar, and she had already accepted a ride home from one of the other young men there by the time Alfred asked her to dance, remembering her from their brief encounter at the drive-in. Doretha, looking back at the moment, laughed and said, "I didn't know he couldn't swing. I guided him. You better believe it. He could slow dance but he couldn't swing." Alfred asked if he could drive her home, and she agreed, knowing well she would offend the person from whom she had already accepted that same offer.

Alfred later ran into Doretha at the bus station where she worked as a waitress, a job she landed soon after arriving in Fort Pierce. She served black people in their designated section, in the back of the building, far behind the white patrons' dining room. It was a safe place for the under-age girl to work, away from scrutinizing eyes. He went there to get something to eat. Alfred told his friend Sol, "I kinda like her," which was quite a compliment coming from Alfred. They double-dated, Alfred with Doretha and Sol with her sister Sarah. Things were just getting started.

Over the years they became friends, and Jimmie Lee worked for Barnes until Barnes retired. They became so close that Barnes would buy Jimmie Lee a new car every two to four years. On weekends Jimmie Lee worked as a barber in a shop at the Gifford theater complex. Soon the family moved from The Groves, and years later, Barnes gave them his parents' home.

Mattie attended Gifford High School. It was segregated and the only school in Indian River County for black students. "That's where I met two of my lifelong best friends. I was an honor student throughout school, had great teachers who were very interested in educating the 'whole child.'" She earned titles and participated in extracurricular activities. Mattie, class valedictorian, was voted and crowned May Queen of Gifford High School and Miss Gifford High School Attendant. She made the honor roll and National Honor Society and was recognized with academic awards on the school's Annual Awards Day; she also held various class offices, treasurer and vice president among them. She excelled on the girls basketball team and was a member of the Student Council and the Library, Home Economics, and Math Clubs. Mattie also acted in school plays. Hers was a blessed youth, about which she said, "I will always cherish the beautiful memories made there."

Alfred and Mattie met at a football game in Vero Beach; the Gifford and Fort Pierce teams were rivals. He played on the Fort Pierce team, the Greyhounds, and she was a majorette in the Gifford High School band. They talked casually on the telephone for a few months because she was not permitted to date until she turned sixteen. Mattie's oldest sister, Addie Thornton, invited Alfred to a surprise sweet sixteen birthday party she gave for Mattie at the Gifford High School auditorium. "It was a magical night with a popular live local band," Mattie recalled. "The lead singer, a high school friend of mine, dedicated two beautiful songs to me: 'You're So Fine' and 'Only Sixteen.'" Alfred and Mattie had their first dances to those songs.

Alfred was her first date and the first and only boyfriend she would have until years after their children, Bonita and Kelvin, were born. "He even came to my house to meet my parents and pick me up," Mattie exclaimed. And Alfred took her to his prom as his date. This is especially notable because during that time only eleventh and twelfth-grade students were allowed to go to proms, and she was in the tenth grade. Mattie's best friend was dating Alfred's friend and managed to get permission for this break in protocol. Mattie explained,

> My best friend and I both asked our teachers to give permission for us to attend the prom at Lincoln Park Academy in Fort Pierce. We were both well liked and respected by our teachers, so they granted our request. It was not that we were too young but were both only in tenth grade. During that time you had to be at least a junior in high school to attend prom. My best friend then and now is Mary Louise Jones [Atkins]. Mary's escort was Maurice Calhoun, a friend of Alfred's who is also deceased.

ALFRED HAIR
"Banana Boat"
Football 6; Basketball 2; Baseball 1;
Handicraft 3; Science Club 1.
Hobby - Hot Rodding
Ambition - Artist

Meanwhile, Doretha and Alfred were becoming an item. But the relationship "went back and forth. . . . He was young; I was young. It was much too early," Doretha acknowledged.

Doretha graduated from high school two years before Alfred. "He was a boy's boy," she explained. "Alfred was older than me. When I met Alfred I was sixteen in 1959 and he was eighteen. He was going into the eleventh grade and I had graduated high school. Alfred told me the teacher flunked most of the boys in his class. But he wasn't likely ready to move on." Because his teacher left town that summer, Alfred didn't have the chance to complete or make up any deficient work, so along with others he was held back.

Doretha was grieving over the tragic loss of her mother, while Mattie, popular, attractive, and studious, was coming into her own. Alfred, still in school, was taking Saturday-morning painting classes. He was on the school football, basketball, and baseball teams. He was in the handicraft and science clubs. According to his yearbook entry, Alfred's hobby was hot-rodding, and his ambition was listed as "artist."

Alfred was Mattie's date to her junior prom. Bean Backus was fond of Alfred and lent him his car. He didn't want Alfred to drive Mattie in his own car with the flames painted along the sides, a decoration that was inspired by the band the Famous Flames, with whom James Brown began his career in 1956.

In her senior year, Mattie became pregnant with Alfred's child. Alfred chose the name, Bonita, for their baby. Due to her pregnancy, Mattie chose to attend adult high school and therefore could not deliver the valedictorian speech at Gifford High School. Mattie recalled,

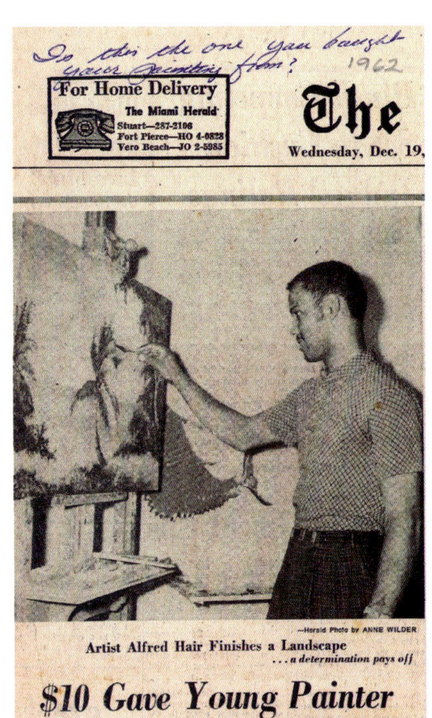

Is this the one you bought your painting from? 1962

For Home Delivery
The Miami Herald
Stuart—287-2106
Fort Pierce—HO 4-0828
Vero Beach—JO 2-5985

The

Wednesday, Dec. 19,

—Herald Photo by ANNE WILDER

Artist Alfred Hair Finishes a Landscape
. . . a determination pays off

$10 Gave Young Painter Boost Toward A Career

The only positive about this decision was my best friend became valedictorian and another good friend moved up to salutatorian. Relinquishing the title I earned as class valedictorian was one of the most regrettable events of my high school years. As a senior, with my parent's blessings and support, I just couldn't face going to school during the day, so I elected to complete the last two and a half months of my senior year at the nearest adult night school in Fort Pierce, where Alfred lived. I knew my parents were totally heartbroken and devastated but did not convey it to me. They loved me regardless of the circumstances. One of the most challenging things for me at that time was living with the pain I felt for disappointing my parents. They continued to love and care for me and my daughter, Bonita Donnette Hair. In addition to my parents, my oldest sister, Addie, was always there for me like a second loving mother. I also had the loving support of my two older brothers and their wives. No young girl going through that much could have hoped for a more understanding and loving family.

Indeed, Alfred and Mattie had a storybook romance, but it was not destined to last. It couldn't, although they would soon have two children. Mattie gave birth to Kelvin slightly more than a year after Bonita was born. It seems, though, that Alfred was destined to marry Doretha, and perhaps she him.

Alfred and Mattie enjoyed one another's company, but they had different outlooks as to how they wanted to live their lives. Mattie was a hometown girl with hometown values; Alfred's fast-paced lifestyle wasn't what she wanted for herself or their children. Down the road in Fort Pierce, Alfred was starting to tear things up on the streets, in the studio, near, far and wide; he was earning lots of money from the sales of his paintings and living the high life. As predicted by his popularity and activities in high school and by his own ambition and diligence along with the training he received in Backus's studio, he was on the brink of success, and money would be its measure. Everything led to fast times and to Doretha. Soon after Mattie's pregnancy with Bonita had become known, Doretha told Alfred's mother that she too was pregnant by Alfred.

Sol Knighton recalls Alfred looking dejected; he confided in his friend, telling him, "I'm in trouble. Doretha's pregnant, and the worst part is Mattie Pearl is too." He sounded resigned when he said, "I guess I'll marry one of them." Sol responded, "I'm glad I don't have to make that decision." Alfred made a pro/con list but then turned to his friend and asked, "Which one would you marry?" He said, "Mattie Pearl. She is a gentle woman and she really loves you. Doretha throws daggers at you when you're flirting."

Alfred Hair Jr. was born in Fort Pierce on October 10, 1963, and Doretha returned to her classes at FAMU in January at the start of the new semester. Her sister Christine kept the baby in Fort Pierce while Doretha was in Tallahassee. Doretha was earning a degree in business education with a minor in art education, and she would go on to earn a master's degree in elementary education. Doretha's sights were set on her career, and her plans had not included having a baby.

Alfred was ecstatic at the prospect of being a father, Doretha said, much happier about parenthood than she was. After the birth, Alfred gave Doretha an engagement ring purchased from Gordon's Jewelers just in time for Christmas. She wasn't ready for this, either. He wanted more children, but Doretha did not. Doretha remained a reluctant bride. "I couldn't do it," she said. "It ruins a very good relationship. I want somebody to be with me because he wants to be with me. . . . I didn't want to be like my mother, having a baby every year. Your life is raising children all the time. I couldn't see myself doing that." However, she was on that path, a young woman whose memory of her mother's brutal death at her father's hands was still fresh, in college and fiercely independent, presented with a baby and an engagement ring.

Months after Doretha graduated from FAMU and returned to Fort Pierce, she was pregnant again, and the couple bought a newly constructed house on Dunbar Street in Fort Pierce. This was in October 1965, and by then Alfred's enterprise was eminently successful. While she was away at college, he and his artist friends were selling their paintings with ease. The creative atmosphere rose in pitch and even became competitive, with one trying to outsell the others. Money flowed, and Alfred's business momentum no longer needed to be disturbed by trips to Tallahassee. Alfred soon painted murals on the living room walls of their home, an ocean scene with breaking waves and large palm trees against a blue sky. Perhaps these were celebratory paintings, his own welcome-home gifts.

An easel, a tree, or the side of a building no longer sufficed as an art studio. Not content with laboring on a single painting, Alfred worked on multiple boards at once. For a while he painted in the laundry room adjacent to the carport of their home. But he needed more space in order to expand his practice or, one could say, spread his wings. So Alfred enclosed the patio of their home, blocked it in, and put a roof over the new room, which became his studio. In lieu of easels, he attached 2-×-4's to the rafters to make a structure long enough to hold ten pieces of Upson board, on which he painted, on each side of this interior partition. He kept paintbrushes, linseed oil, and turpentine on a wooden stand. The room had fluorescent lighting and was bare except for a portable radio.

Alfred's confidence in his capabilities had grown to the point that he felt he was no longer practicing his art, no longer preparing for success. He was ready to conquer the world, or at least his part of Florida. He would paint en masse, as the radio blasted soul music, often James Brown, his favorite. Brown and other African American musicians performed in Fort Pierce, which was once a center of black culture. "He liked Joe Tex, Otis Redding, Wilson Pickett, Sam and Dave, and Jackie Wilson," Doretha recalled about the sounds coming from Alfred's studio. He loved listening to the Drifters and was often humming the tune from the song "Banana Boat," with the lyrics "Day-o, day-o/ Daylight come and me wan' go home."

Although using the same subject matter as Backus, Alfred did not take the elder artist's advice to slow down. He did just the opposite. He worked feverishly on two, five, ten, or even twenty paintings all at once. He would go from one to the next. If, for instance, he had mixed the green he wanted for grass, he would paint the grass on all the boards while he had the hue mixed. This saved paint but more importantly, it saved time. And time is essential to understanding Alfred Hair. He was always on the go, wanting to experience as much as could, to enjoy and to share. He was not rushing to his destiny; he was living life like he painted landscapes, passionately and in the moment, as if there was no tomorrow.

With the birth of their daughter, Sherry, on April 7, 1965, Doretha said, Alfred was insistent that the couple wed. But she still did not share Alfred's enthusiasm. Fortunately for her, the impediment to their marriage continued to exist: her lack of the required legal identification. Though she drove, she had no license. Driving was more important to her than marriage, she said. Doretha remained a reluctant bride.

Alfred was determined, and Doretha accepted the engagement ring he had purchased after the first child's birth. She did not know then that it was half of a set until he came to Tallahassee two months later and brought the wedding band with him. He also brought along "Little Al" from Christine, Doretha's sister, who was caring for their baby in Fort Pierce while Doretha was away at college and Alfred was out selling paintings.

Marriage was getting closer to becoming reality for the couple. Doretha explained,

> When Alfred came to Tallahassee, where I was attending college, in February 1964, with our baby, Alfred Jr., we attempted to get a marriage license in Thomasville, Georgia, but because I had no identification to prove my age, we were turned down for a license. He got us a house in Frenchtown, and we began living together, and I started using the last name "Hair." I did not think about a formal marriage. I really did not care for marriage, a piece of paper that changes a relationship. Why change the way things are?
>
> We came home for the summer and stayed with his mother until it was time for me to go on my internship in Eatonville, Florida. He found a house where we could get a room. We stayed with a family and went out to eat every evening at the local black restaurant because we did not have cooking privileges. When I graduated in December of 1964 we returned to Fort Pierce, where we rented a one-bedroom duplex on Avenue E and Eleventh Street in our common name of Hair. We bought the house on Dunbar Street on October 16, 1965, as husband and wife.
>
> I had an accident on Twenty-fifth Street and Orange Avenue in 1966. I was not at fault, but because I did not have a driver's license I had to go to court. Before appearing, I had to get a driver's license and was able to obtain a license using my college records. We used to go to West Palm Beach often, and one day we ended up at the courthouse. Alfred said it was time we got married, as everyone thought we were married anyway. We got the license and we went to Vero Beach and got married.

Alfred was a married man, but otherwise nothing else changed much. He loved his children and carried on.

A SECOND COMING

Business was brisk to fever-pitched for two decades. But when the artists ran out of customers in the early 1980s, their activity virtually halted. Most of the painters drifted apart or away or returned to or found steady employment then, except for the original cadre who set the pace and the aesthetic. Besides Hair and Newton, Livingston Roberts, Roy McLendon, and James Gibson defined Highwaymen art, and these painters did not abandon art making and resort to job hunting. The second tier of the core artists, who are more integral to the story than to defining the art, are Al Black, whose sales acumen set the fast pace, Mary Ann Carroll, whose color sensibility extended the visual parameters of the oeuvre, and Willie Daniels, an exceptionally talented artist whose paintings best illustrate the shared aesthetic. These eight people continued to practice their art to an increasingly indifferent clientele. It was all they knew; painting was their life and provided their livelihoods. Most of the rest of the twenty-six Highwaymen ceased painting.

And when their activity went dormant, it was as if it had never happened. The paintings then hung, aged and were ignored. Around the turn of the millennium, people began noticing the seemingly ever-present but taken-for-granted art when Jim Fitch, a gallerist from Sebring, got wind of what had happened and dubbed the then anonymous painters "the Highwaymen." Then, suddenly, with the release of my book *The Highwaymen: Florida's African-American Landscape Painters* in 2001, each and every one of the painters picked up brushes, bought oils and canvas, and began painting again as they saw a new market emerge. Suddenly they went from being painters to being artists, and no longer did they have to run the road in search of buyers. No longer did they have to lug stacks of wet paintings from office to office. Now buyers came to them.

The renewed interest was profound. Many of their paintings had been discarded without a second thought over the years. Many were found at flea markets, scratched and gouged, stained, and otherwise damaged. Large, 3' × 2', signed, and framed Highwaymen paintings could have once been acquired at yard sales for pennies on the dollar of the original $25 selling price. Sometimes people were selling the painters' makeshift frames to which the paintings happened to be attached. Occasionally, people used the backs of the paintings for signs. Some were left behind when their owners moved. Paintings had even been discarded and then rescued from roadside trash heaps.

Things changed in an instant. The paintings quickly went from being sold at flea markets to being sold at antique stores. Now the artists' signatures mattered. Collectors emerged, and they bought voraciously, competing against one another, steadily raising prices to unimaginable heights. Highwaymen galleries opened. Prices escalated like land in a Florida boom as people rushed to get in on the ground floor. The floodgates were opened, and the artists were hailed as visionaries and celebrated as heroes; their stories made for good press in newspapers and magazines. Articles were plentiful. Everyone, it seemed, wanted a piece of the action, and it was soon difficult to find a weekend, especially during the winter season, when there was not a Highwaymen event somewhere in the state. People came in droves for meet-and-greets to have their pictures taken alongside Highwaymen and to purchase new paintings. The book that had rescued the group from oblivion became an autograph album.

The artists churned out paintings to meet the new demand, and most of the growing legion of fans were not nearly as particular as the hard-core collectors who sustained a deeper attachment and found a deeper meaning in the older paintings. These dedicated collectors also possessed a broader discernment of this artwork; they had more than the hyped awareness of weekend enthusiasts. Still, few of the more discriminating collectors were sufficiently well versed in art history to locate, order, and measure Highwaymen painting in the broader social and cultural context, especially as to how this genre fit into contemporary aesthetics. The art did not make it into the big leagues; the museum culture was not yet interested in what seemed to be anachronistic, regional art.

The few better, accredited art museums that included Highwaymen paintings in their exhibitions, among them Jacksonville's Cummer Museum of Art and the Boca Raton Museum of Art, originated intelligent and intelligible exhibitions. They showed the paintings in a new light. But other fine art museums did not follow their cue to study, interpret, and establish a place for the body of work in art history. Highwaymen paintings were mostly seen and celebrated at local venues such as art galleries, regional history centers, and public libraries, and there they were presented without scholarship.

The frenzy of speculation to obtain pedestrian artwork that characterized the new issue of paintings overshadowed the vintage paintings. Aesthetic judgment yielded to mercantile sensibility. Integration into the culture of high art that comes with consideration by curators and the explicating and qualifying of extraordinary work by art historians were lost in the flood of new paintings. Still, change was inevitable, though acceptance of this art in scholarly circles hung in the balance. Fine arts museums that kept a distance from popular art became interested in it, and major Florida art museums curated intelligent, probing exhibitions of Highwaymen paintings, the Museum of Art/Fort Lauderdale and the Orlando Museum of Art among them.

Among collectors this laid the foundation for making the vintage paintings even more highly prized, some more so than others. They even established a point system of sorts to justify prices. A painting by Harold Newton with a person in it was the Holy Grail; his paintings with cows and steers followed. And a "jumbo" painting, measuring more than 24" × 48", the largest size that the artists had typically painted, was an especially prized commodity. "Minis" commanded a pretty penny too. Vintage paintings that had been considered worthless were, within a few years, worth hundreds of dollars, then thousands of dollars, and the most esteemed Newton paintings sold for tens of thousands of dollars.

The artists were back, to even their own amazement, and they were producing and selling paintings. It was like the old days but even better because now people sought them out. They were vending to an audience with an insatiable appetite; it was a dream come true for buyers and sellers. The Highwaymen were inducted into the prestigious Florida Artists Hall of Fame in 2004, a function of the Department of State.

The artists produced new paintings that sold for a few hundred dollars each, and they would often sell out at the events held in their honor. For budget-minded consumers, stacks of giclée prints were available for purchase. Prints on tote bags, computer mouse pads, and the like were available too. It was nothing at all like the old days.

The Great Recession hit in 2008, and pent-up interest grew as sales slowed. It was history in the making again, and as the recession ended, even more people wanted to be included. Collectors bought bragging rights and took pride in the Highwaymen's stories and accomplishments. Once again the artists were driving Cadillacs, this time Escalades instead of Coupe de Villes.

CONSEQUENCES AND CONTEXT

Alfred Hair would not be part of the revival; he would have been both mystified and elated had he lived to see it. Doretha Hair had moved to Fort Lauderdale soon after Alfred's death in 1970. In April 1980, she married her longtime friend John Truesdell. Loyal, pleasant, and happy to remain in the shadows of the Highwaymen phenomenon, Doretha said about her husband John, "If it weren't him, there'd have been no other husband."

Two months later, they relocated to New Jersey. The couple began visiting Fort Pierce after the turn of the millennium and came with regularity beginning in 2006, just after the reconstruction of Alfred's gravesite, for which she was consulted. A mosaic of a flower, copied from a painting of a hibiscus that Alfred had given her, now graces his resting place.

It was then that Doretha committed herself to being Alfred's voice, to tell the truth about his central role and see that he was recognized for it. By that time, Alfred's importance as an artistic leader was being lost in the feeding frenzy. Some of the artists

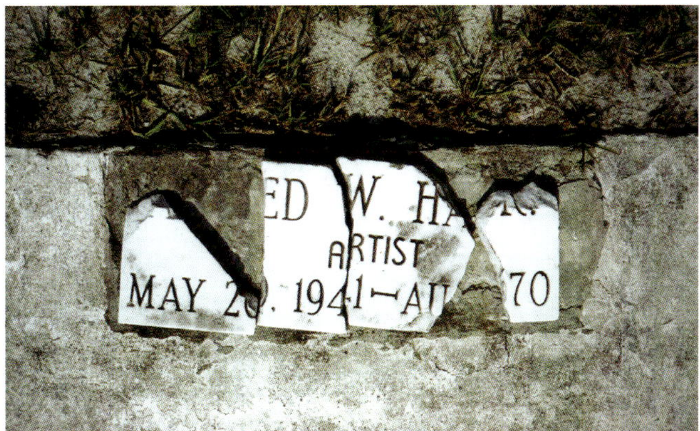

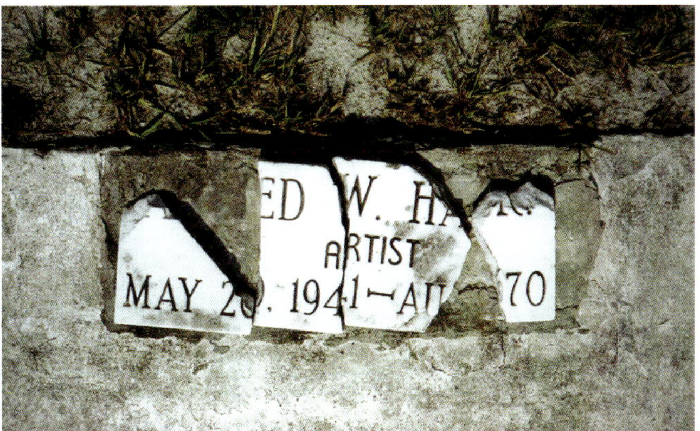

The restored grave (*far right*) and the original.

pointed to Harold Newton as their inspiration, and most collectors favored Newton's more traditional paintings to any of the others' work, including, if not especially, Alfred Hair's fast paintings. Mary Ann Carroll and Roy McLendon were vocal in their homage to Newton, not quite dismissing Hair but distancing him from their successes. Indeed, Doretha's mission was often overshadowed by Harold Newton's popularity among collectors and the aggressiveness that other painters took in hawking their own new paintings. It became every man for himself or woman for herself, in Mary Ann Carroll's case.

Within a few years of the release of *The Highwaymen,* their history was rewritten, as the resurgent popularity of the art led some of the peripheral artists to assume disproportionate roles. Dealers and other painters moved into the market. Misinformation swelled, causing a skew in understanding the actual history of this art phenomenon. It had all the properties of a gold rush.

Kelvin Hair jumped on the bandwagon of revitalizing the Highwaymen in the early 2000s. He began to paint, and given the quality of his art and his being Alfred's son and heir apparent, he received considerable opportunity and attention. Kelvin was a talented painter whose good looks, engaging personality, and entrepreneurial bent were reminiscent of his father's commanding presence. Alfred Hair's other children have that particular bearing as well. But Mattie and Alfred's son, Kelvin, were there on the scene in Fort Pierce and received exclusive recognition.

Residing in New Jersey for decades, Doretha felt excluded from the emerging Highwaymen story, and Alfred Hair's other children were left on the fringes through geography. Learning of the new glorification of the Highwaymen and Alfred Hair's gravesite restoration project from a newspaper exacerbated Doretha's and her sense of her children's loss at being left out, unable to take pride in Alfred's accomplishments from afar.

During Alfred's life, the women and children had a collegial relationship. Mattie and Alfred remained friends as they drifted apart romantically and Doretha and Alfred became a couple. Still Alfred visited Mattie and their children, and he gave her money for their needs. He provided gifts that even Doretha sometimes delivered. In other words, things were harmonious. "I would go to Gifford some weekends," Doretha recalled. "I would take all of the children with me shopping, my children, Bonita and Kelvin, nieces and nephew, and buy gifts for all of them." Doretha graciously took Kelvin and Bonita to Alfred's funeral along with her children, as Mattie was away on her honeymoon in Detroit, Michigan. Mattie said she had no regrets about her time with Alfred or the ending of their relationship. Alfred was doing well, and she was living a more sedate life than he would have provided, the kind of life she preferred.

Yet as the story of the burgeoning renown of the Highwaymen brought increased fame and reward, discord developed as the artists' popularity grew. Doretha's feelings escalated from being hurt to being annoyed and incensed. Doretha claimed Kelvin was opportunistic and questioned his paternity. Kelvin responded equally by questioning the paternity of some of Doretha's children and the sincerity of her relationship with Alfred. The rediscovery that should have brought joy, brought pain.

BLOODLINES

Alfred Hair had so much family in Fort Pierce's Lincoln Park—in addition to the Hairs, there were the Jenkinses, Gilliams, Wrights, and Minuses—that a section of the African American community where many resided was referred to as Jenkins' Quarters. This was bordered by Tenth Avenue, Means Court, Avenue D, and Moore's Creek. Irregularly laid out, paths cut under the shade trees from home to home. The Hairs came from Blackville, South Carolina. In Fort Pierce, Alfred's father, Sam, worked for Velda Farms, and his mother, Annie Mae, drove a schoolbus. Sam and Annie Mae had seven children: Arlena, Samuel Jr., Gladys, Thelma, Alonia, Alfred, and Donald. The family eventually moved into a house on the west side of Thirteenth Street. Alfred would paint a robin and a blue jay beside the picture window. The morning sun illuminated the birds.

"Everyone knew the Hairs," said Sam Gaines, an affable and charming man who knew everyone in the community. "The Hairs were well liked," he readily acknowledged. Like many descendants of enslaved people, the Hairs had white ancestors and were light-skinned.

Alfred's great-grandfather was enslaved; his grandfather was of mixed descent, and his grandmother had Creek Indian in her bloodline. Gaines described Alfred's complexion as "a pleasant, smooth color."

Alfred's high school teacher Zanobia Jefferson said, "Alfred had a personality that people liked even as a child. He came from a good family." In the Hairs' tightknit and loving family, two members of the extended family stand out as social and cultural role models.

People looked up to Alfred's uncle-by-marriage Estes Wright. He was not submissive to white authority during a time when it could be dangerous to stand up for one's inalienable rights. Before acts of defiance reached the required tipping point to usher in the civil rights movement, Estes was a lone warrior. He once drew a pistol on three white men who sought to run him off the bridge where he was fishing. He refused to wait in a "colored" line until all the white customers were served. He walked proud, and this was anathema to the white supremacists of Fort Pierce.

In September 1935 Estes Wright saw white men berating a frightened black man, Frank Ricks, at the scene of a fender-bender at Avenue D and Seventh Street, and he intervened. Ricks ran away as police officers approached. An altercation ensued, and Estes, beaten unconscious, was borne away by the police. The official report dismissed the incident as a case of Estes Wright interfering with the law. He fell, according to the police report, and struck his head against the curb, causing his skull to fracture and leading to cerebral compression. The few black witnesses who observed the altercation disputed this version and pointed out that there were no curbs at that intersection. The police delivered an unconscious Estes Wright to his home at 713 Thirteenth Street the night of the incident. His wife, Margaret Hair Wright, was pregnant with their sixth child. She and their five children, neighbors, and curious onlookers were made to stand across the street across from the house and kept at bay by the authorities until Estes was placed in his bed.

Then, in military fashion, a convoy of automobiles pulled up in front of the Wrights' house. A white man dressed in white with a black tie and wide black belt emerged from each vehicle, one after the other in an eerie, silent sequence. Each man carried a shotgun. Only after the last man got out of his car did they form a line and proceed into the house single file. They walked by Estes's dying body in his bed, then continued out the back door and around the house to their cars. Gazing slightly over the heads of the intimidated onlookers, the men entered their cars and drove away. A word was never uttered. They did not have to say anything. Fear of the Ku Klux Klan was embedded in the consciousness of the dark population. Margaret and others crossed the street and entered the house to find Estes unconscious in his bed. They tended him until he died the next morning, September 15, 1935. There was no further investigation, and no one was charged.

Police cars cruised by the Wrights' home often. Residents of the neighborhood felt their presence. Estes was buried the following day, but no one recalled a funeral, and no one knew where he was laid to rest. Although a death certificate was filed in Tallahassee that came to light recently, there was no record of Estes Wright's death in St. Lucie County court records or the mortuary files. Only one distorted photograph attests that this man ever lived.

Estes Wright was, according to the historian Jean Ellen Wilson, a "lonely, early advocate for justice" during a time that resistance by a black man could result in becoming one of the era's "disappeared." He was a larger-than-life, death-defying individual who questioned authority that denied equality before the notion was widespread; like too many others, he would give his life in the pursuit of human dignity, his own and others.'

Another of Hair's uncles gained more widespread fame. James Hair was the most renowned of the Hairs. He was also "a devilish one," according to his sister Carrie Ellis. This may have been because, having suffered from diphtheria, he was not disciplined like his twenty-one siblings, of which he was the nineteenth. The family resided on Avenue E near North Twelfth Street, and James starred on Lincoln Park Academy's basketball team. Sister Carrie related, "When he wanted the ball he'd holler like Tarzan and people would throw money to him on the court." It appears that Alfred shared this trait.

James attended Bethune-Cookman College, where he was class president, and later received his degree from Xavier University in New Orleans. In 1942, at the height of World War II, he joined the Navy and served as a seaman, as had many other colored sailors. Still segregated when he enlisted, blacks served as stewards, cooks, and deckhands. But in 1944 James Hair, along with twelve other black sailors, became a member of the Golden Thirteen, the first African American officers in the US Navy. The sailors were so named because of the gold stripes they aspired to wear. He and his fellow officer candidates were determined to prove the ability of African Americans. They covered the barracks windows with blankets when it was lights-out and continued to study. Their scores were so high that skeptical Navy officials ordered them to retake the exams. Their second scores, averaging 3.89 out of 4, were even higher and the highest ever recorded at the officers' school at Naval Station Great Lakes in Illinois.

Carrie recalled that during the war her brother would show up unannounced at home and leave unexpectedly a few days later. When wartime restrictions lifted, he explained that his visits were stealthy because his ship was at the Port of Fort Pierce and he had a few hours of shore leave. He pushed boundaries. James was so light-skinned that he appeared to be a white man. Donald Hair said James was able to stay at hotels that allowed whites only. He even got away with registering his niece by telling the desk clerk that she, a dark-skinned woman, was his "keeper." James entered the Wrights' home to view the dying Estes Wright the night he was attacked; James said he thought he was able to do it because whoever was keeping all the blacks out thought he was white.

In 1945 James was promoted to lieutenant and assigned to the destroyer escort USS *Mason*, which until then had an all-black crew led by white officers. The ship, nearly 290 feet long, had a complement of 156 sailors. Honorably discharged in 1946, he earned a degree in social work from Fordham University in New York City. There he was a caseworker and supervisor for thirty-one years. James Hair died in Manhattan on January 3, 1992, at age seventy-six.

The character and accomplishments of his kinsmen inspired young Alfred. Their stories seem like polar opposites, but indeed theirs were only very different less-traveled roads. Alfred may have had more of James Hair's conciliatory traits than Estes Wright's confrontational intervention style, but both elders sought to break the color barrier by leading moral lives.

Carrie Hair was married to John Ellis Jr., and in the 1950s their Ellis Barber Shop was a center for community action and a place for plotting during segregation days. If it wasn't the only barbershop in Lincoln Park, it was *the* barbershop. Carrie became the first female barber in St. Lucie County in 1949. The shop was modern, with multiple barber chairs, and had an alligator mounted on the wall. It was a cool place for students to get their haircuts as well as a popular place for respected police officers to get theirs. Ellis Barber Shop, Zanobia Jefferson said, "was like a beauty parlor in that the men gossiped as much as women." She added, "The family was very well respected," and they were central to a very respectable community.

BEGINNING OF THE END

Alfred had been spending more and more time with his father in Hallandale, where he was identifying sales opportunities. No longer would selling one painting at a time suffice, not if he were to make his million dollars. He would have only six years left to realize that dream. This amount of money was, especially then, like an exclamation mark, a metaphor for the good life. Alfred was living large; he had a succession of luxury cars, dressed to the nines, and was surrounded by women who were attracted to him and by men who admired him. He would reach out to anyone he encountered. He loved his children. On August 9, 1970, he was in Fort Pierce to see his daughter Bonita. It was her birthday. It was also the day he would die. He was twenty-nine years old.

That morning, Alfred drove from Hallandale to Gifford, where Mattie lived with their children, Kelvin and Bonita. After spending time with them, he drove to Fort Pierce, to the home on Dunbar Street that he shared with Doretha and their children. Doretha recalled that it was a gathering place, with artists, salesmen, and friends continuously dropping by to spend a few hours working or just visiting. For a brief time Alfred had rented a building on Avenue D in which he planned to paint prodigiously. But given its central location in the community and the pool table he had brought in, socializing competed with production, and soon he reverted to working in the studio he had built in the back of the Dunbar Street house.

Doretha wasn't expecting Alfred that day, and if Kelvin Hair's version of events is correct, she was not expecting him at all. Perhaps she was looking forward to a Sunday dinner with him. What is certain is that, Doretha said, "things died with Alfred." She lamented telling him it was all right if he were to go out socializing with Livingston. How different things would have been had she told him to stay put, but she was not about to clip Alfred's wings. That was unimaginable but not as unimaginable as what did happen.

It was a frenzied time, and money and emotions flowed like the paint used to create the steady stream of paintings that guided and defined Alfred's life. Family matters pale now in retrospect, blurred by faulty memory or confabulated by fresh recollections if not informed by wishful thinking.

The sun was in Sol Knighton's eyes while he drove along Avenue D. Alfred was driving in the other direction as they saw one another, waved, and slowed down to a stop. "Hey Banana Boat, What's up?" Sol asked. "Just trying to sell some paintings," came the reply. Alfred said that he would be going to Eddie's Place, the happening juke joint on Avenue D. It had been a profitable week, so Alfred was going to set up the bar for his friends. He said he would go to the Greenleaf Bar in Gifford after that. Sol was sure he planned to see Mattie Hunter in Gifford. "It never stopped," said Sol, referring to Alfred's romantic escapades. Infidelity was no secret. Alfred never made it to Gifford; he didn't leave Eddie's Place alive.

Alfred was at home with Doretha when Livingston Roberts came to the back door late that afternoon. Alfred was working in his studio when she saw Livingston walking toward the house, cutting through the neighborhood the way he often did. Livingston asked Alfred about going to Eddie's Place, also known as Eddie's Drive-in and Eddie's Bar. Alfred asked Doretha if she would mind, and although she might have wanted to tighten the proverbial leash, she said she did not mind. After all, the two men were best friends, they had spent the weekend selling paintings, Eddie's was the local hangout, and it was Sunday night.

The businesses along Avenue D were mostly closed, so Eddie's must have appeared like a beacon aglow. Inside, young people cavorted in the crowded space while Eddie, rolling a cigar in his mouth from side to side, served drinks from behind the bar. The bar was lined with stools, and there were also round tables where people sat and drank. There were two jukeboxes, and both were often simultaneously playing records. A dance floor and pool tables completed the layout. The small washhouse on the side of the building must have seemed extraneous that night, as it did most nights. On the other side of the building was a dirt parking lot.

Eddie's Place was the place to be, and this night was like other weekend nights—hopping. There might have been, hanging over the laughter and relaxation, the sense of anticlimax in that the weekend was ending and soon most of the patrons would be returning to a week of labor with little promise of ever escaping a life of drudgery. There was little discretionary income flowing in the Avenue D section. Blacks earned livings doing hard work in the fields and groves. The western lands produced a bounty of vegetables and citrus, and hands were needed to tend and pick the crops. Field hands would regularly congregate at the loading zone on Avenue D in the lot by the Lincoln Theater and Margarita's Grocery Store, at 3 a.m. Buses would line up and load the laborers—men, women, children, and entire families. Truckloads of sleepy workers were driven west on Okeechobee Road. A worker would make a dime for filling a bucket with tomatoes. A diligent worker could make an average of $10 a day, but it was a long, back-breaking day under the glaring sun.

Alfred and his painting associates were glaring exceptions. They had extra money to spend, and they did, especially Alfred. Gertrude Walker, wife of Highwayman Charles Walker and sister of Livingston Roberts, said Alfred would customarily buy drinks for others, including the women who were with other men. "Alfred was a ladies man," she said. "He had a nice car and money. He was good-looking. All of them [women] were after him." Sam Gaines said Alfred "knew how to play them," too. "Alfred was, during his time, the Don Juan of Lincoln Park Academy," Gaines said. His buying rounds of beer might have aroused envy. But Alfred was not at all arrogant; to the contrary, he was open-handed and gregarious. His brother, Donald, put it this way: "Alfred didn't have a mean bone in his body. If he had $20, he'd gladly give it away. He knew he could make more. He was just unique." Donald and Doretha agree about that. She said, "We gave away a lot of money because it was easy to make. Alfred was very generous with the money we made. We didn't think about the money drying up. We made it and we spent it."

It might have been his generous nature that made Alfred Hair a target that fateful night. Police reports chart how the night unfolded at Eddie's Place, how an agitated Julius Funderburk became a murderer. It is impossible to know precisely what happened as the beer flowed around the unfolding events. The juke joint noise got louder and louder. The barroom became increasingly crowded and smoky and hot inside on that summer night. People came and went. It was clearly a sociable place, until a few minutes past 11 p.m. A few hours later Dr. H. L. Schofield would remove a single bullet from the body of Alfred Hair.

Livingston Roberts arrived at Eddie's Place alone just as night fell, he told the investigating police officer. He said Alfred arrived soon thereafter with Alonzo Pratt, a friend and salesman who sold their paintings. Alfred's car was parked out front, a light blue Lincoln Mark III.

Given the ever-changing scene inside, with young people mingling and moving about, forming and reforming constantly into temporary groupings, witness memories were bound to be somewhat amorphous too. Nevertheless, various memories agreed that Alfred Hair, Livingston Roberts, and their friends were sitting at or near the bar, filling glasses from quart pitchers of Budweiser. Julius, "JL," or "Jel" Funderburk was there too; he may have been a familiar face, but he was not part of the in-crowd.

Mary Barnes said Alfred "was talking, acting lively, friendly," and invited her to have a beer. Livingston, she recalled, sat with them, too. The police report noted that Barnes noticed Beneva Murray "trying to attract the attention of Alfred Hair but did not appear successful." Carolyn Greene recalled that Beneva was sitting between Alfred's legs earlier, as he sat on a barstool.

Born on March 9, 1939, in Sumter, South Carolina, Julius Funderburk was thirty-one years old when he shot Alfred Hair. Having completed only four years of grade school, he was nearly illiterate. He and Lucille Wyche, nicknamed Lilly, began living together in 1957, and the couple had six children, ages two to ten at the time of Alfred Hair's death. They wed some three years before JL killed Alfred Hair. He was described as short and dark-skinned, and that night he was wearing a small, black hat. Until being charged with murder, Funderburk's only offense had been reckless driving.

Funderburk denied having had an intimate physical relationship with Beneva, telling police that he knew her only casually. He said the disagreement between Alfred and himself that night was a "friendly argument." It led to his raised voice, then to tussling and ultimately gunfire. Still Funderburk denied that it "concerned any disagreement between the men and Beneva," according to the detective's write-up of the interview the following day, soon after Funderburk turned himself in "at about 5:28 a.m."

Alfred's friends and others had formed a lynching party. They went looking for Funderburk with a rope in hand. When Funderburk turned himself in, a soft-spoken sheriff's deputy, Lieutenant Pat Duval, had to stop the angry mob from storming the jail.

Within hours of shooting Alfred Hair, Funderburk admitted that Livingston Roberts and he argued. He told Duval that Alfred Hair "butted in" and they began to have words. He got his gun from his car. He walked up to Roberts and told him that his friend should not butt into their argument. "Castro [Roberts's nickname] and I got into a scuffle. Hair was standing behind me when I hit Castro. When I turned to hit Hair with my left hand the gun went off. I still had the gun when Hair and I went out the back door. We both fell to the ground and the gun went off again. I got up and ran." He further explained, "Alfred must have been shot when we fell outside. He fell on top of me. I did not mean to shoot him."

Funderburk pleaded to second-degree murder, and on November 23, 1970, he received a life sentence. Soon thereafter, on December 3, as inmate 028638 he entered the Lake Butler Reception and Medical Center. On September 6, 1977, Funderburk was paroled. Then he moved inland from Fort Pierce, settling in Belle Glade by Lake Okeechobee, where he had family. Bean Backus told Doretha "not to worry about Funderburk returning to Fort Pierce." He may have been warned to stay away.

Beneva Murray was twenty years old at the time, unwed, with a six-year-old child. She told police she had known JL by sight for three or four years but was uncertain of his last name. She added that "she had never had a lot of conversation or personal relationship with JL and never had a date with him." JL, she told the detective, "had never asked her for a date, offered to buy her a drink or shown any interest in her whatever."

Street gossip in this small community, according to Eddie Asbury, the proprietor of Eddie's Place, was that JL and Beneva were having an affair. But if that had been the case, it would not be the only illicit relationship either would have. Terry Stevens, a fifteen-year-old tenth-grade student whose family moved to Fort Pierce from Tallahassee about a year prior, knew that Funderburk was married and had a family. She admitted having dated and had sexual relations with him. Beneva Murray, meantime, had known Hair and was aware that he was married and had a family, and she admitted having dated him since November of the previous year, acknowledging that they had a sexual relationship. Alfred had told Beneva that they'd better "slack off," and this ended their intimacy after a few months.

All except Julius Funderburk were having a good time at Eddie's that night. But by 11:15, the scene of revelry had become the scene of a murder. It would become a night that those involved and those affected would remember vividly for the rest of their lives. Alfred's memory still haunts the community. It was more than anyone could reckon then or now.

Beneva Murray and Mary Barnes were sitting at the bar, and Livingston was next to them, but he was facing the other direction. Alfred was nearby, socializing by a jukebox. Julius Funderburk approached Beneva. According to witness testimony, he was angry. His hands were raised above Beneva, and his fists pounded on the bar as the two spoke. She told him to get his hands out of her face. He responded that they were not in her face, as he became more agitated and increasingly incensed. "Nasty" is how Beneva would describe his behavior.

Funderburk walked away then, likely with humiliation stoking the anger he was already feeling. Alfred bought the women a round of beer. Beneva saw Funderburk and Amos Lundy walk outside, and she followed them, perhaps sensing Funderburk was cooling off. There she apologized to JL "for fussing at him." They talked and shook hands. She returned to her seat by the bar.

Earlier Livingston Roberts or Beneva herself might have told JL that she had feelings for Alfred or inferred it. It wasn't much of a secret, as the two had carried on for a while. Funderburk said, "I heard Alfred's been seeing Beneva," to which Livingston had replied, "None of my business." Then, Funderburk knocked Livingston's drink off the counter and stormed off, leaving the premises.

Funderburk came back inside, and this time he confronted Livingston. Despondent, he said to him, "I thought you were my friend." Taken aback, good-natured Livingston replied, "Yes, I am your friend. What are you talking about?" Funderburk responded, "I thought you were my friend. Why don't you treat me like I treat you?" Livingston asked him to clarify what he meant. "He didn't know whether he wanted him to buy him a beer, loan him some money, or what?" reads the police report. Complicating this was a purported aside about the kind of beer Funderburk drank. Most patrons preferred Budweiser, but Funderburk preferred Schlitz. His uncertainty about what he was drinking or if had he been served Bud could have added to Funderburk's feeling alienated.

Meantime, Livingston, still trying to figure out what was bothering Funderburk, asked Eddie for change of a ten-dollar bill and received a five and five singles. Then he laid them side by side and told Funderburk to choose either the five-dollar bill or the single dollars. Funderburk, perhaps confused by the odd gesture, grabbed the five-dollar bill, crumpled it, and threw it on the counter. Now Funderburk was annoyed that he had failed to get whatever he expected from Livingston Roberts. It was clear that in the midst of the noise and smoke, he was becoming increasingly agitated.

Mary Barnes thought JL pulled some money from his pocket and said, "Can't nobody take nothing from me." He said it loudly and repeated it a few times. From behind the counter Eddie Asbury heard Funderburk say something about "using his dust," a reference to Livingston's money. He mumbled something to Alfred, something that did not appear to be argumentative, as he again walked out of the bar. Barnes said Funderburk knew how close Livingston and Alfred were. Swinoil Armstrong, though, saw it differently. Armstrong said JL took a few steps toward Alfred when he was finished with Livingston, and he thought that indeed JL was upset and angry and had words for Alfred. Jackie Gaskin, Alfred's cousin, said while they sat "laughing, talking, and having fun" by themselves in a corner of the bar, Funderburk approached and said something that was threatening to Alfred. Jackie said Alfred just asked him, "What's wrong, man?" He never got an answer.

Funderburk walked out of Eddie's, crossed the street to his car to retrieve his .32 caliber, chrome-plated, short-barrel revolver. Some witnesses said Alfred walked over to the jukebox, dropped in coins, and played the hit song "War." From that point on, few words were spoken.

Mary Jennings, Terry Stevens, Fannie Stevens, Annie Belle Baker, and Shirley Travis were outside the bar getting some fresh air. Noticing Funderburk remove the gun and put it in his pocket as he approached Eddie's, Mary Jennings intervened, asking him what was wrong. With mounting anger turning to rage, he said he was tired of being mistreated, of "people pushing on him." Seeing that JL was so upset, she asked him not to go back inside. Terry Stevens asked Funderburk to leave, then to take her for a ride. He refused. Fannie Stevens said Funderburk "more or less pushed them away" as they tried to keep him from returning to the bar. She saw him remove the gun from his pocket, and as he went inside Eddie's, Annie Belle Baker heard him say, "I am going to kill some M.F. body tonight and do me some time." The gun was in his right hand.

Funderburk walked up to the bar and hit Livingston on the side of his head. Some accounts say he struck him with the gun. Others claim he hit him with his left hand; one account holds that he had a bottle in that hand. Livingston, reported Mary Barnes, was "knocked back on his stool" when Funderburk grabbed her by the front of her dress and pushed her back. Livingston did not strike back and ran out of the building.

Funderburk turned toward Alfred, who was standing a few feet away by a jukebox, and struck him. Most accounts say that he hit Alfred with his empty hand on his arm or hand, knocking Alfred's glass of beer from his hand. Swinoil Armstrong offered that Funderburk slapped Hair on the forehead with the gun. This would account for the bruise the coroner later noted on Alfred's forehead.

Willie Joe Westley said that Alfred might have stumbled as he dodged another blow. Upon regaining his balance by holding onto the bar, Alfred rose to his feet and ran toward the back door. Funderburk pursued, firing his first shot as Alfred turned the corner of the bar. That bullet missed him.

Funderburk lunged at Alfred as he pushed through the back door. Then the two men tussled. Jackie Gaskin said Alfred tried deflecting Funderburk's gun hand, and "they were down on the ground scuffling." It is uncertain who was on top. Armstrong "saw Hair fall to the ground after he was outside." They fought, and Armstrong reported, "JL was on top straddling Alfred. Funderburk later claimed that Alfred was on top of him, but more than one account puts Funderburk on top of Alfred. By that time, Funderburk had fired again, maybe more than once, as various people reported hearing three and even four shots. Up until then, Funderburk would claim, the two of them were engaged in a friendly argument.

Thomas Gaskin had warned Alfred to "watch it. He has a gun," as they struggled. Alfred, he reported, said, "Yes, he has shot me." Jackie Gaskin confirmed that Alfred said, "Man, I am shot." He was getting weak and losing his grip on Funderburk. Funderburk broke away and ran, ditching the gun as he fled. The weapon was never found; presumably someone picked it up. The shooter claimed that the shots were accidental and that he was the victim, fearing that Alfred was coming to Livingston's defense and that they would "double team" him.

Alfred managed to make his way back into the bar. The jovial atmosphere turned to horror as the wounded Alfred Hair stumbled through the room, out the front door, and toward his car. He did not make it, though.

Testimonies in the police reports are as follows:

Willie Joe Westley: Alfred staggered back inside the bar bleeding, at which time he knew Alfred has been shot.

Armstrong: Alfred finally got up from the ground, ran back through the bar and out the front door. He ran up to his car, apparently tried to get inside but fell by the car. It was apparent that Alfred had been shot. He said he has never seen or known anything definite regarding JL and Alfred's girlfriends, but the street talk was that JL has been using dope and JL and Alfred are interested in the same girl.

Shirley Travis: A few minutes later, she saw Alfred Hair stumble in front of Eddie's Bar and fall near his car.

Terry Stevens: A few minutes later, she saw Alfred Hair stumble out the door, it looked like he hit the side of the door, fell, then got up, went on in front and fell by his car. She was near enough that she could see blood on Alfred and assumed he had been shot.

Jackie Gaskin: Alfred got up from the ground and ran to his car. When he got around to the door, he collapsed.

Annie Belle Baker: At this time, she saw Alfred Hair run between two cars and fall to the ground.

Mary Jennings: A few minutes later, she saw a man struggle out the front door of Eddie's Bar and fall to the ground. She was told by someone, does not recall who, that the man who had fallen near a car in front of the bar was Alfred Hair and that he had been shot.

Fannie Stevens: A few minutes later, she saw Alfred Hair stumble out the front door of the bar, more or less hit the door as he was stumbling, then stumble on to a car and fall near it.

Carolyn Green: After the shots, she came out of the storage room, saw Alfred Hair coming from the back door through Eddie's Bar, going out the front where he fell by some cars.

Eddie Asbury: Shortly after hearing the shots outside, he saw Hair run back through the bar, out the front door and fall by his car.

Beneva Murray: After coming out of the ladies' rest room, everyone apparently had scattered out of the bar and someone said Alfred Hair had been shot. She walked outside to the front and saw Hair lying on the ground near a car and he apparently had been shot.

Thomas Gaskin and Livingston Roberts picked up a dying Alfred Hair and rushed their friend to the hospital. It was about 11:15 and a few minutes before blood would fill his chest cavity fatally.

Gertrude Walker said her brother, Livingston Roberts, told her that he had administered mouth-to-mouth resuscitation to Alfred as he bled profusely. He held Alfred in the backseat of the car. Livingston, she said, was soaked in Alfred's blood and had cried all night long. He told her that he thought the hospital staff did not do enough, that they laid him on a cart and let him die, but these may be the sentiments of a man who just lost his best friend.

At 6 a.m., Arthur Murray, Beneva's uncle, who was also Charles Walker's uncle, knocked on the Walkers' front door. When the door opened, all he said was, "Beneva got Alfred killed last night."

Dr. Schofield's anatomical protocol read in part that "this is the body is [*sic*] a very well developed colored male of light color and characteristically presenting those ethnic characteristics of the Negro race." Completing the autopsy, he continued,

> The chest plate is removed and a very marked amount of blood clot is present within the left chest cavity and a considerable amount of blood clot is present in the right chest cavity. . . . The passage of the bullet has been made through the upper lobe [of] this left lung adjacent to the fractured rib as it lies against to pass in the pericardial sac near its base and projects into the direction of the great vessels as they leave the heart. . . . It is the passage of the bullet which is recovered, through the left chest wall then through the left upper lobe of the lung, through the pericardial sac where it has torn the pulmonary artery and out the cardiac sac through the right lung, bruising the inner surface overlying the fourth rib in a posterolateral position, bouncing back into the right chest cavity where it is found supported in a fairly large amount of blood. This man bled to death. . . . Findings are such that one would presume that death came about rather rapidly because of the massive bleeding.

Schofield placed a crude "H" on the base of the bullet, sealed it, and presented it to Lieutenant Duval of the Sheriff's Department of St. Lucie County, who would enter it into evidence for use by State Attorney Charles Carlton.

"Things died along with Alfred," Gertrude commented.

THREE SIDES OF THE SAME COIN

Julius Funderburk never knew his biological father. His mother worked as a domestic. When she injured her hand, she could no longer perform those duties and took to migrant labor, bringing Julius with her as she followed the crops. They settled in Fort Pierce in 1952. Julius skipped school to earn money for his mother by working in the tomato fields, but he didn't want her to know he was working when he should have been studying. She cried when she found out that he labored in the fields. Julius's path was set. A good worker, soon after getting a driver's license he was promoted to driving a truck, and he was taking it up Avenue D to pick up migrant workers before the sun rose.

Julius met and married Lucille Wyche before his twentieth birthday. With a growing brood of children, Julius was a responsible man. He grew a vegetable garden and raised chickens at the house the family rented at 908 North 17th Street. Funderburk was earning good money, at $50 a week. He paid off his car loan and the balance he owed Badcock Furniture; he was paying down his finance bill, too. He was a family man, and things were looking up for the Funderburks. He was going to close on a house within the week when things fell apart, before, as he put it, he "got in trouble." As he saw the killing and his incarceration, it was just a fluke.

Fifty years after that awful night, Funderburk did not deny killing Alfred Hair but recalled it differently than has been recorded. Perhaps his version was confabulated, adjusted over time to meet the needs of his family's lore, and lost to the fog of adrenalin and fear. He spoke with care if not empathy. "Things like that happen so fast, there's not much to say," he explained. He did not express contrition. He did not know Alfred Hair as an up-and-coming artist; he was more familiar with Livingston Roberts. "It was not my intention. I hardly knew the guy," he said of Hair.

Funderburk claimed not to remember what they argued about, who initiated the dispute, or why it happened. He knew that Alfred and Livingston were tight, and as Livingston's goading escalated, he got his gun from his car. Was he showing off when he exposed the gun to them? Was it to ward them off? He said Alfred "tied me up," meaning he got close to keep the gun by his chest so that Julius could not aim it at him or anyone else. There was a slight struggle, and the gun went off. The bullet that ripped into Alfred Hair was an accident, Funderburk maintained. The argument was "not much of anything," he said, adding that he did not run outside and shoot Alfred, as had been reported. In this scenario Hair was a guy in a bar who grabbed for his gun, and it went off accidentally. He was not even arguing with him.

As Funderburk fled the scene, he wondered, "How did this happen? My wife and children . . ." He may have wondered that for years. He did not consider that he and Alfred each had a wife and six children. He showed little remorse, not necessarily because he was a bad man but because he believed Alfred Hair's death was circumstantial. He turned himself in and prayed as his mother had taught him to do, and he asked the Lord for forgiveness. He believed the story he told the Lord. But "they had so much on me, like I was a desperado," he lamented. It was in his apartment, somewhat barren but with a TV on which a western aired.

Funderburk entered the prison system in December 1970 at Lake Butler Reception and Medical Center, where he and other prisoners were assessed. Elvis was on the radio singing "Blue Christmas," a fitting song for the season and the occasion. He quietly sang, "I'll have a blue Christmas without you" and smiled slightly. He thought back to how he played Santa Claus for his children every year. He drew reindeer tracks and sleigh skid lines in the dirt. He said Beneva was an attractive woman, but they did not have a relationship. Although married, he admitted to having girlfriends. He wouldn't, he pointed out, have brought one to Eddie's; doing so would have engendered talk around town. He was there to relax with the guys before the work week began.

"I didn't know what I was fixin' to go through [in prison]," he said. While incarcerated he told his wife, "Honey, this is not your fault. This is my fault. I don't know if and when I'll get out of this. You're free to move on with your life." The only codicil was that she was not to get pregnant should she want to continue their marriage after his release. Lilly stood by him.

Julius Funderburk was imprisoned at the Glades Correctional Institution. He was a model prisoner assigned to work on nearby farms; he drove the prison bus that transported inmates to night school and other county prisons. Upon release, he said, he and his wife built a home in Belle Glade, "across the ditch," a canal beside a mostly African American neighborhood of low income. Lilly passed away in 2006. Julius's health soon began to fail. He became confined to a wheelchair and lived in a bleak apartment a stone's throw from Highway 441, where trucks from the surrounding fields zoom by. He remained convinced of his innocence and that the incident in 1970 was a bad day. He was candid and seemingly genuinely interested in telling his story, a version of which he could live with.

Funderburk said, "I didn't go out looking for someone to kill. I went out for a Sunday evening, before I go to work." His story was tempered by his observations on hard luck. "I came up the hard way all my life. People that had something, they moved on," he said. He could more easily rationalize his life than escape what he considered being held down by it.

Whether accepting his life begrudgingly or not, he offered, "It's a hard part to take out of your life living with the fact you know what happened and there's nothing you can do about it. It's hard." He said he didn't carry a grudge and wasn't jealous. Whether he felt that way fifty years earlier is another matter.

IN RETROSPECT AND MEMORIAM

Things indeed died with Alfred Hair then, but the painting enterprise continued. Highwayman Hezekiah Baker said, "There was nothing to shoot for when Alfred died. He was the glue holding things together." But there was momentum with the enterprise, and painting and selling at that point were in high gear. Life changed but went on, and their paintings continued to sell for another decade. Then the landscapes disappeared as quickly as they had appeared. As the paintings seemed to lose their appeal and fade from view, the anonymous artists were rendered inconsequential. Their names did not merely fade from public consciousness; rather, it was as if they had hardly existed and ever painted.

Yet, many paintings continued to hang in homes and offices, their bright colors losing their edge to sunlight and nicotine. Like so much decorative art, they became fixtures on the wall, taken for granted, like white noise. Some still maintained their appeal, that special place in the hearts and minds of their owners. A few of the artists kept painting, but for fewer and fewer consumers. The exception was Harold Newton, who was always in his own orbit and possessed exceptional talent. The others never equaled his skill, and those who tried emulating him generally failed. George Buckner, who professed a reluctance to knock on the doors of strangers to hawk paintings, made an effort to paint with Newton's fastidious reserve. He came closer than any of the others but despite his excellent skills fell short of accomplishing Newton's flair.

Alfred Hair had no need to work at achieving flair. He had it from the start. His style came to him naturally, without effort or any affectation and without emulation. He enhanced the spirits of his fellow painters, liberating them spiritually, artistically, and financially. Doretha Hair summed this up well: "No one made a good living until Alfred came along." Zanobia Jefferson observed, "He was there from the beginning and almost to the end.

They took what Alfred did and added on and on to it." Flair was his artwork's trademark, but his paintings possessed pathos too, a quality by which a viewer did more than look passively at the landscape: it was as if one *saw* it, connected with nature personally.

Alfred wore hats that concealed his receding hairline. He set crab traps from his motorboat and loved to fish and cook. He made sure others were enjoying themselves, gladly buying beer and serving it freely. He feigned annoyance at friends who brought food to his home when they came to visit; he wanted to feed them. Alfred and his family were well known and liked. "He was prime," Sam Gaines said about Alfred. "He was an inspiration." Gertrude Walker offered, "Alfred was very nice, very personable, and very ambitious. He certainly wanted to make something of himself and his art—to get rich."

Alfred Hair wanted to live richly; money in itself meant little if anything to him. His goal of being a millionaire by his thirty-fifth birthday is best viewed less as a target than as a metaphor. He lived life fully, always in the moment. He was on top of the world when he died. But it was like that every day and night for Alfred Hair. He was also on top of his game, the father of six and living his dream. "He didn't know when to come home," Doretha lamented about that night he would not come home at all.

Seeking comfort, one could say that he went home to the Heavenly Father that sad summer night. Trying to make sense of the senselessness, one could argue that he was too good for this world. Bewildered by the tragedy, one could imagine that the Lord works in mysterious ways. But all those claims fall flat in the face of what was and what might have been.

Stone Brothers Funeral Home was in charge of the arrangements. Alfred's body lay in the casket, open for viewing, the day before he was buried. People came to pay their respects that day and the following morning. Later, at 3 p.m., the proceedings moved to the Friendship Missionary Baptist Church. There Pastor Henry W. White eulogized him. A. E. Backus and Zanobia Jefferson spoke to an overflowing congregation. In fact, during the service the overflow of people extended outside the church. Cars were double-parked in both directions from the church door. Alfred had innumerable ties to his community and beyond, with friends everywhere. The mourners were both black and white.

The procession to the Pine Grove Cemetery seemed long, and there, in the neighborhood where he was born and grew up, Alfred Hair was laid to rest. The unceremonial marker was placed in the ground and blended in with those marking the other nondescript gravesites in the segregated African American cemetery. Like the paintings, it too would lose its luster. It would remain there ignored as lawnmowers ran it over, season after season, chipping it until it was worn and weathered so badly that parts of the stone were missing, resembling an uncompleted jigsaw puzzle.

"Who would have thought his name would be like it is today?" Sam Gaines asked, as he reminisced about the times when Alfred was in high school and would come see him and say, "I need some money for canvas and paints. Sam, come here and take a picture. Which one do you want?" Gaines knew that resistance was futile, nor did he want to refuse his friend. He would reply, "Just put it in the house." A smiling Sam Gaines added, "Alfred was charming."

Donald Hair reflected on Alfred and his art: "There was no violence, no roughness. It was always about water, clouds, and sunsets out there. I think he was trying to find inner peace and was figuring it out in his painting." Perhaps this is exactly what Alfred was doing as a man and as an artist. It might well be that his paintings are not solely about the scenes he depicted or even the painterly qualities by which he realized the locales.

Doretha Hair Truesdell reflected, "Alfred's life had a purpose, and he has never stopped living even though he is no longer with us in a physical form." He indeed left a legacy both tangible and intangible, a transcendent trove of art created by himself and by those he inspired. The paintings took on lives of their own, inspiring still others as they lived and worked in the glow of the images' bright skies and breaking surf, illuminating the ubernatural settings of a dream-inspired Florida.

An intangible quality informs and sets his paintings apart from those of his friends and all other artists. It is not as simple as tranquility, for beneath calm waters torrents swirl. It is not a theme in any sense; that is too reductive. Rather, I think his paintings are infused with his tender conscience, a way of being more than of knowing the world, with compositions reflecting an inner balance continuously righting itself in an unbalanced world.

Alfred Hair made no claims about understanding a chaotic world but was, with each painting, in the process of finding the order and the harmony that he depicted in his artwork. His work was a testimony not to the land of promise that he painted for others but to his own inner worldview. His images reflected his dreams for improving that view, for making the world even better than how he saw and lived life, with zest and vitality.

Zanobia Jefferson summarized what is certain: "Alfred had blazed a trail for other black men." Indeed he did. Generous of spirit and handsome, Alfred Hair was living his dream while Martin Luther King was penning his memorialized speech. Both men possessed the audacity of hope long before Barack Obama wrote about it. An unwitting trailblazer in race relations, Hair sold his resplendent paintings to a white clientele as he drove down the road to riches. He drove a Cadillac, though when selling paintings he drove a humbler car. Social progress was not a part of his agenda, yet change did happen because of him. He was on equal footing with those who had the upper hand in a segregated society. Character, not skin color, defined Alfred Hair.

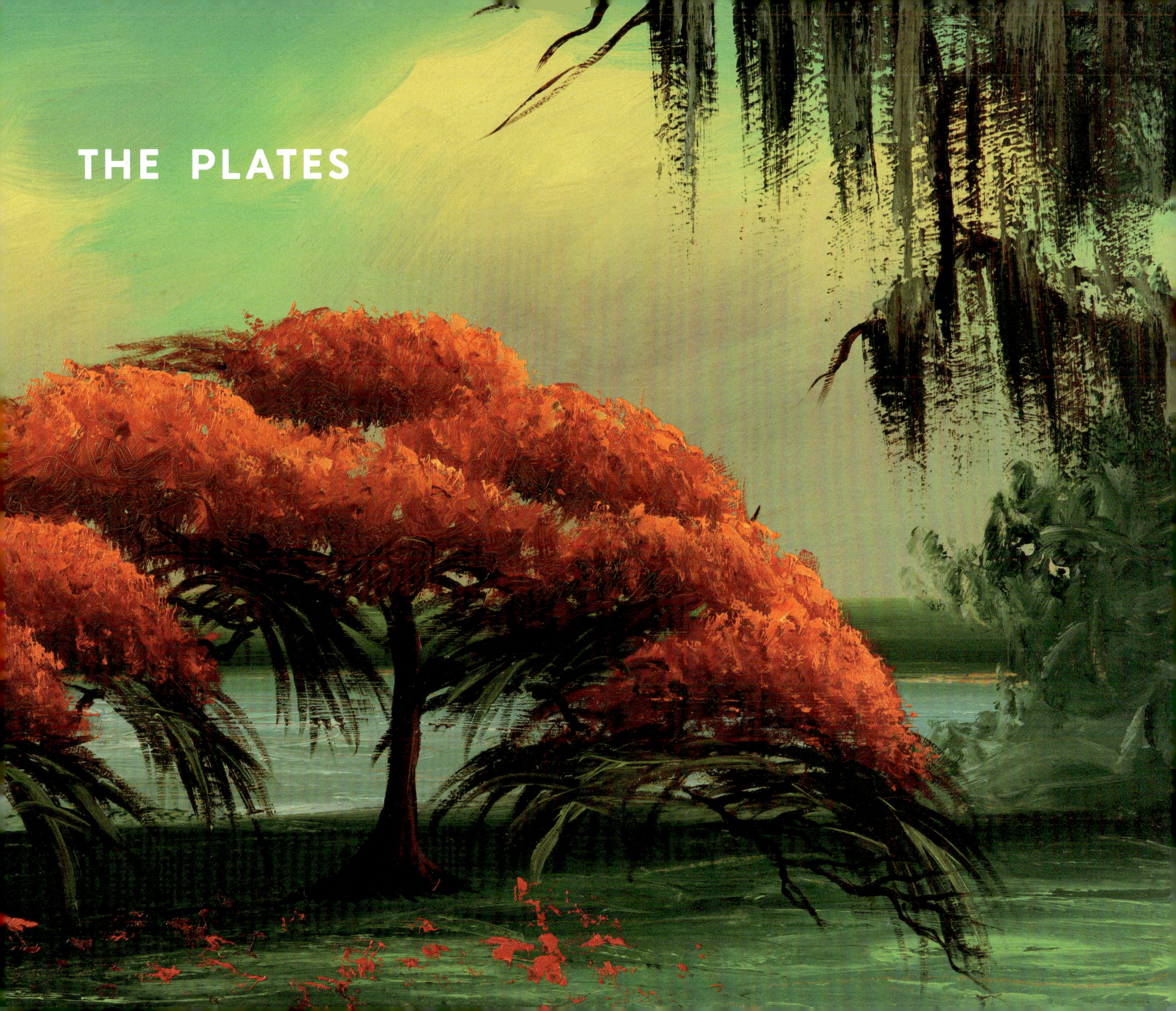
THE PLATES

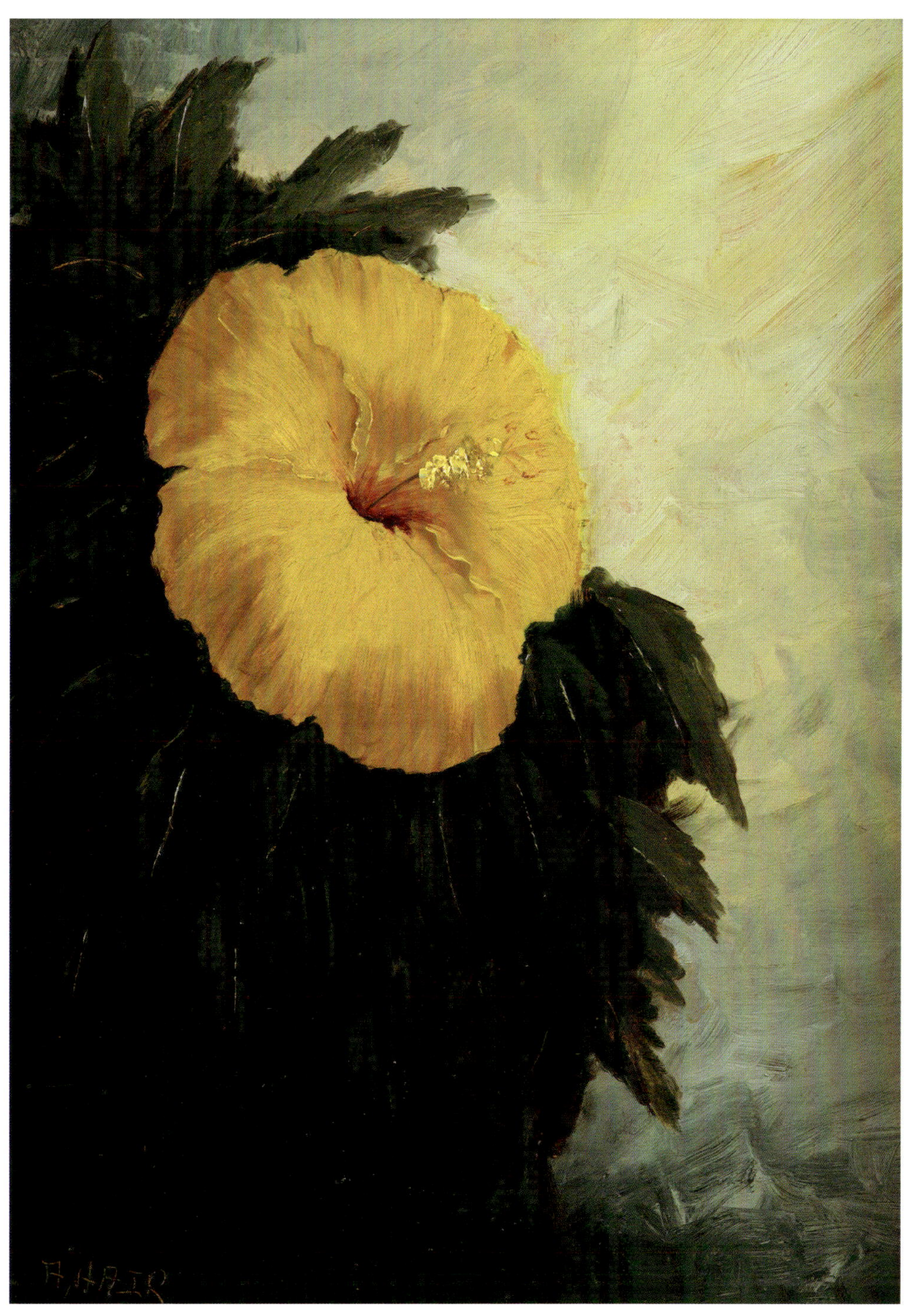
A.HAIR

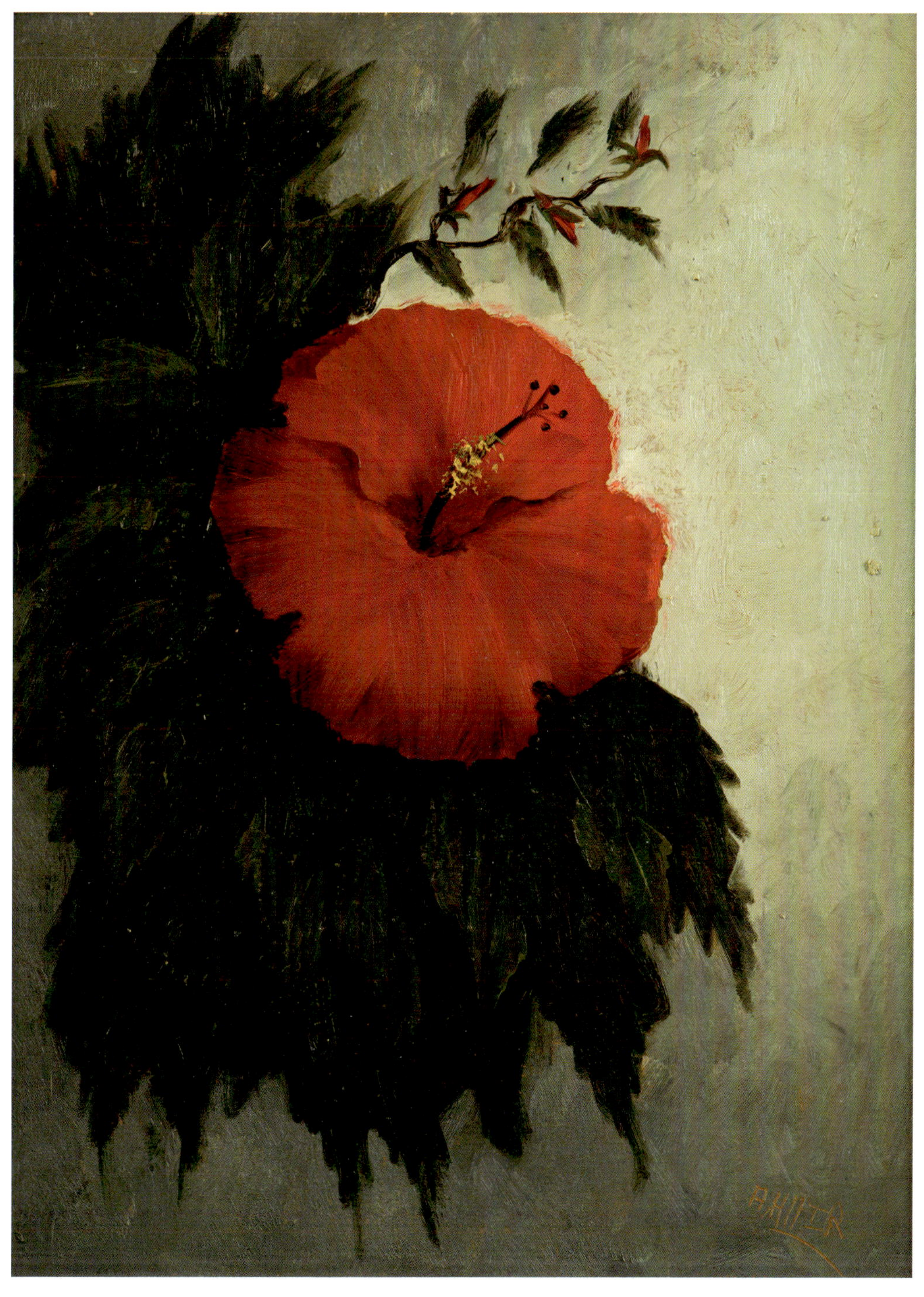

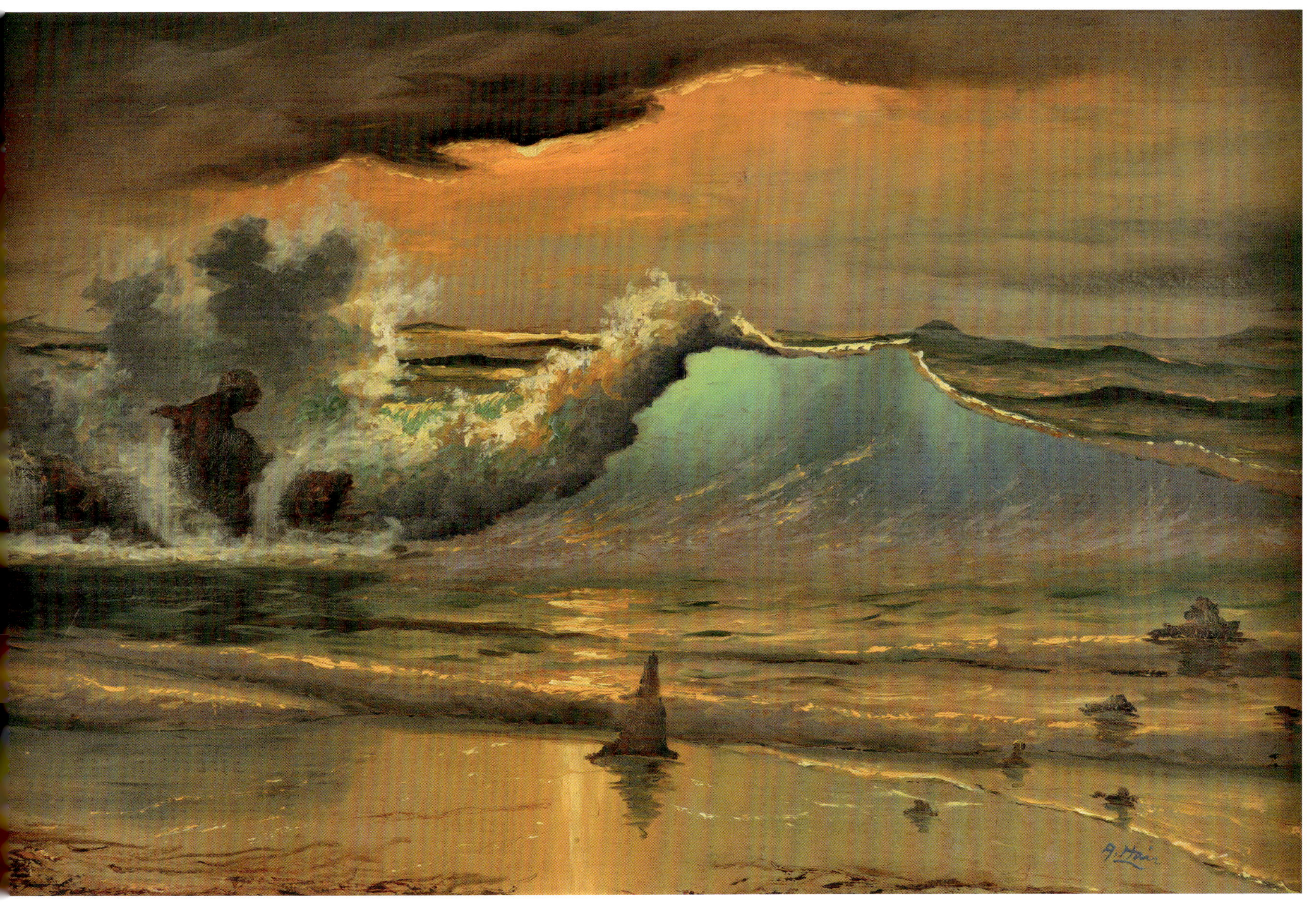

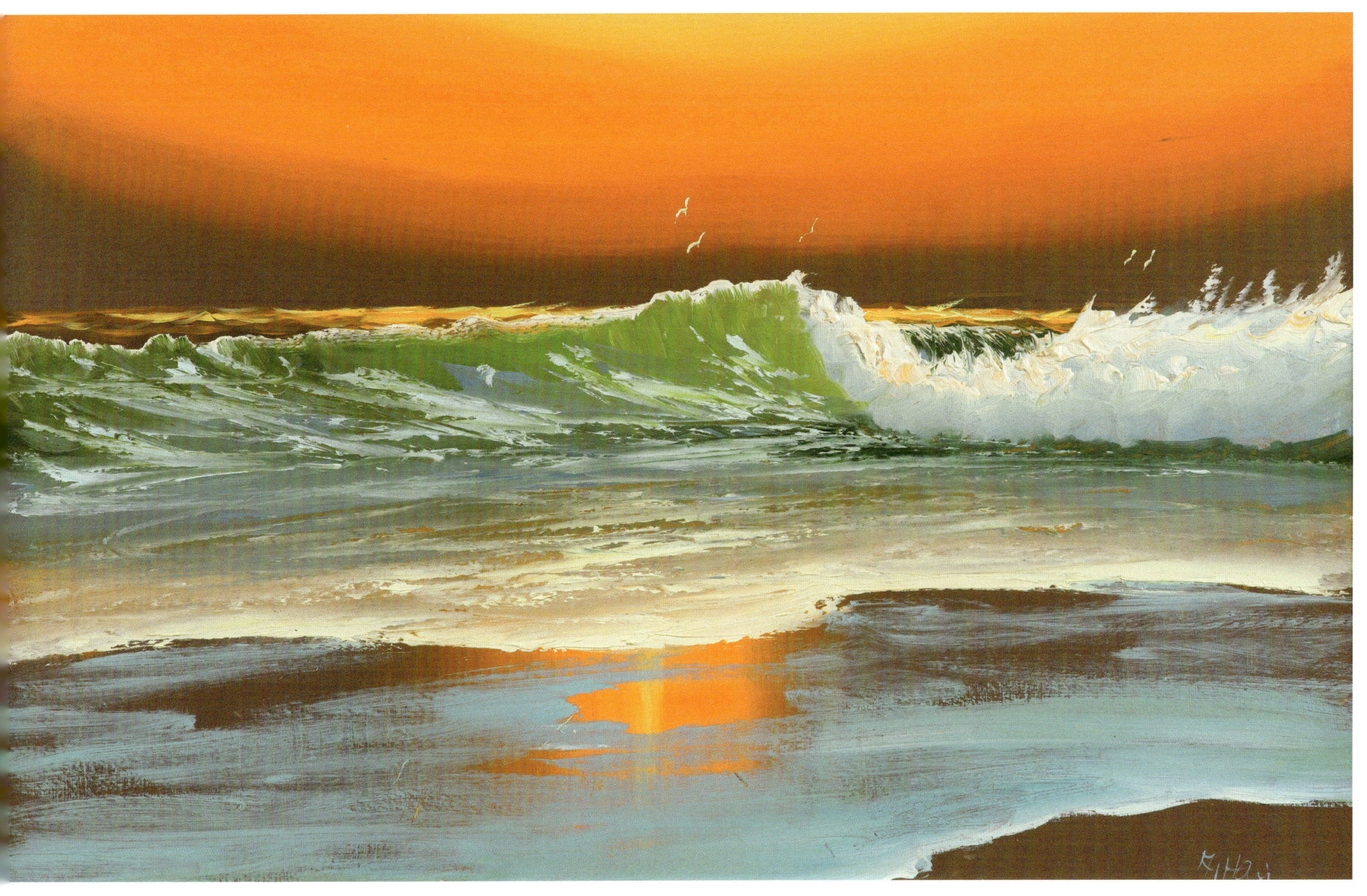

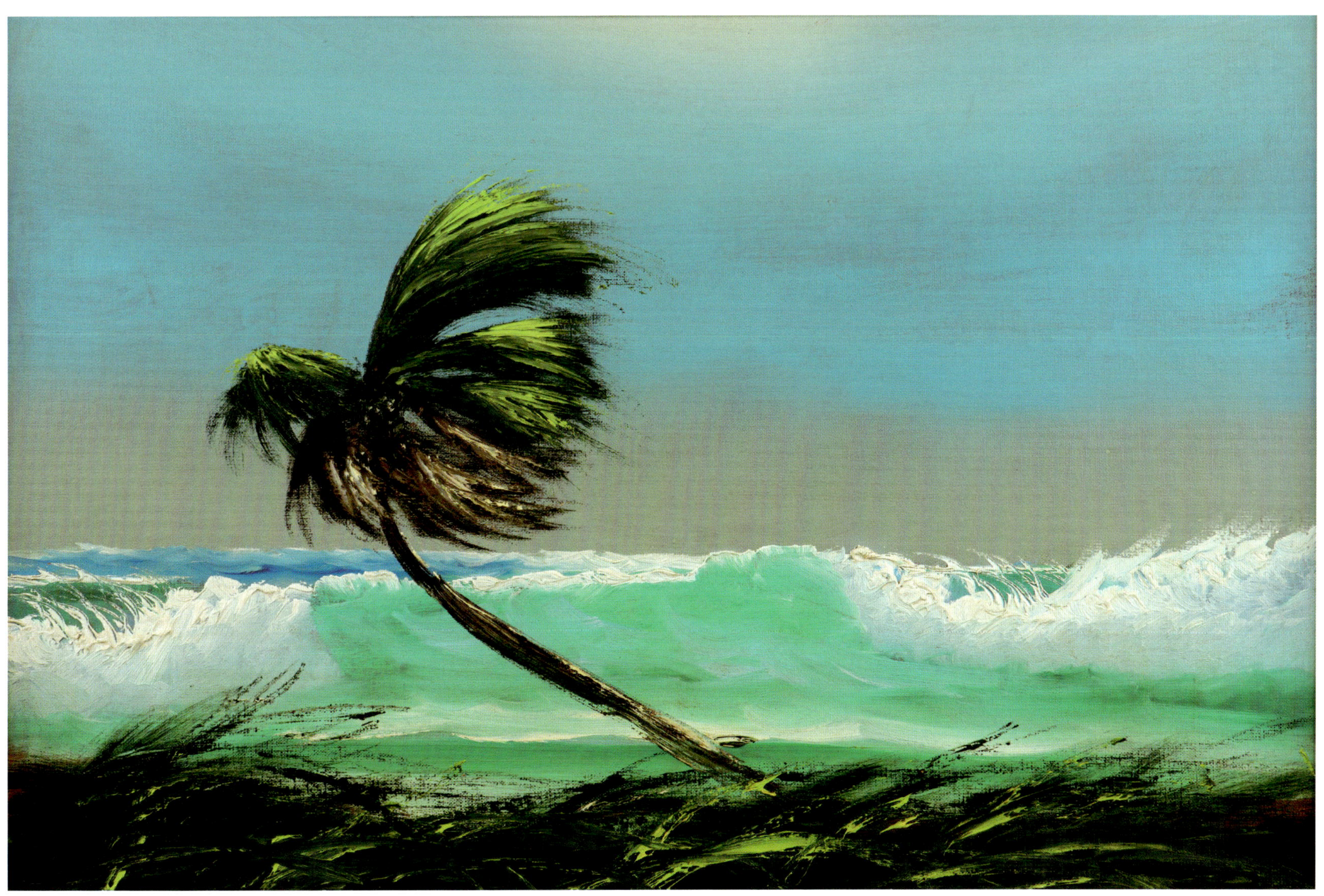

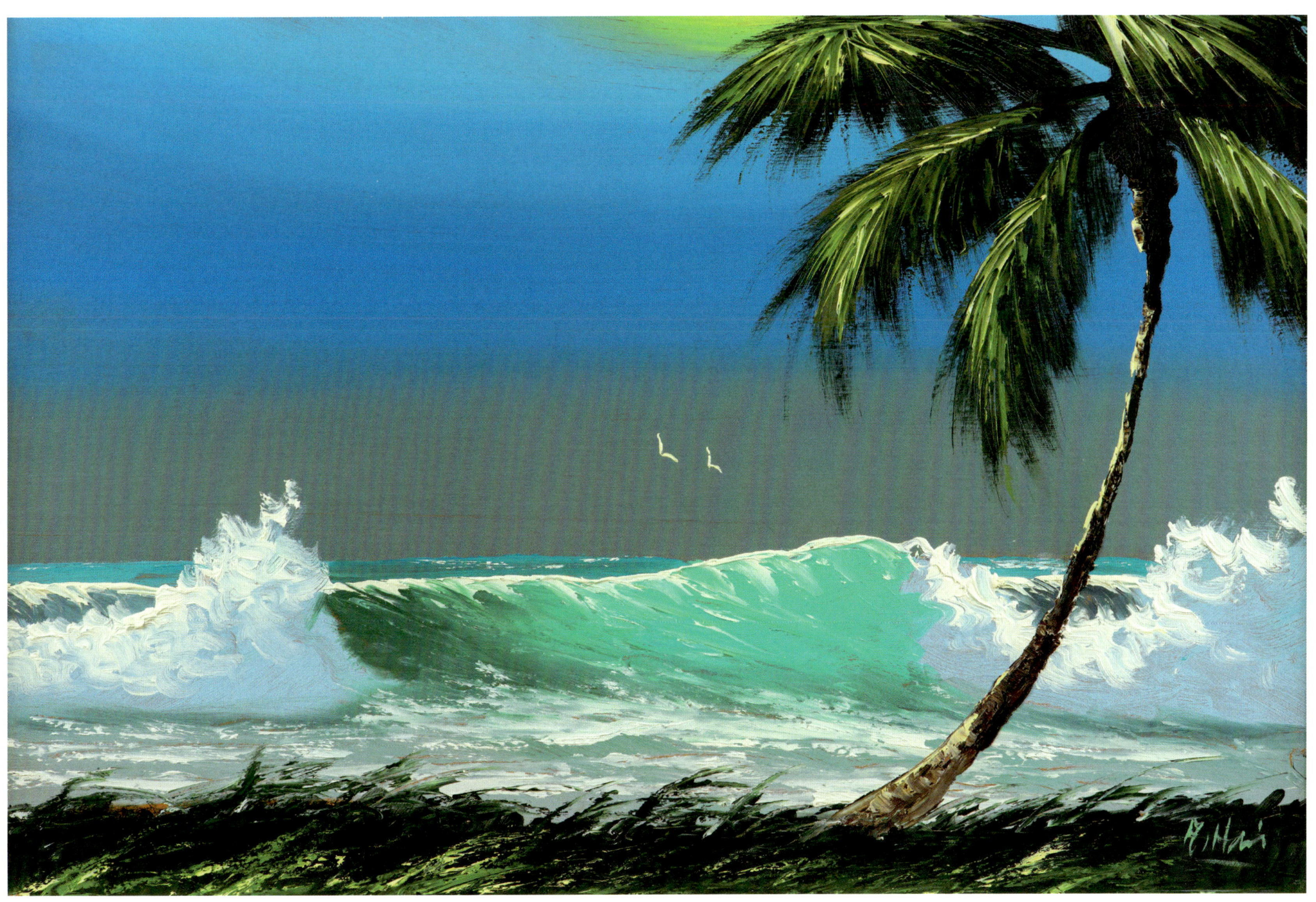

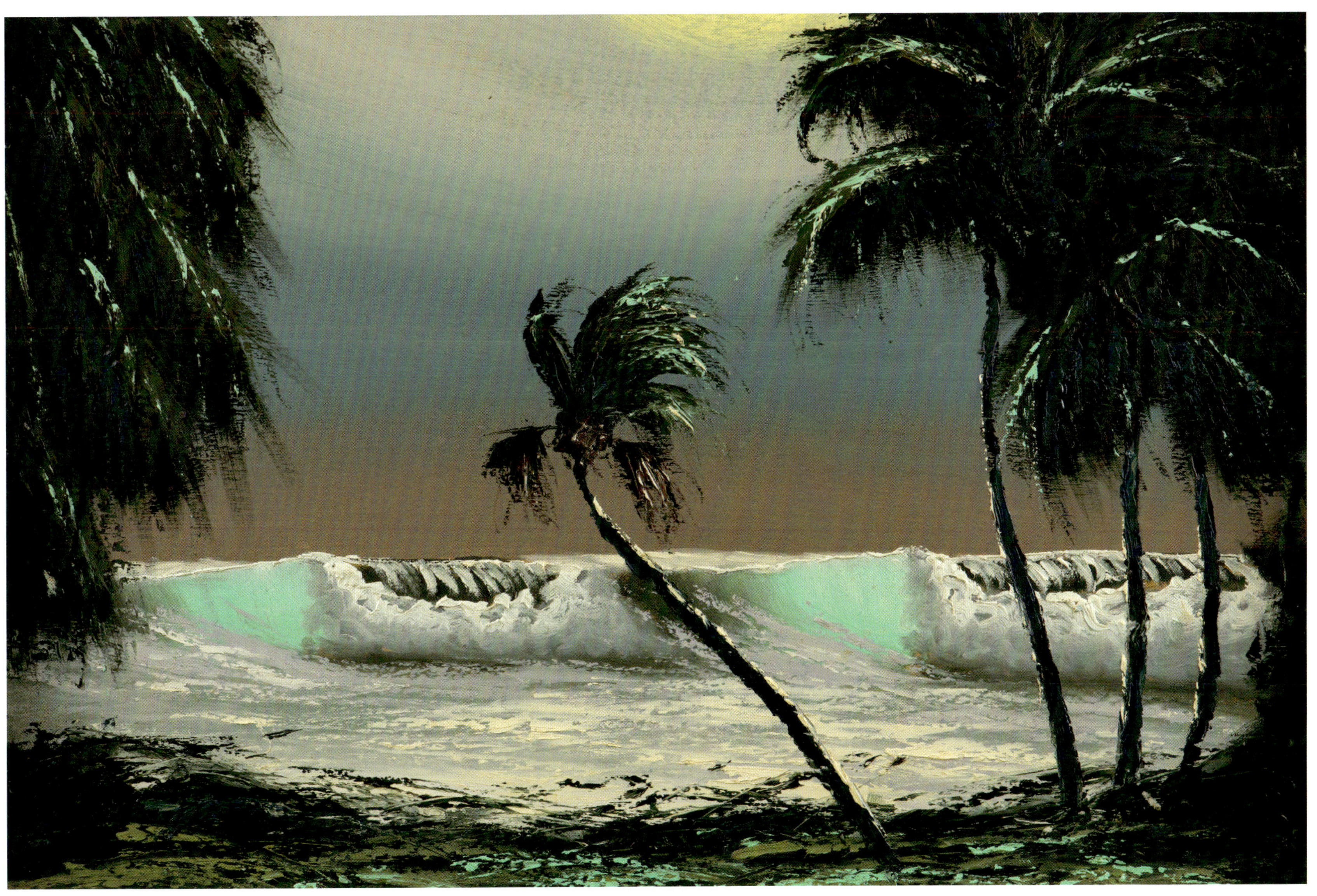

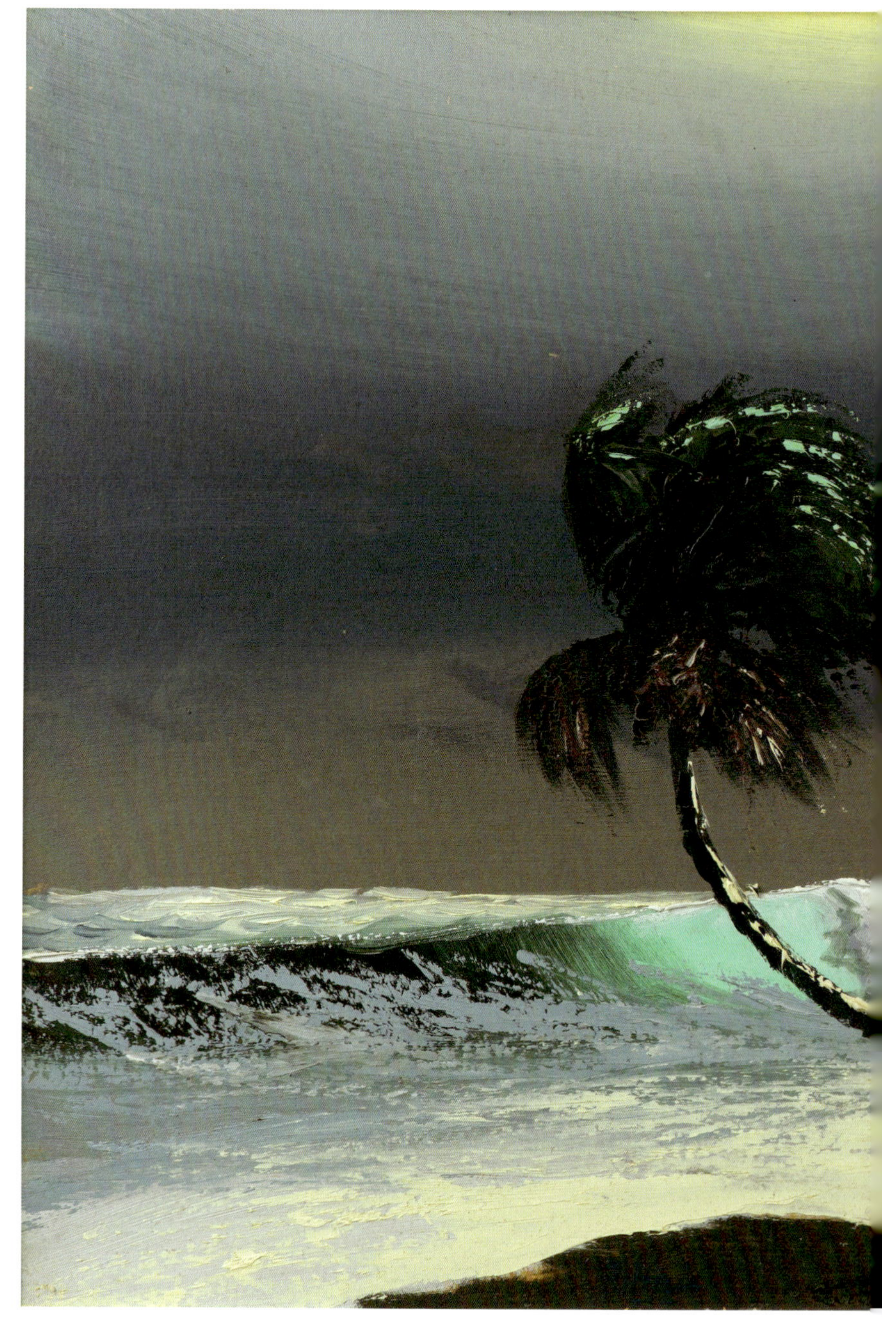

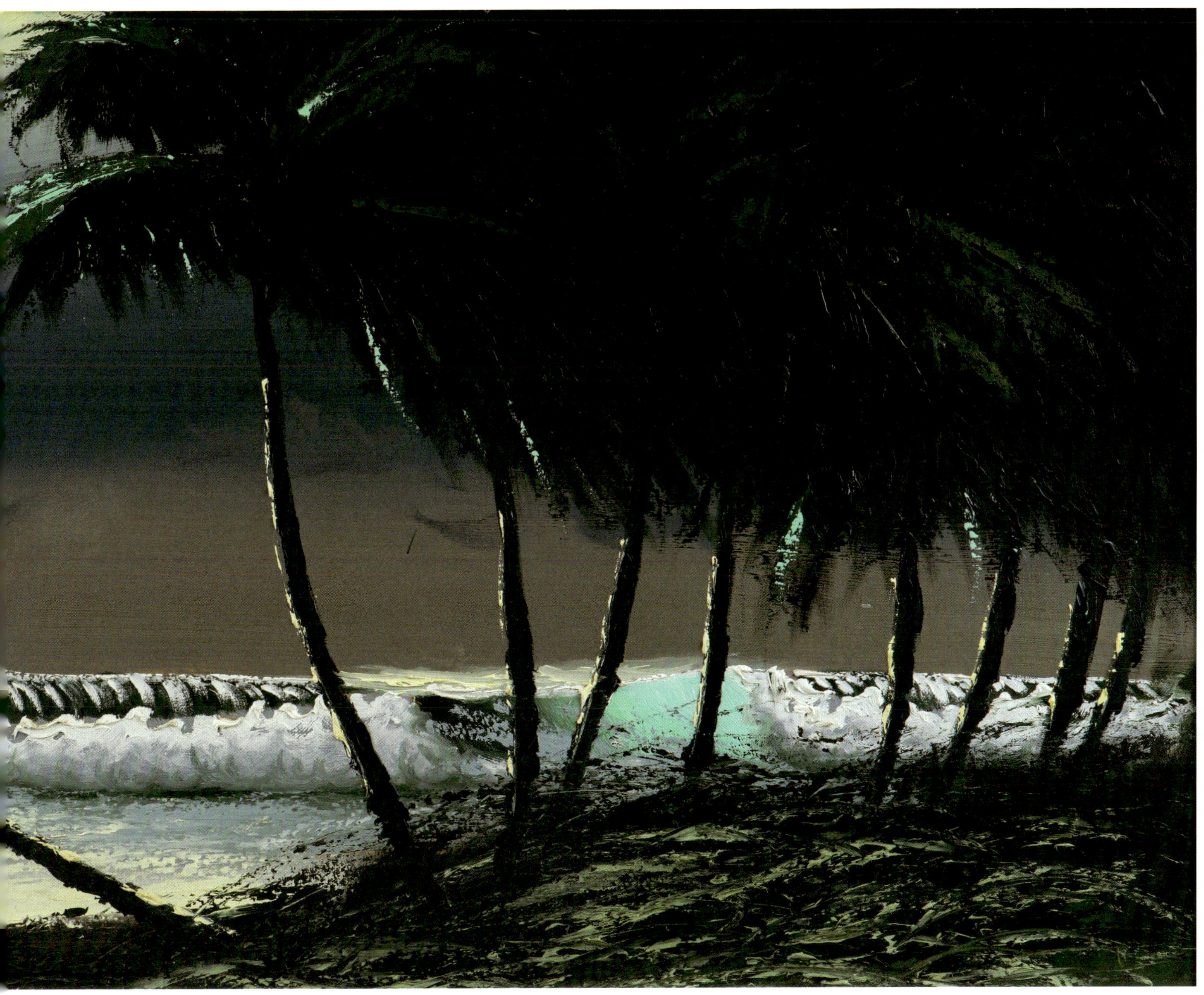

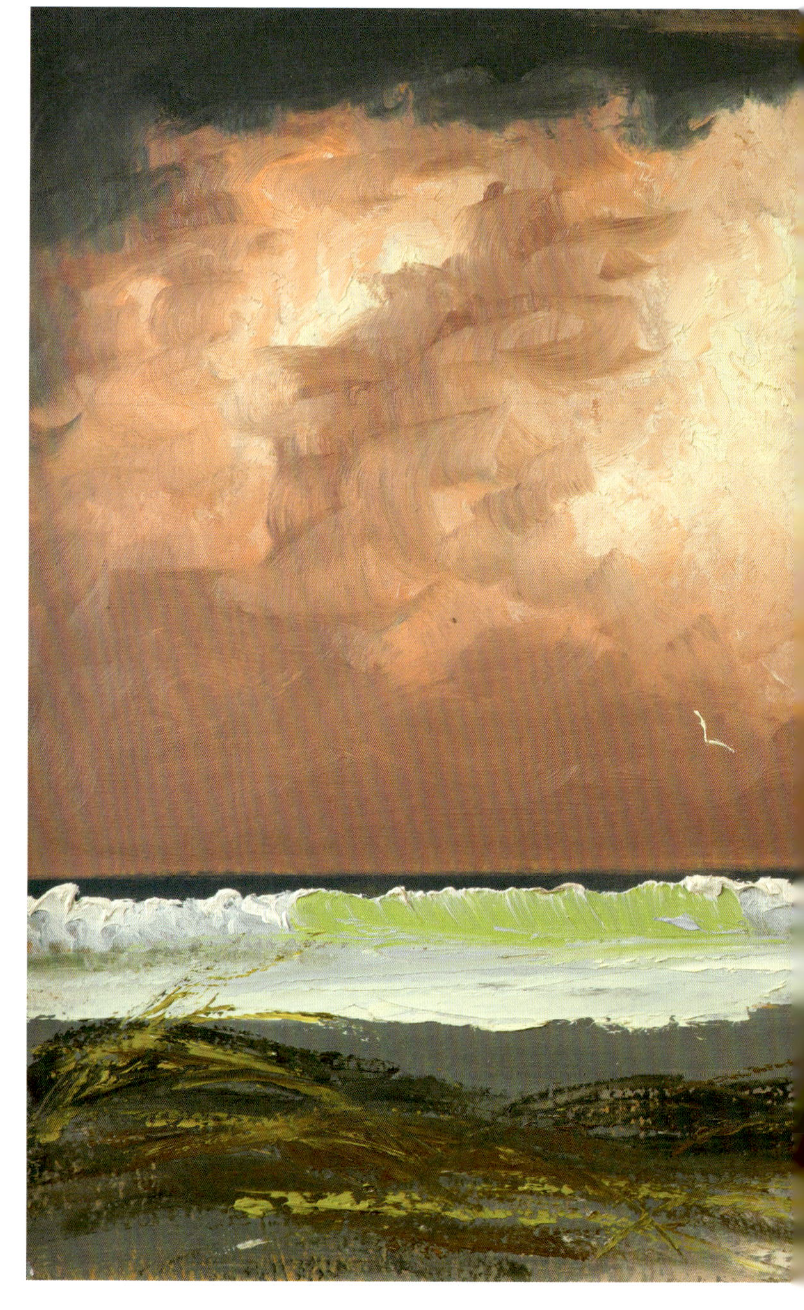

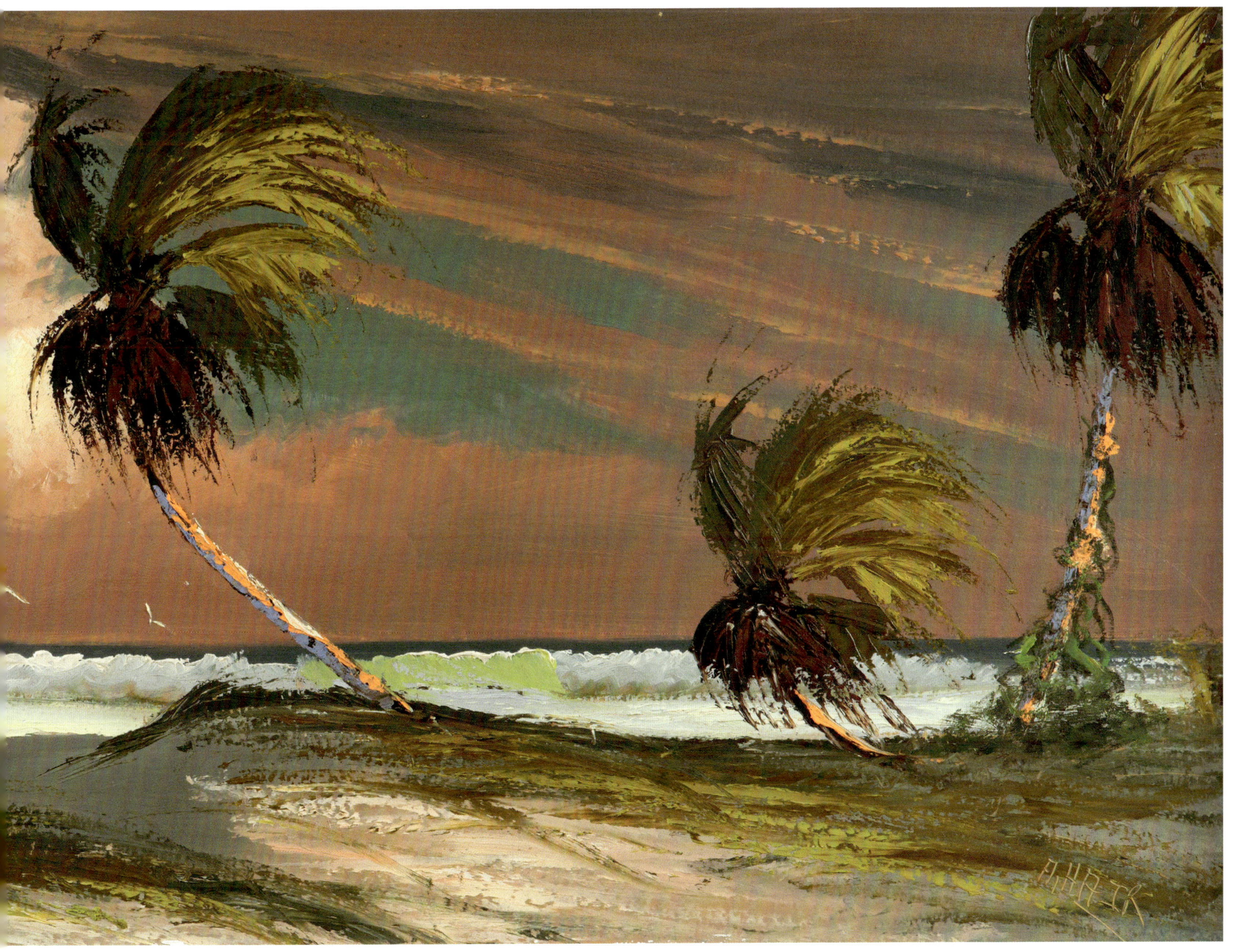

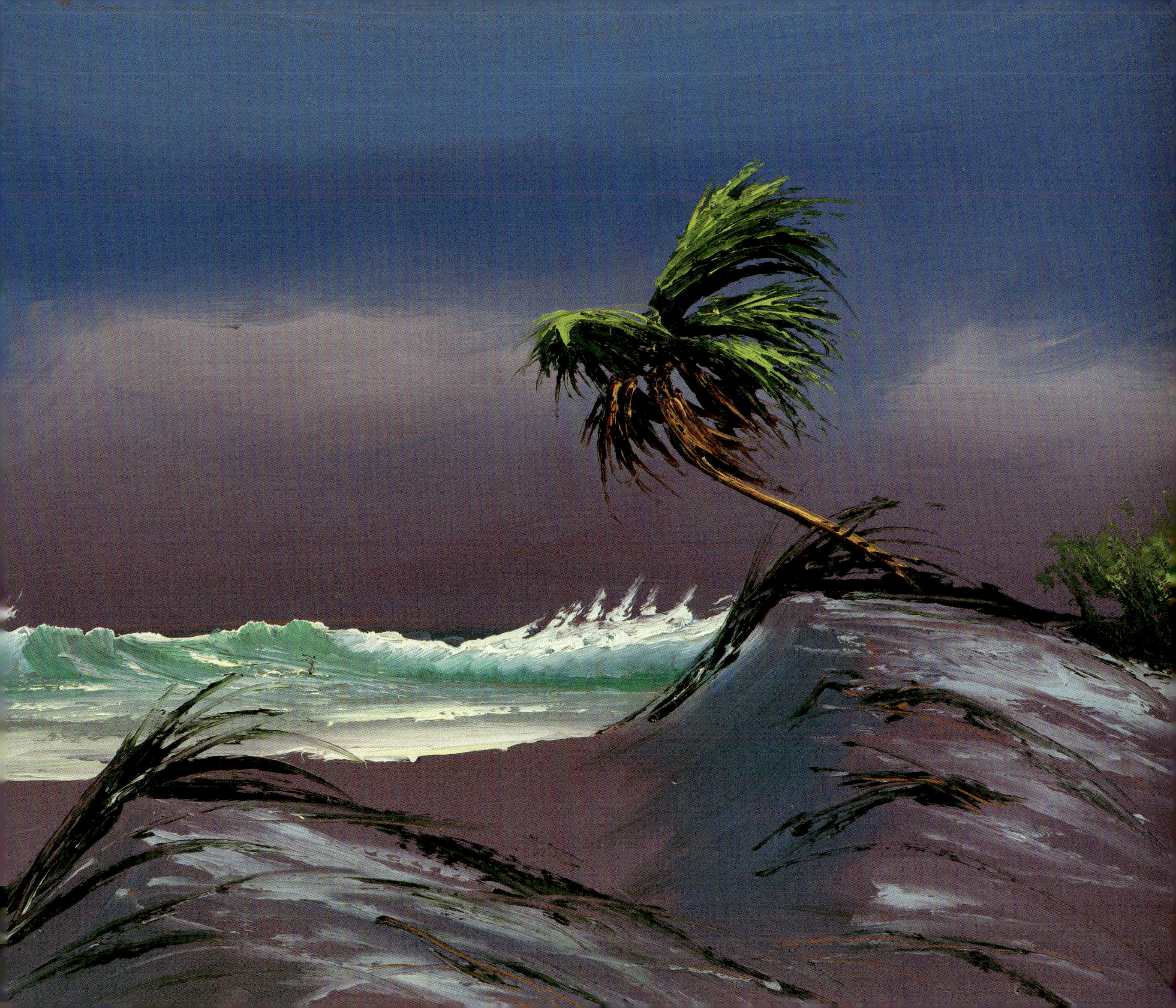

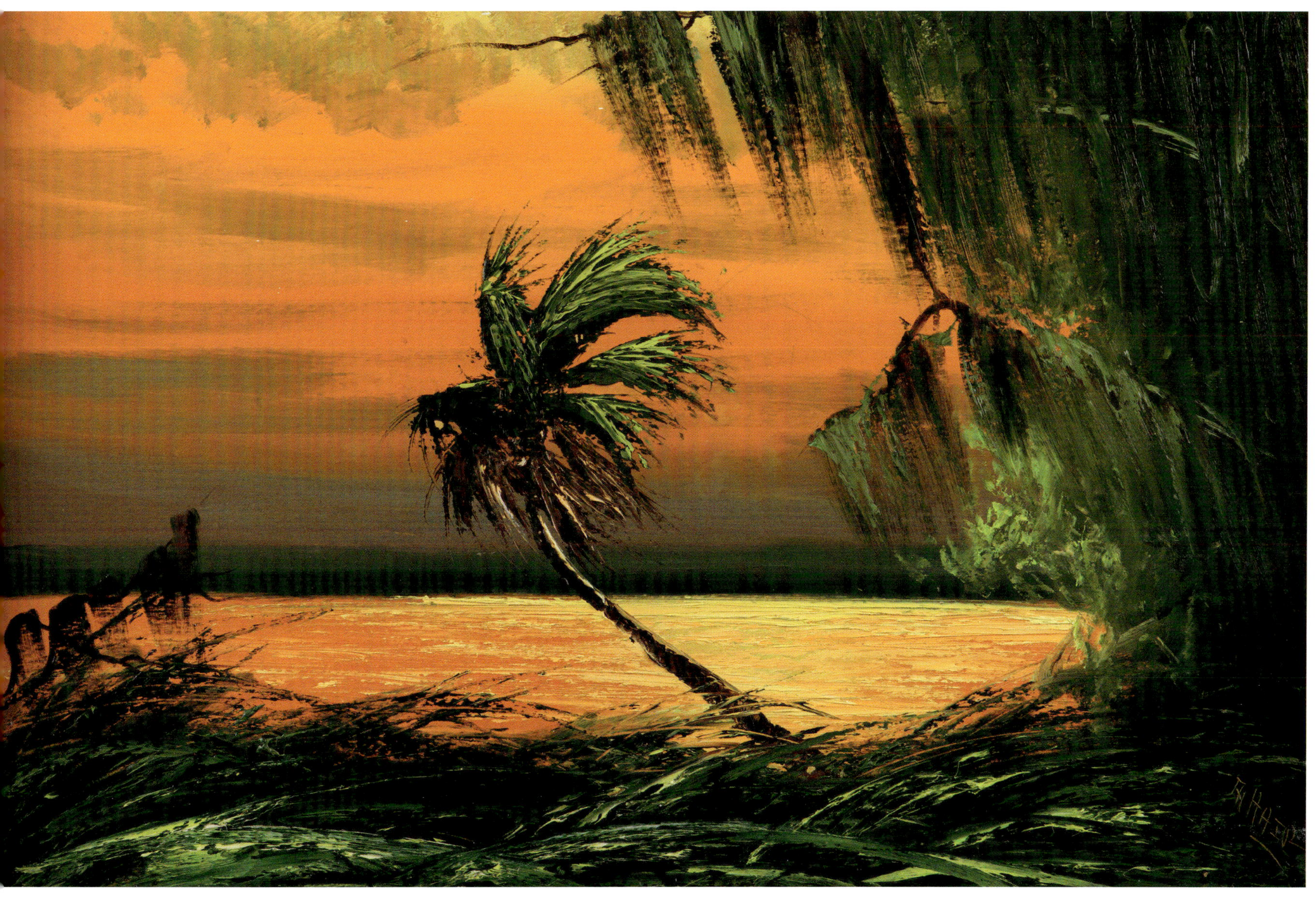

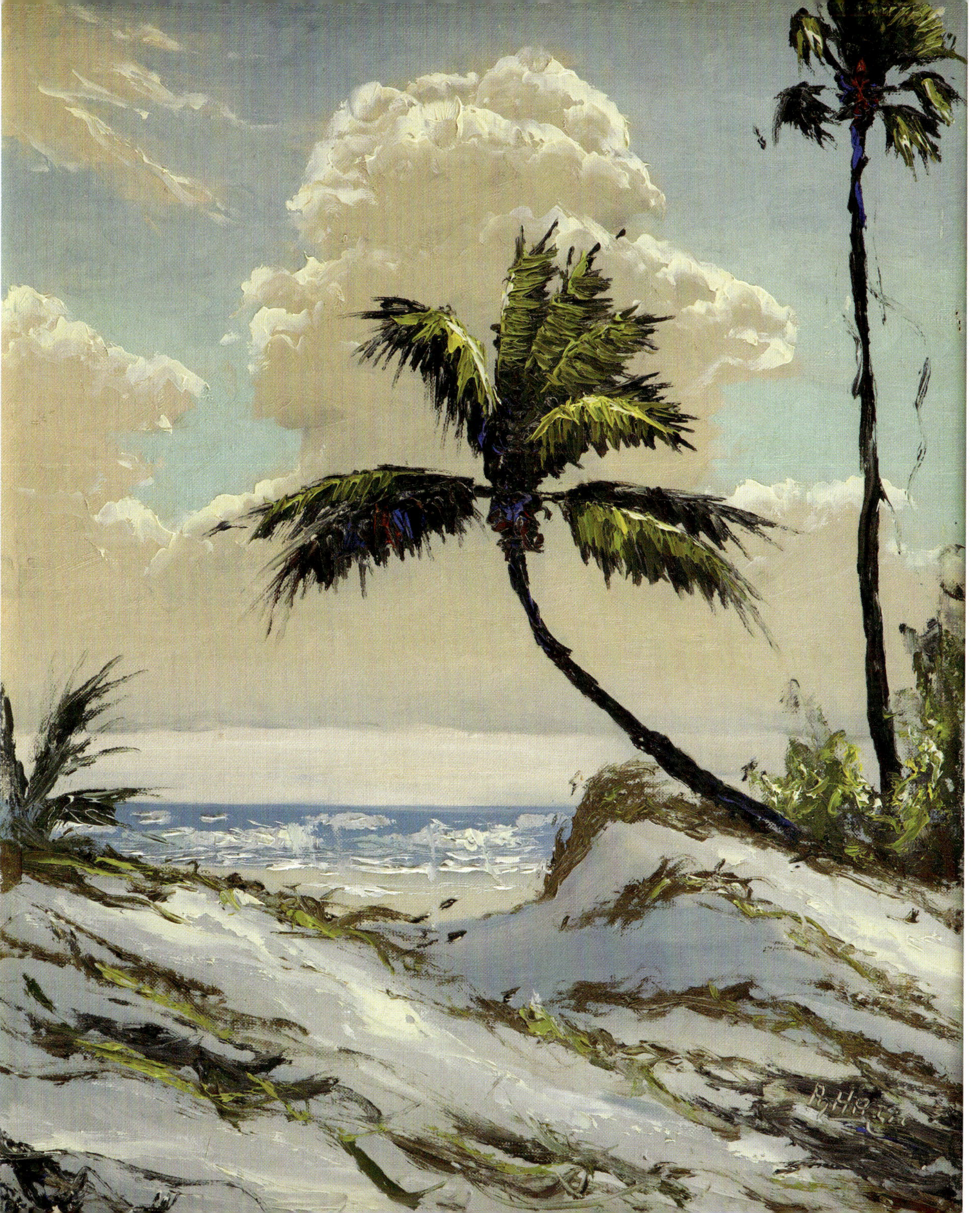

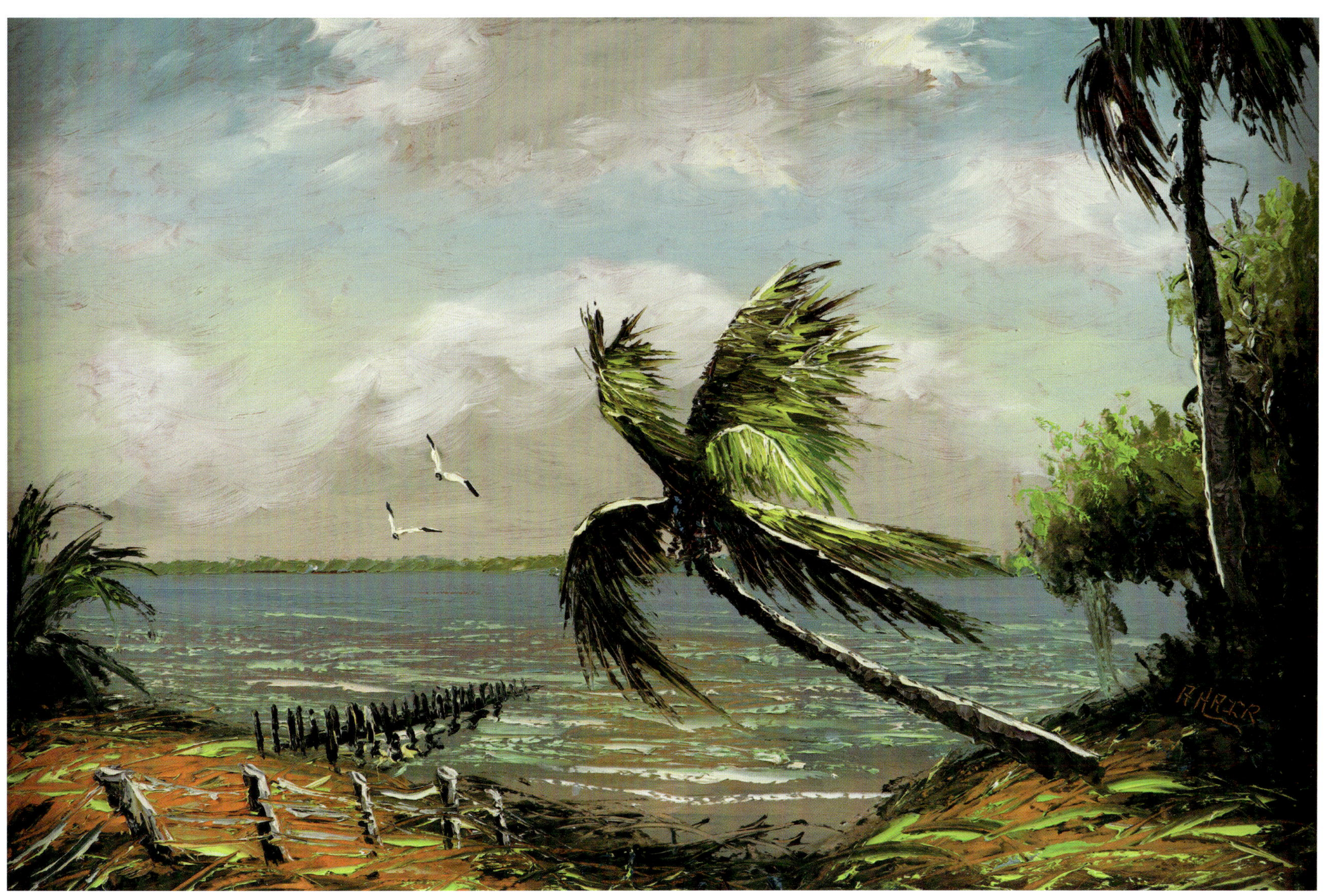

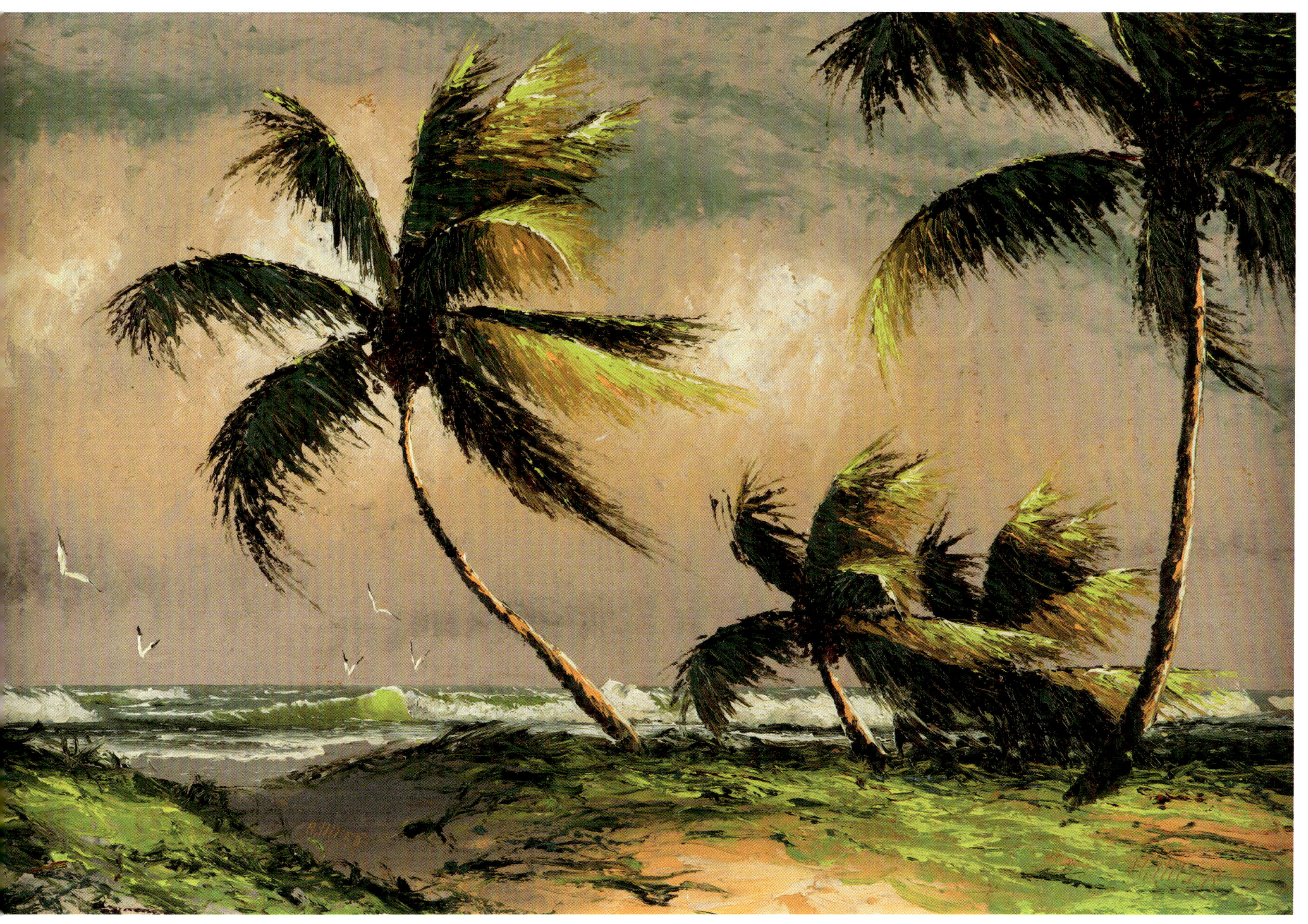

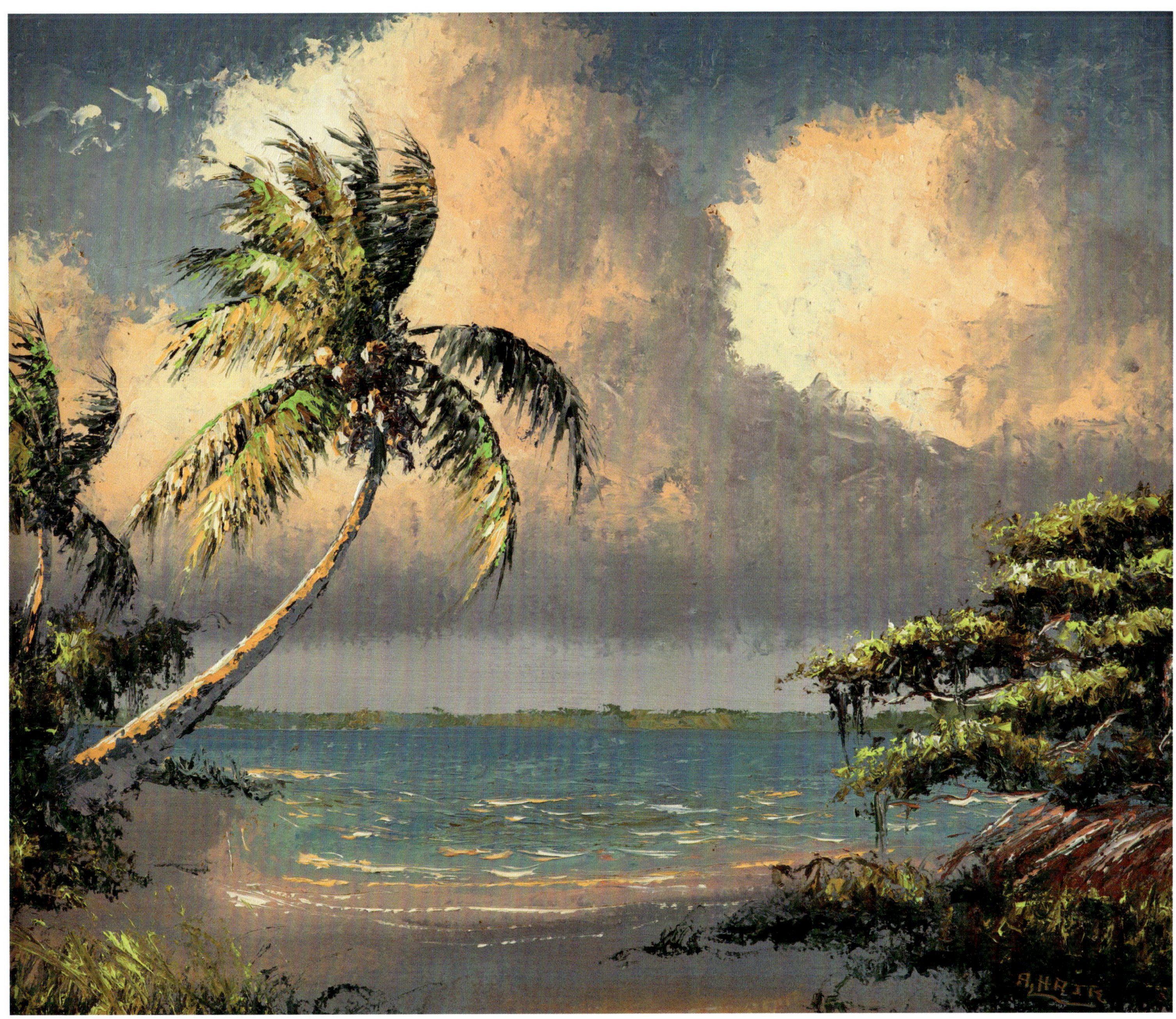
A.HAIR

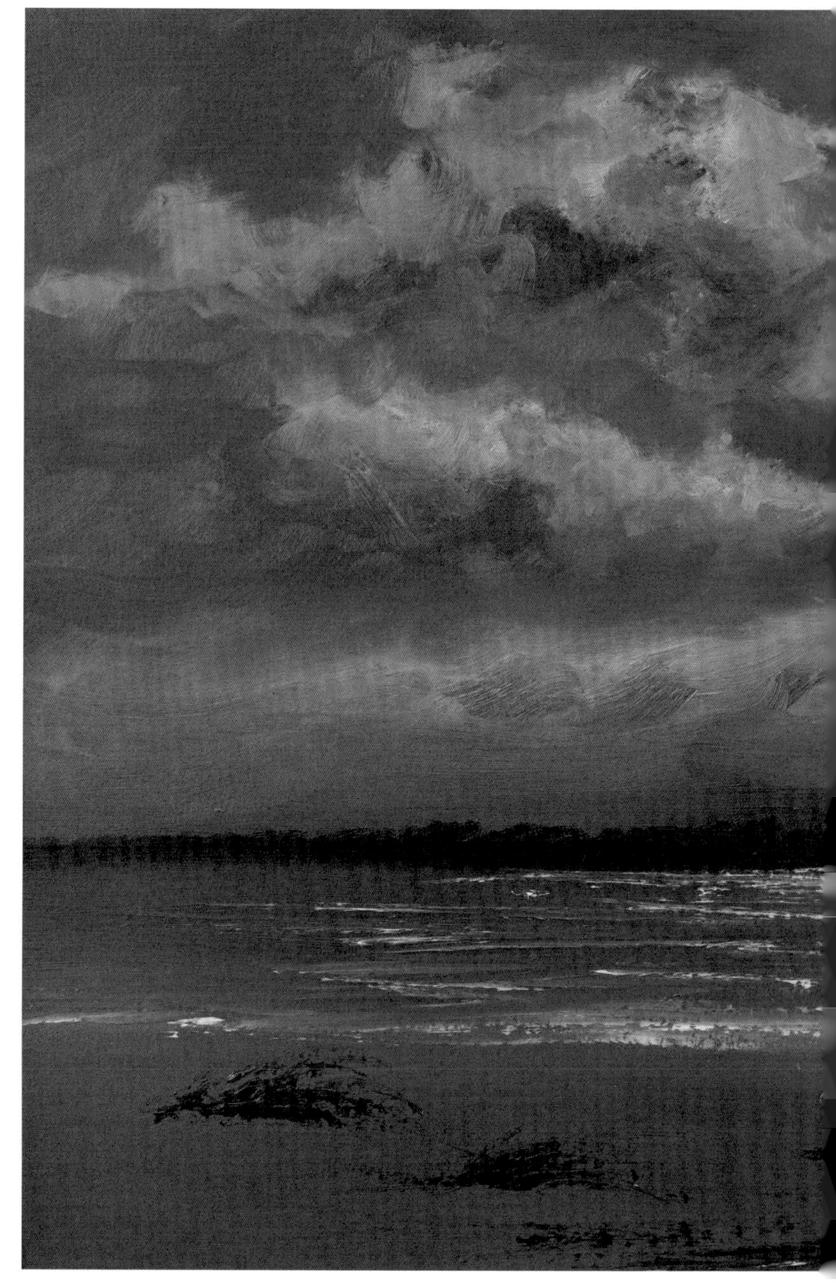

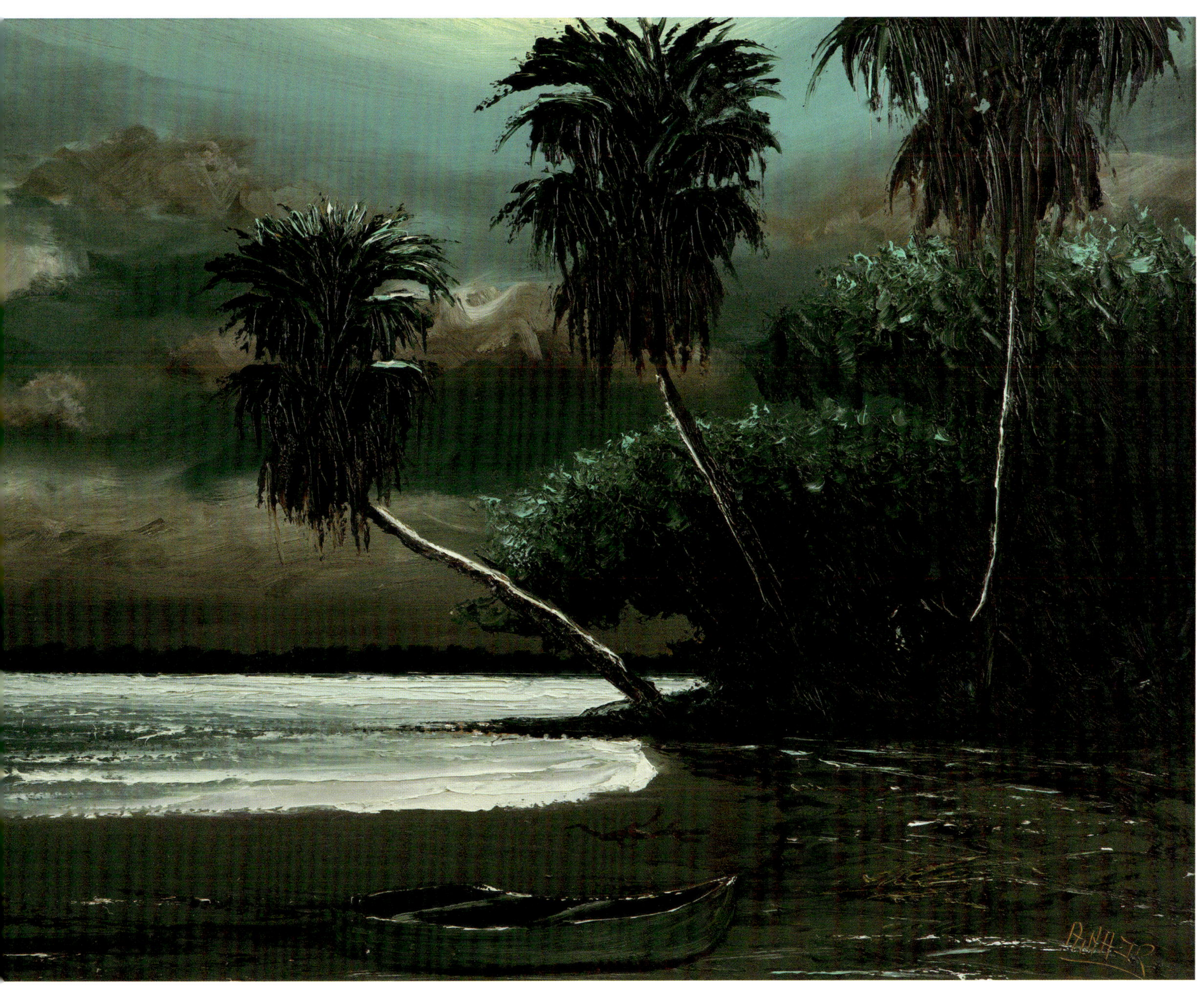

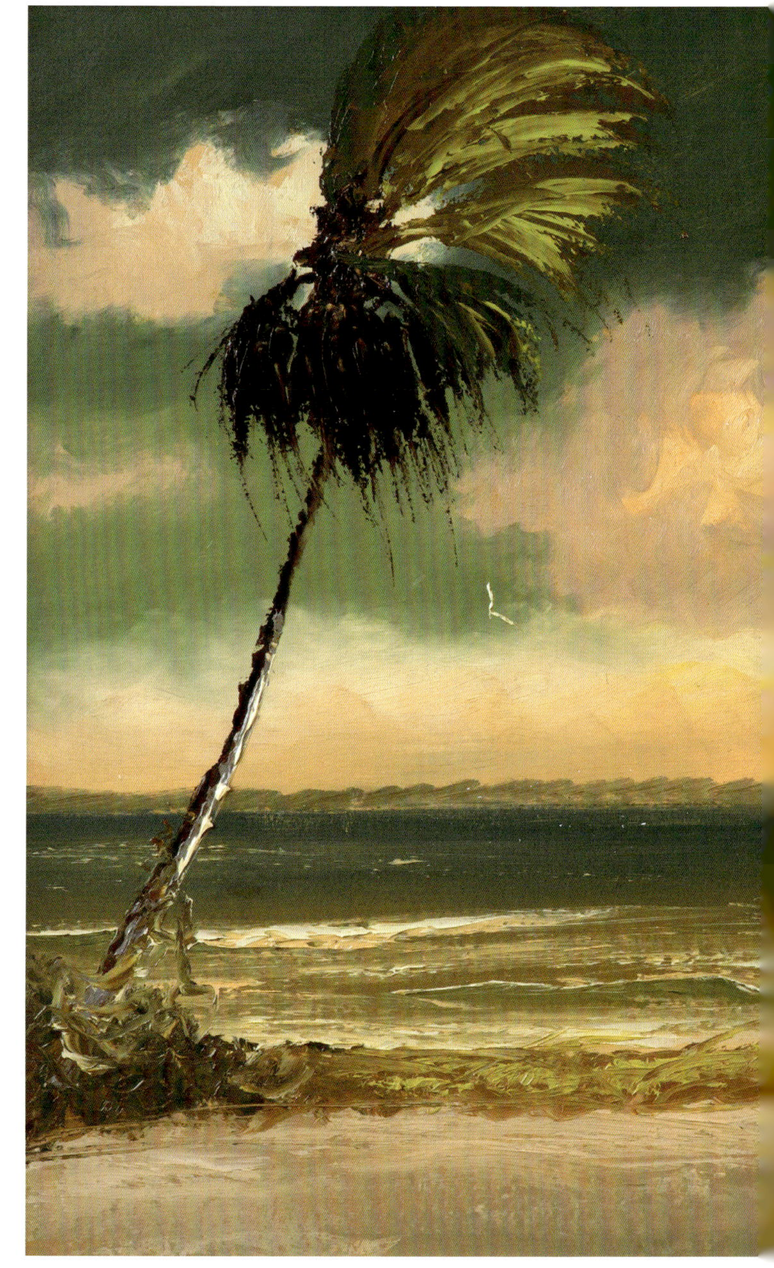

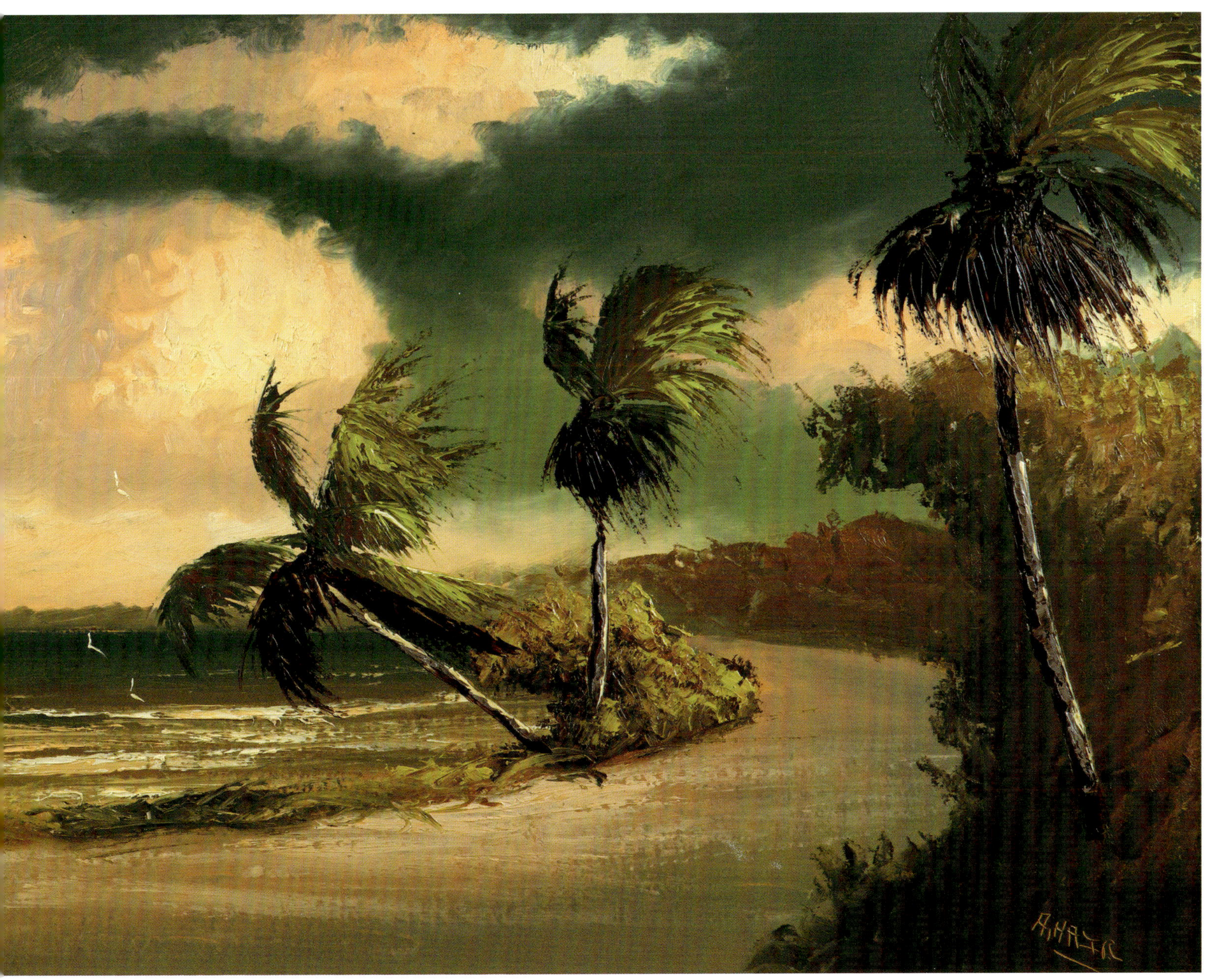
A.HAIR

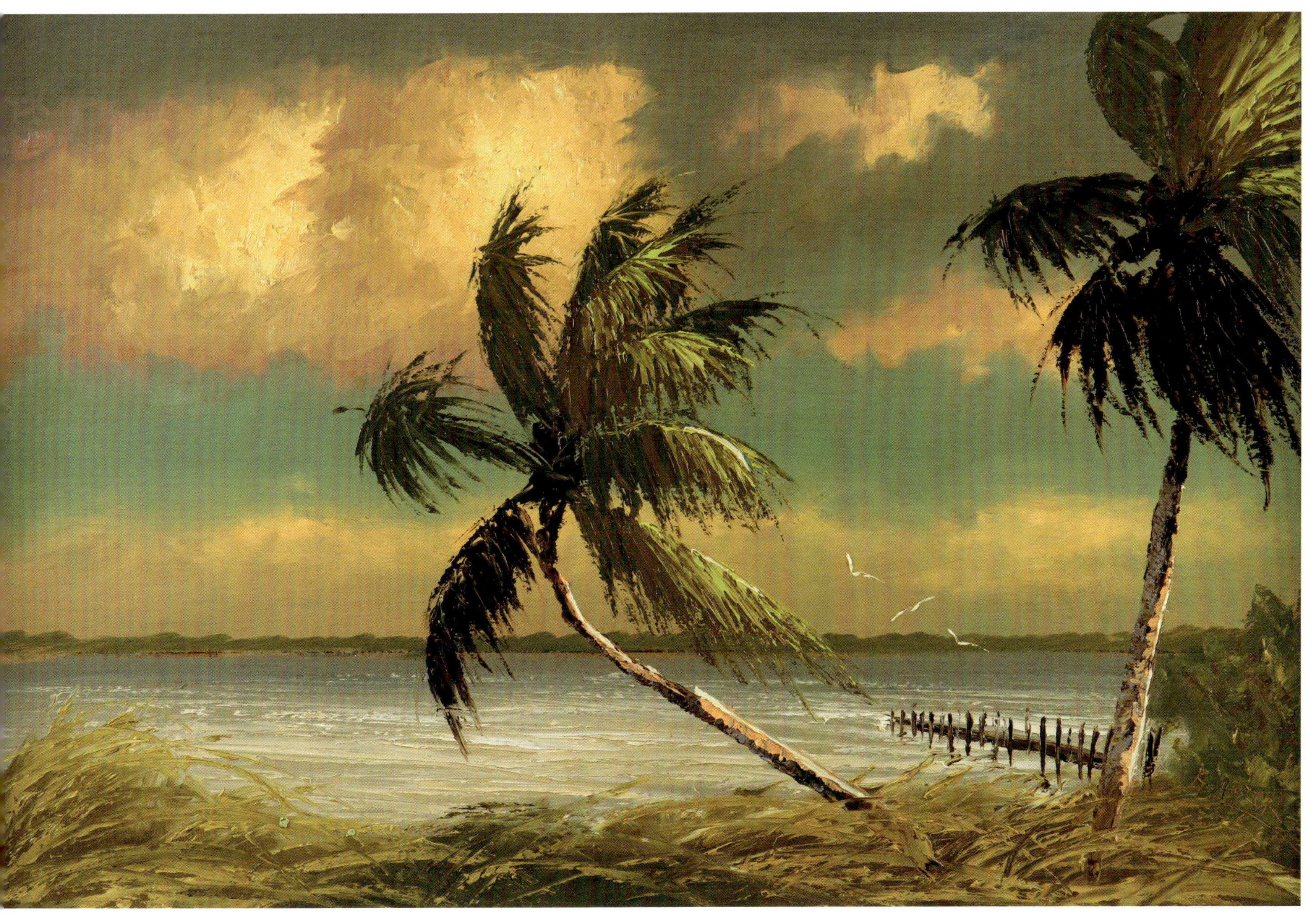

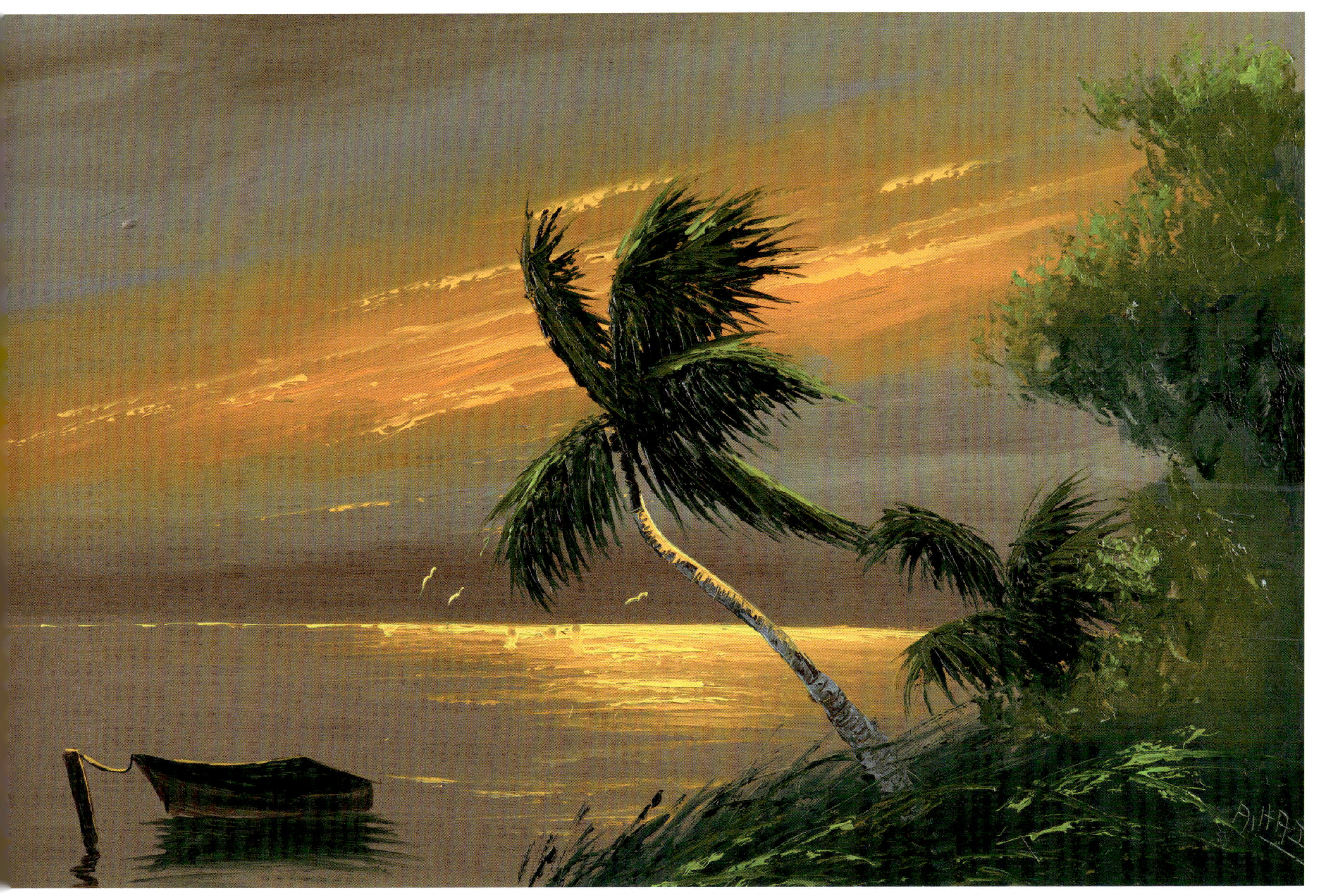

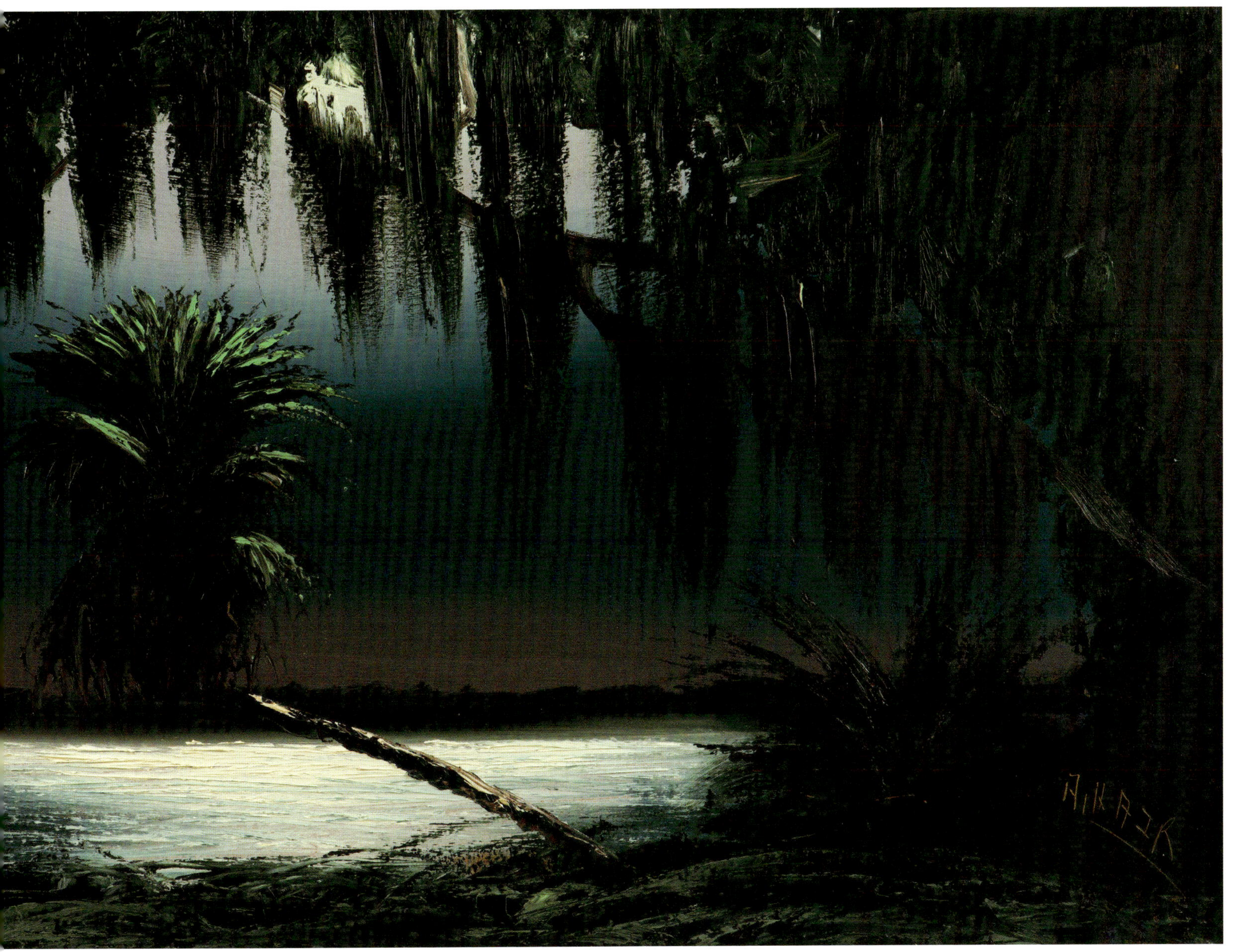

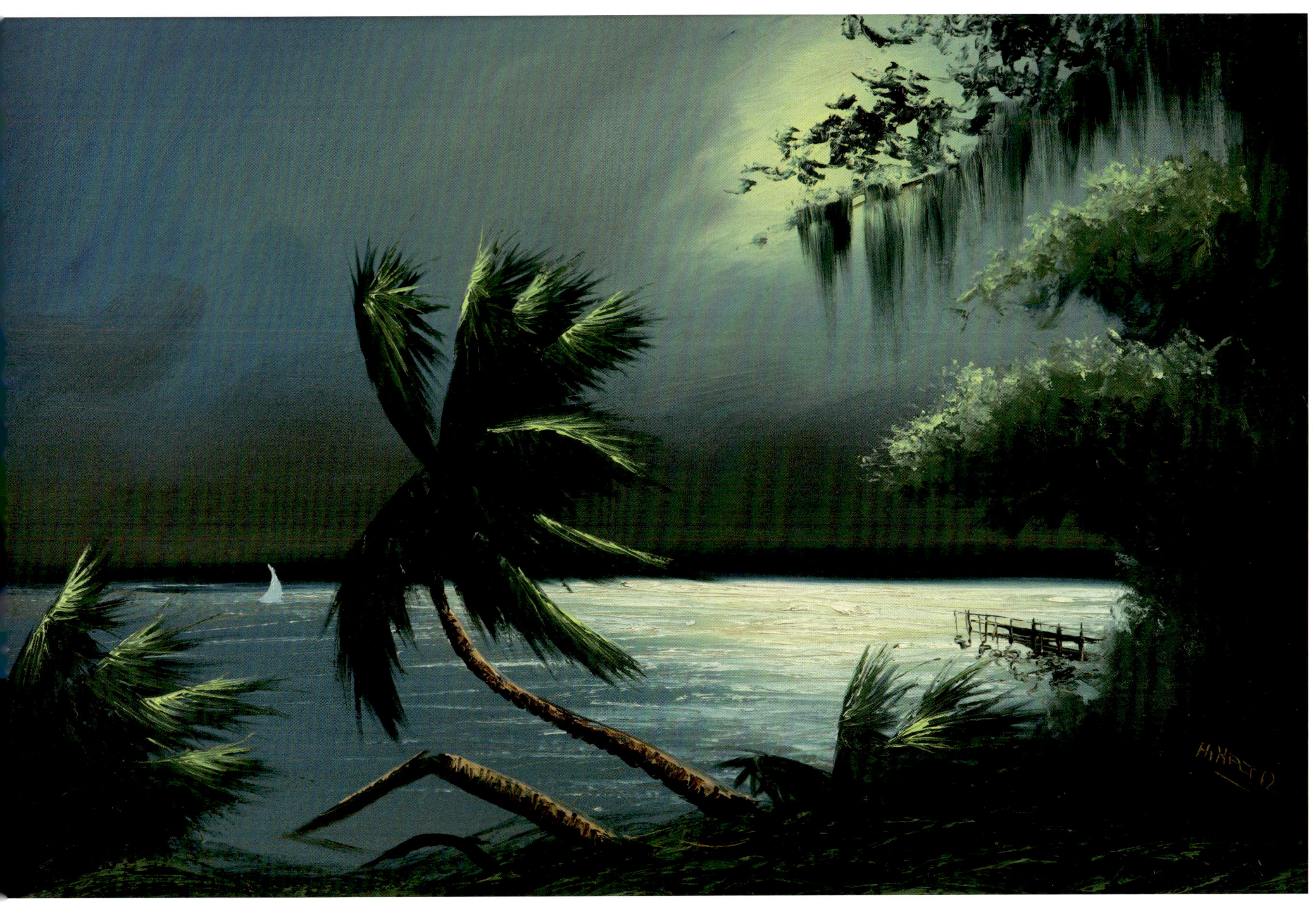

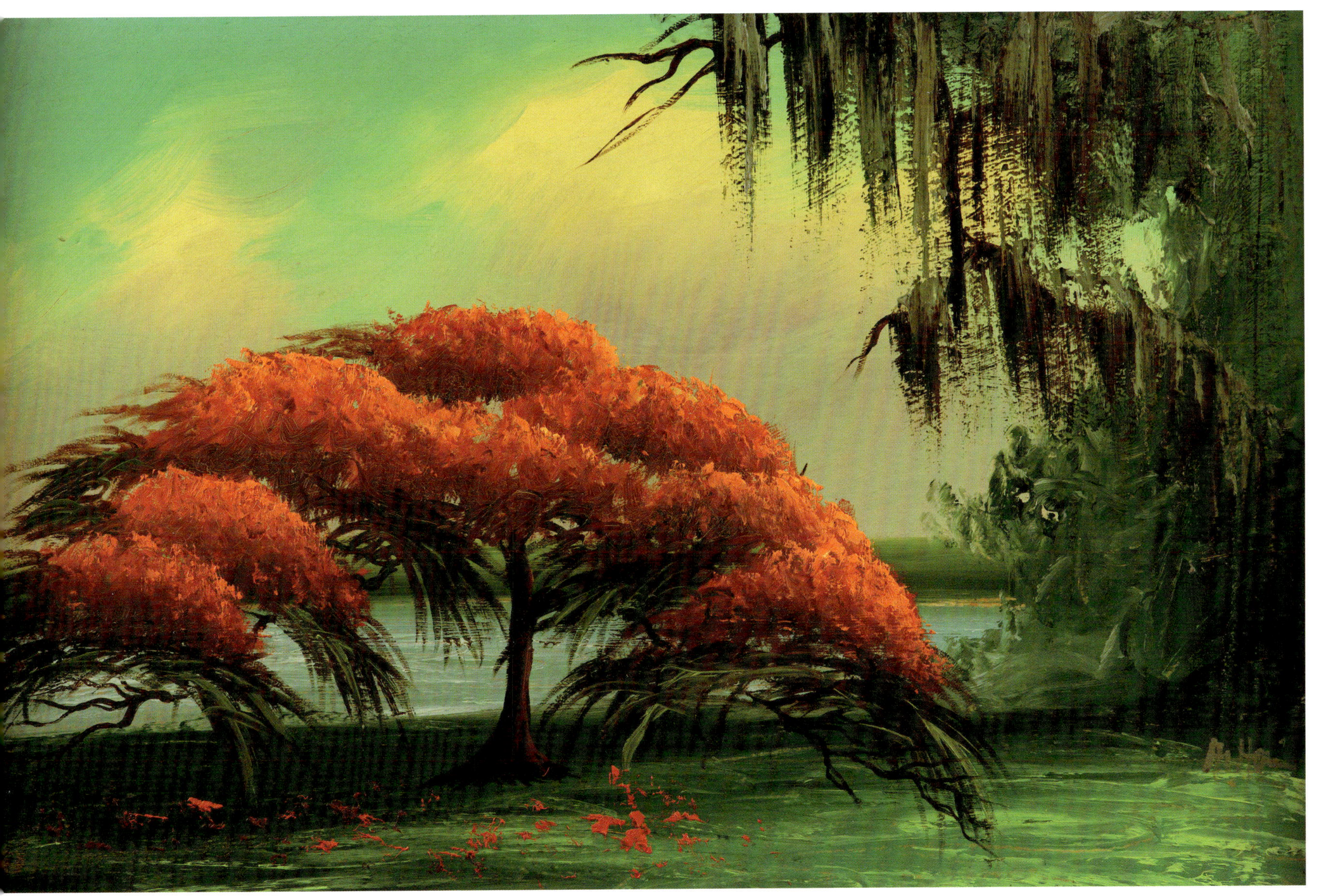

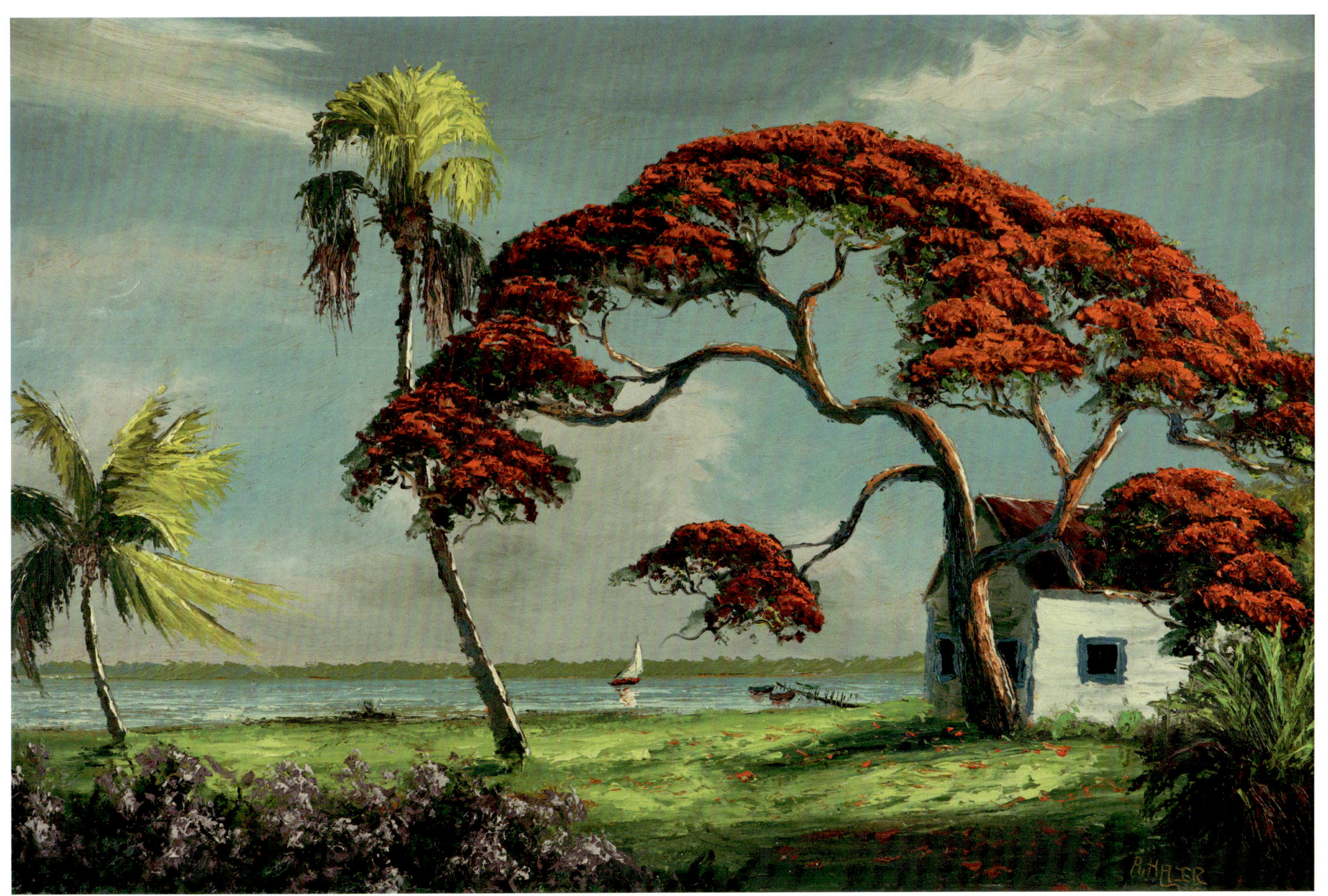

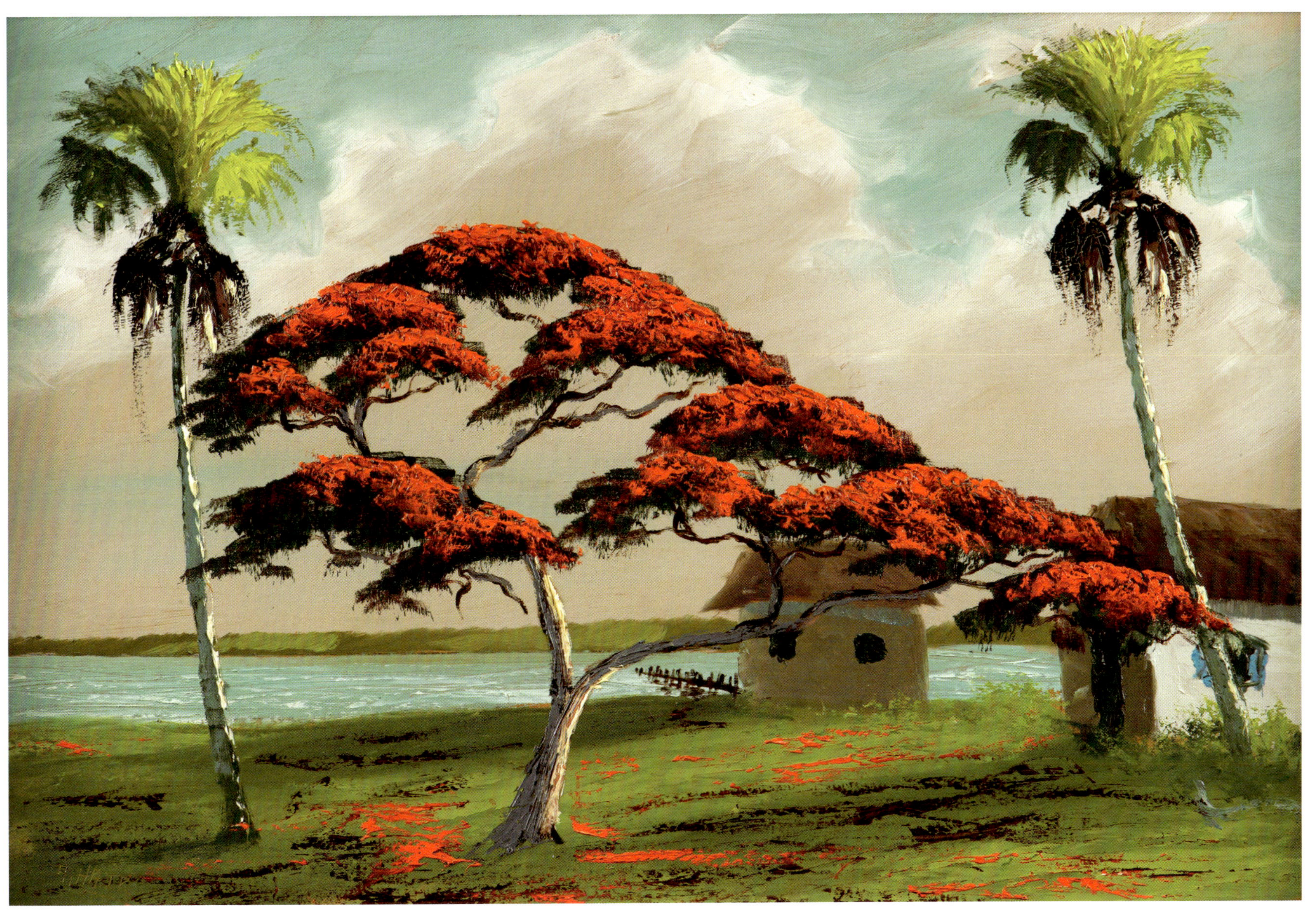

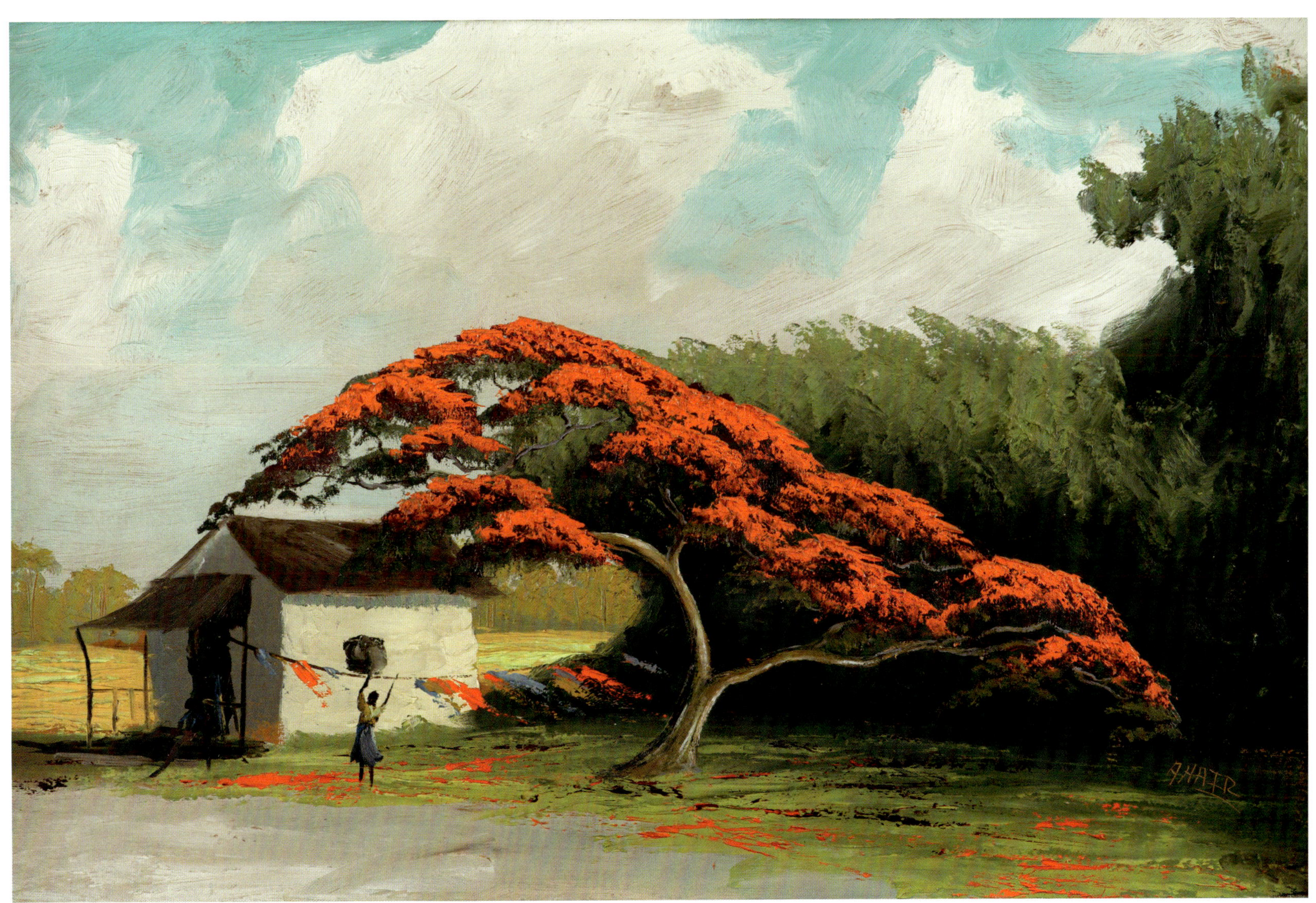
AHAIR

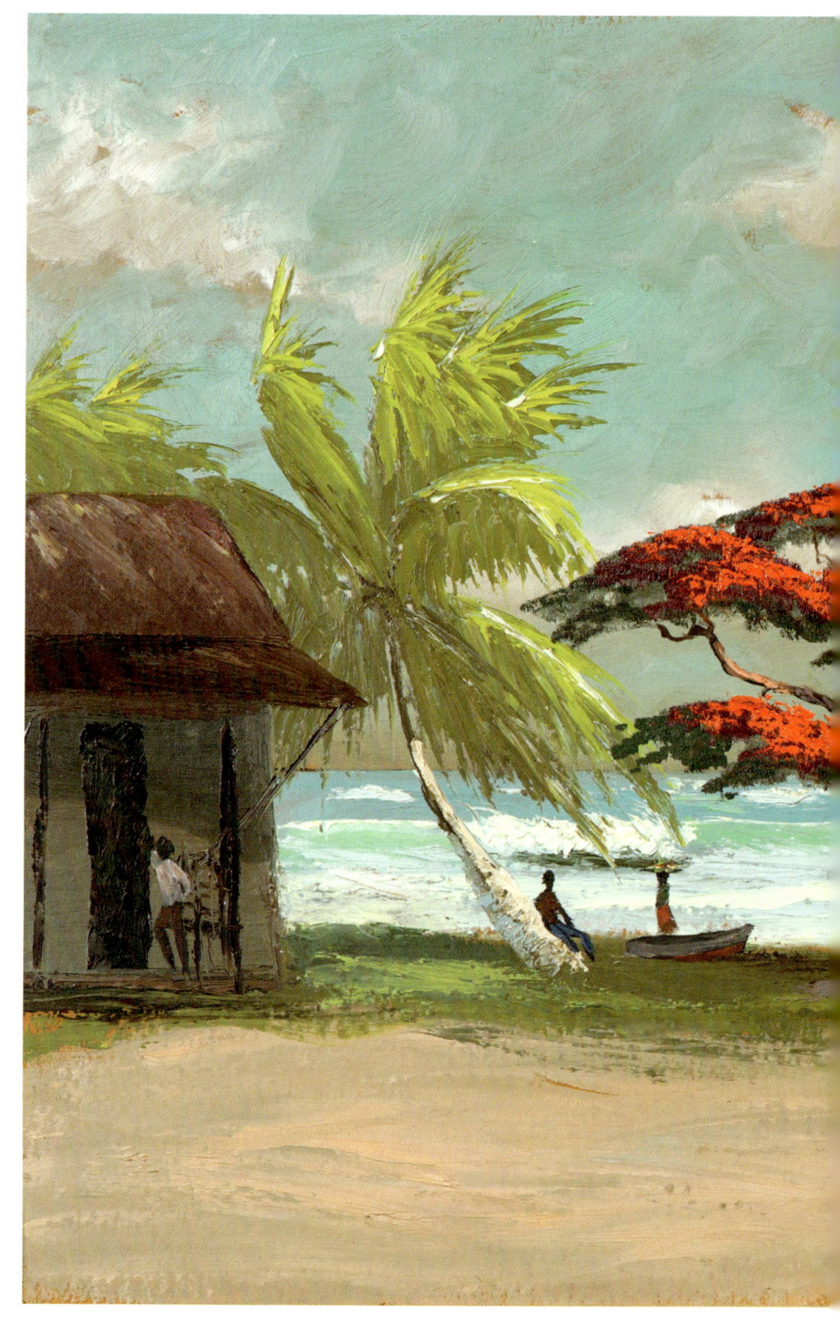

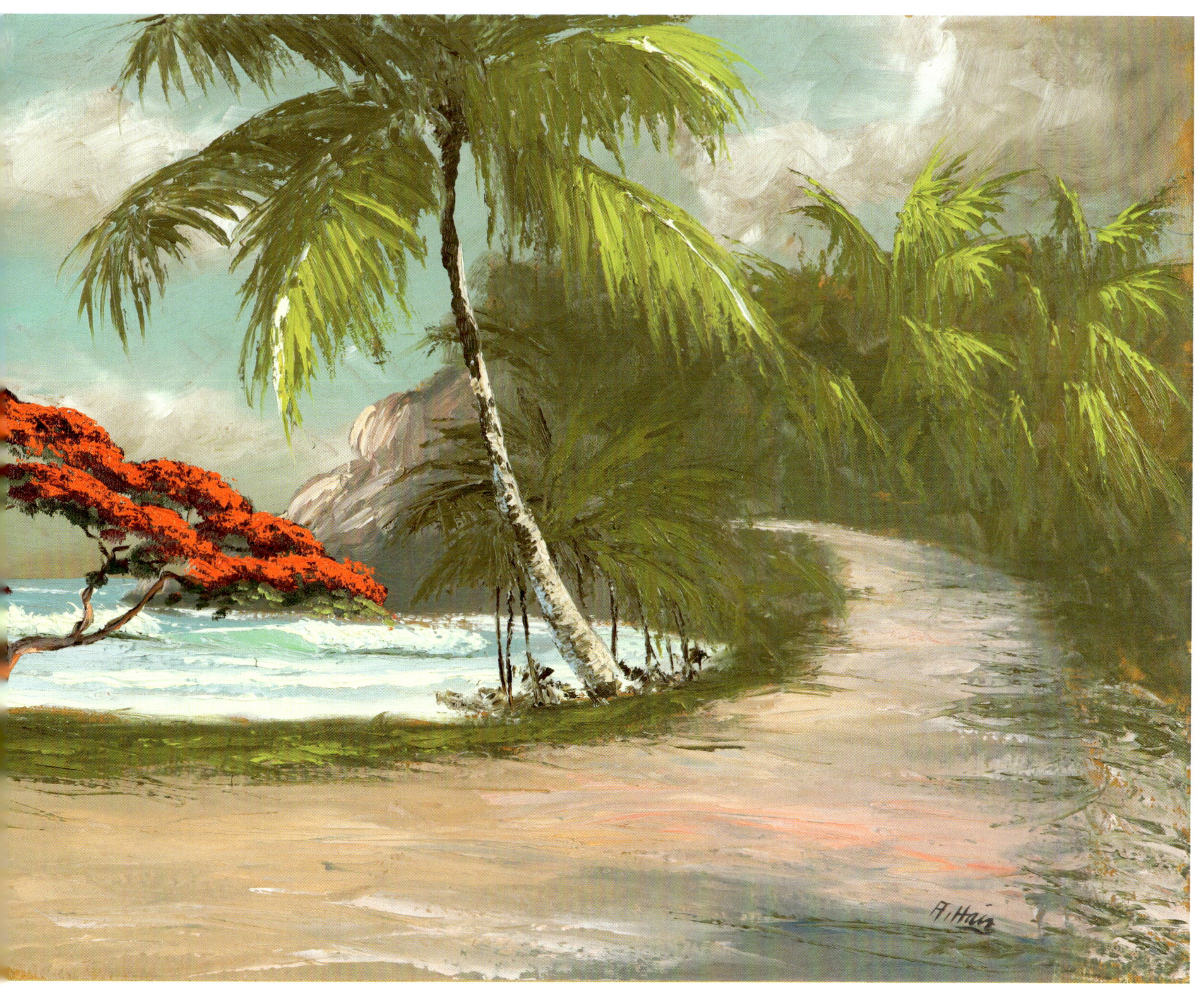

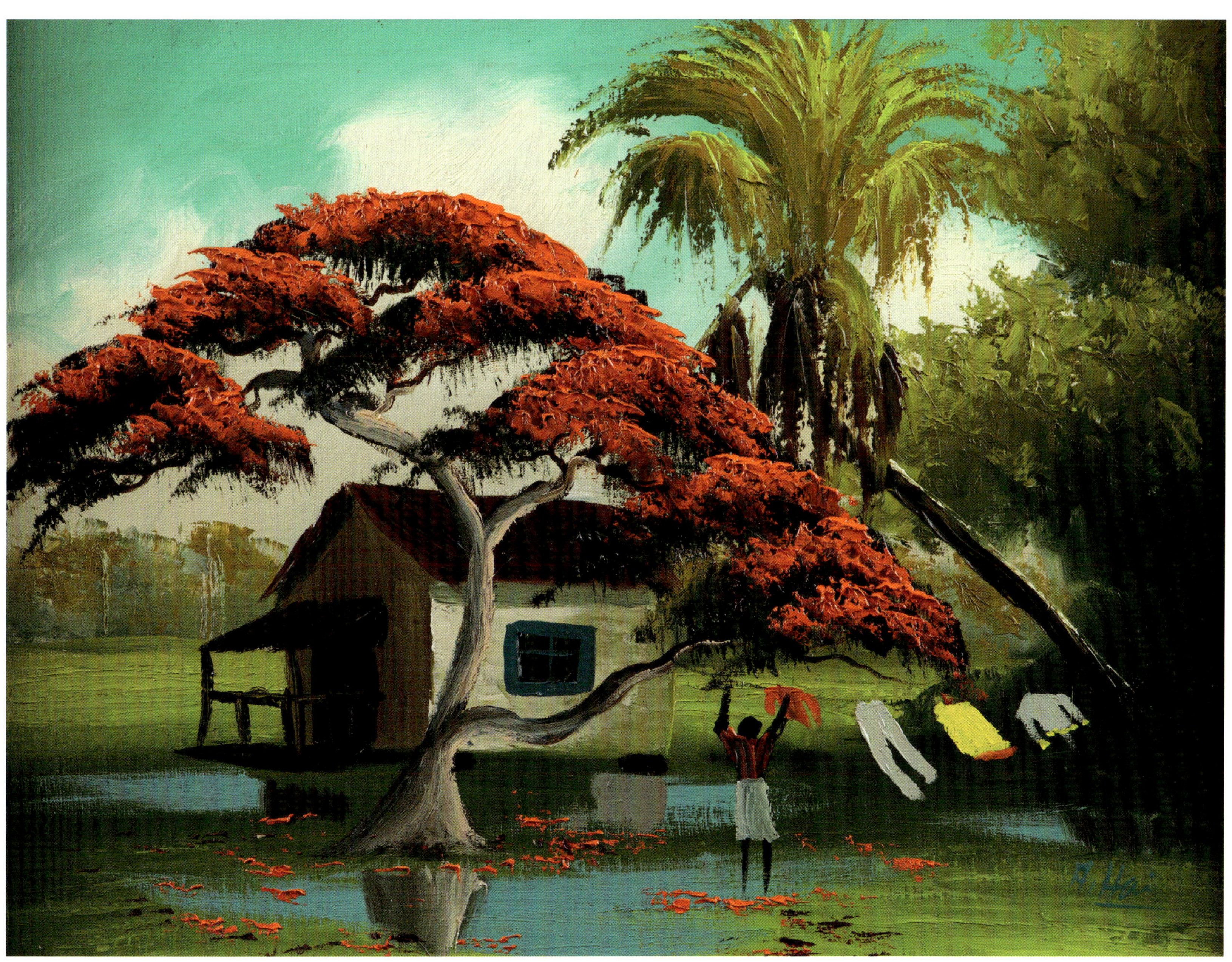

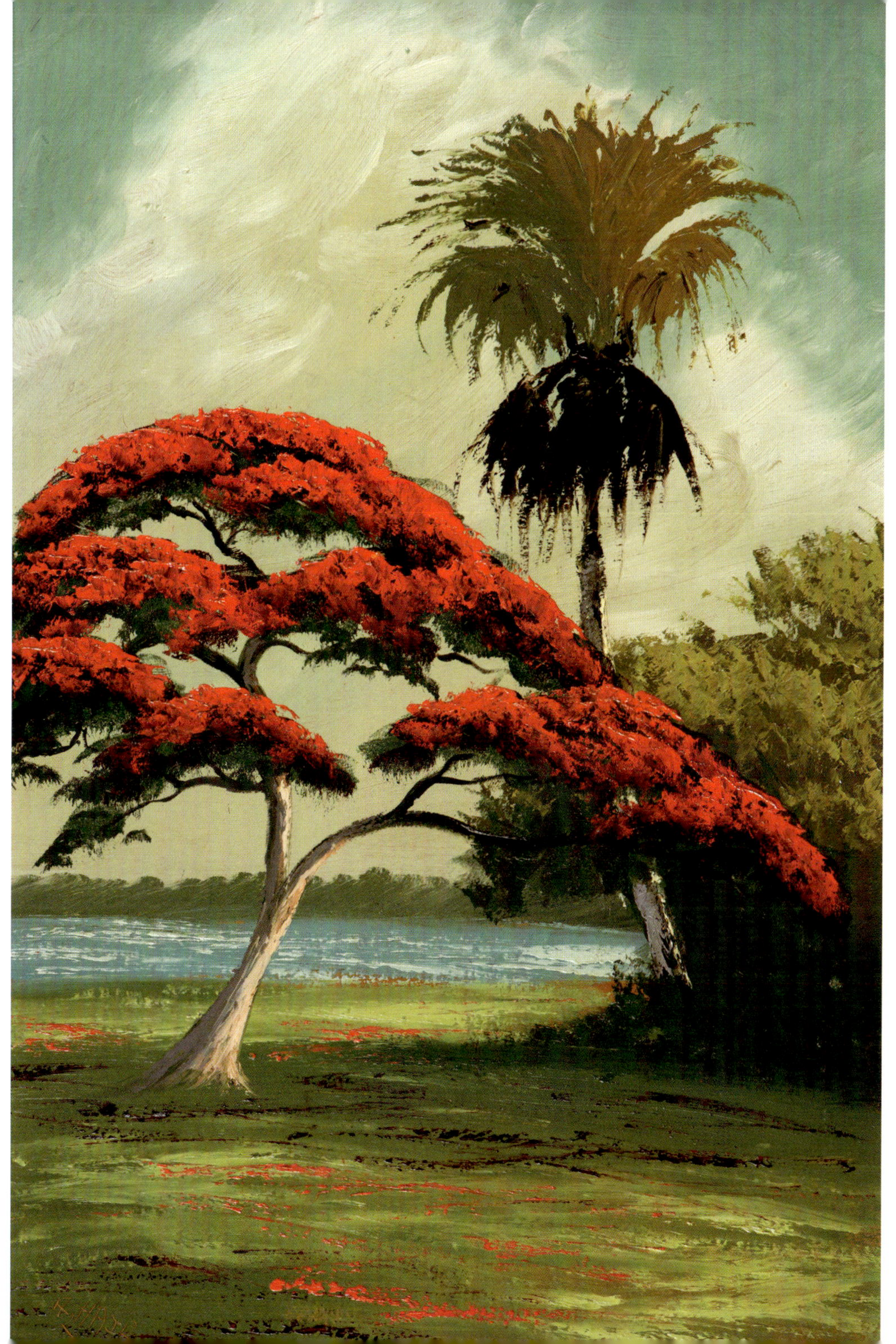

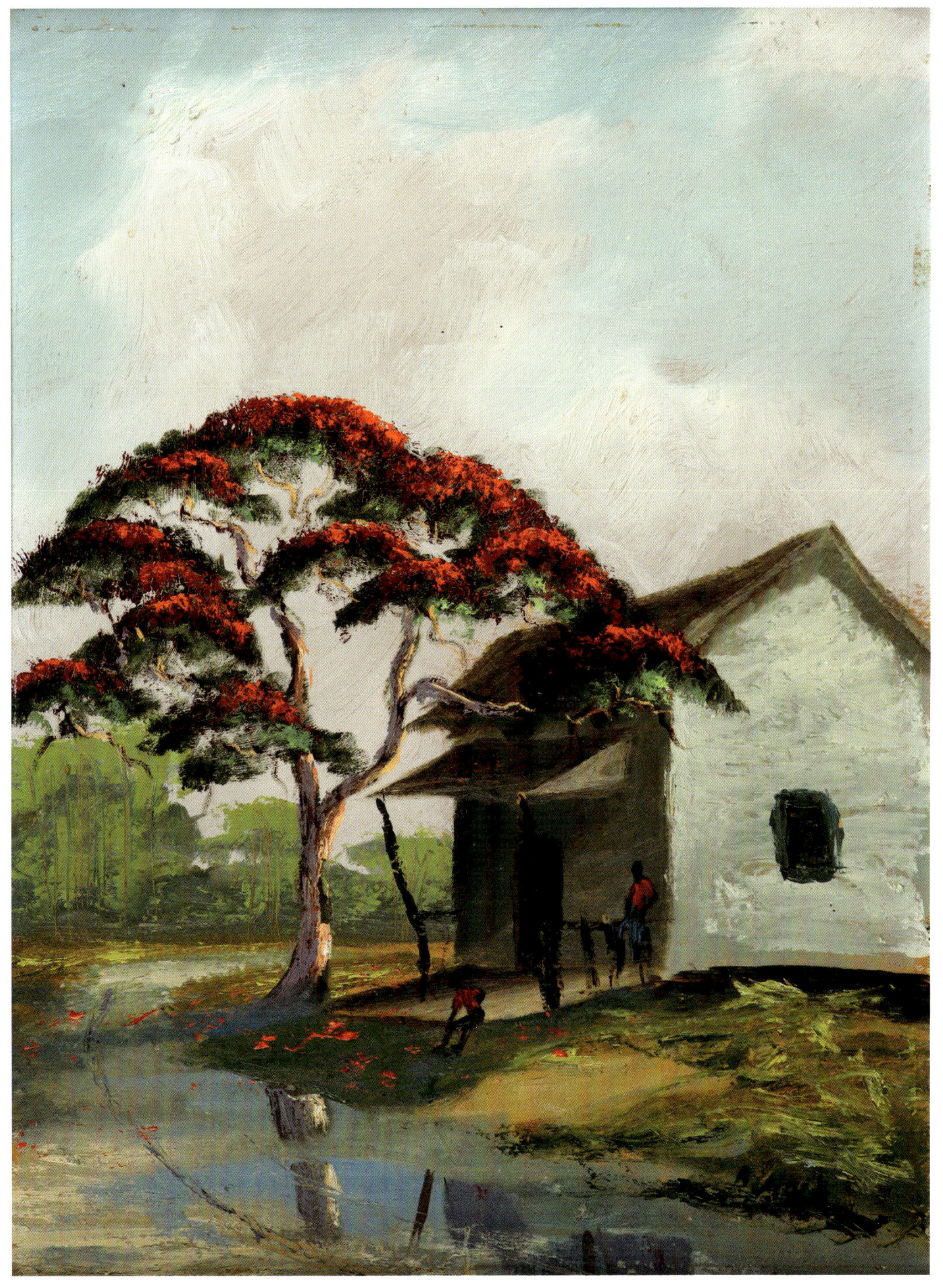

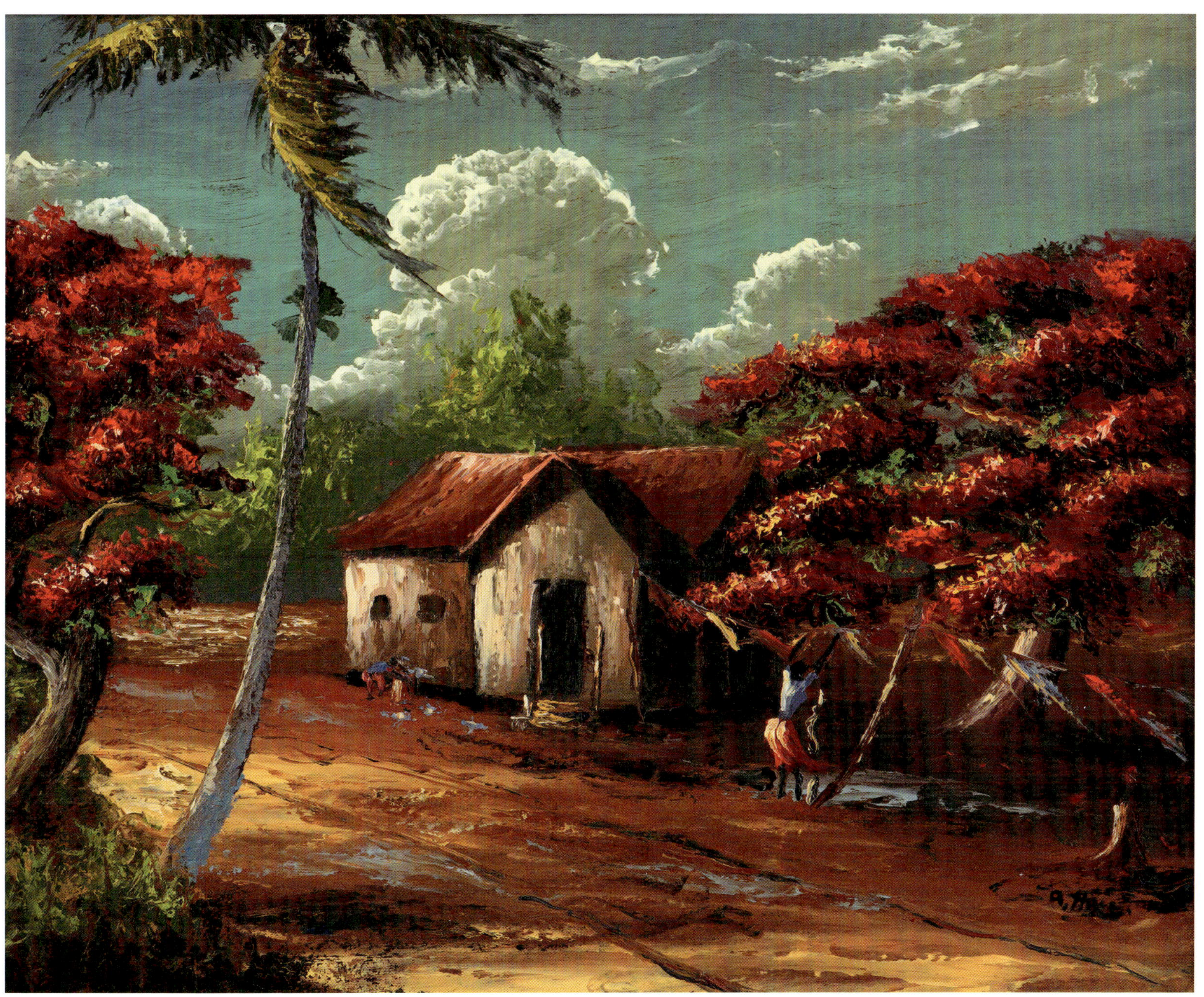

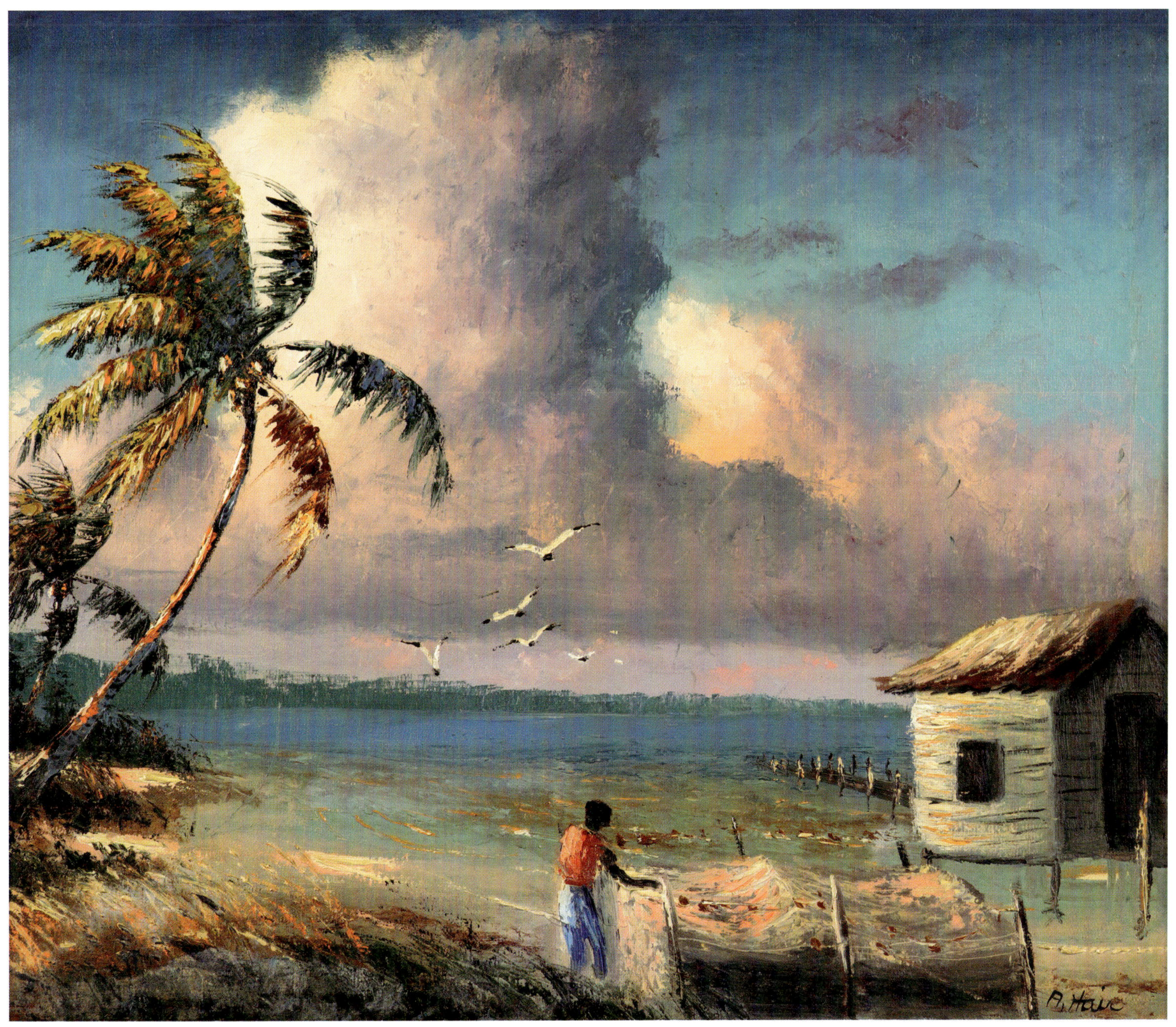
A. Hair

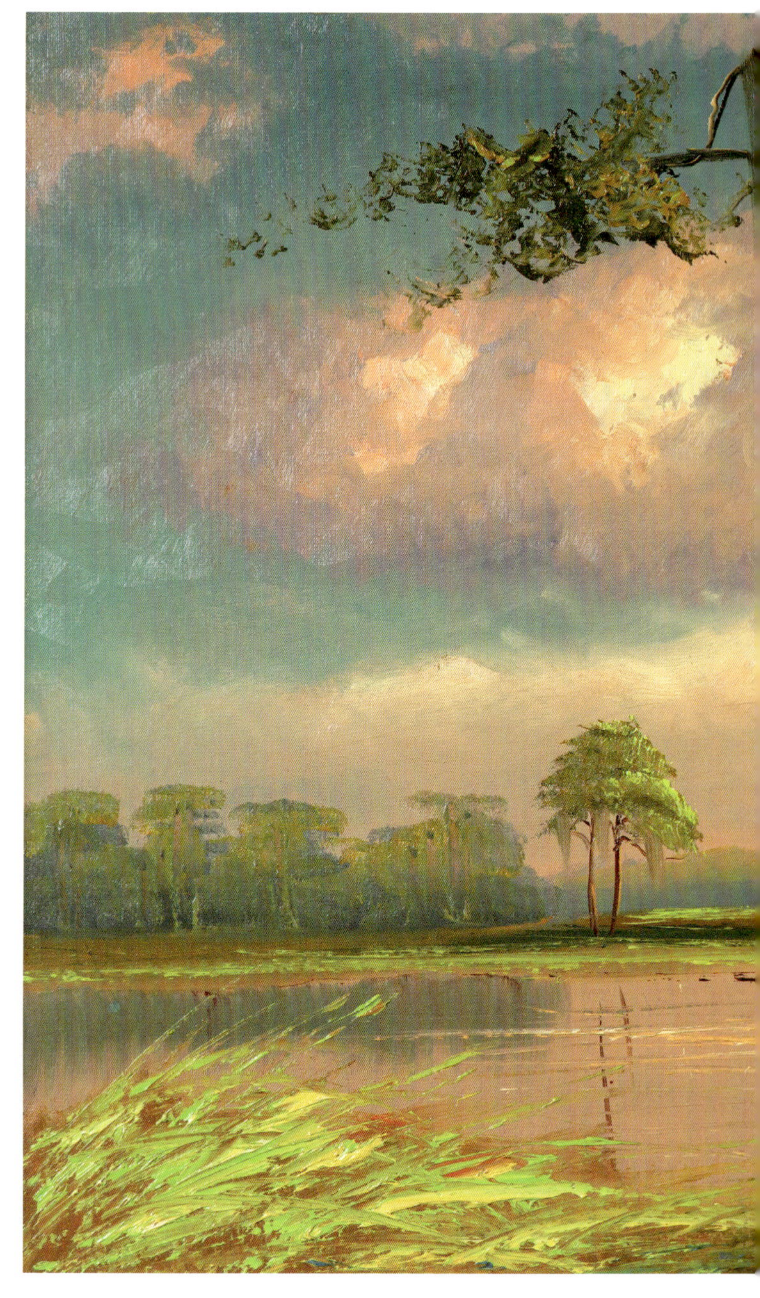

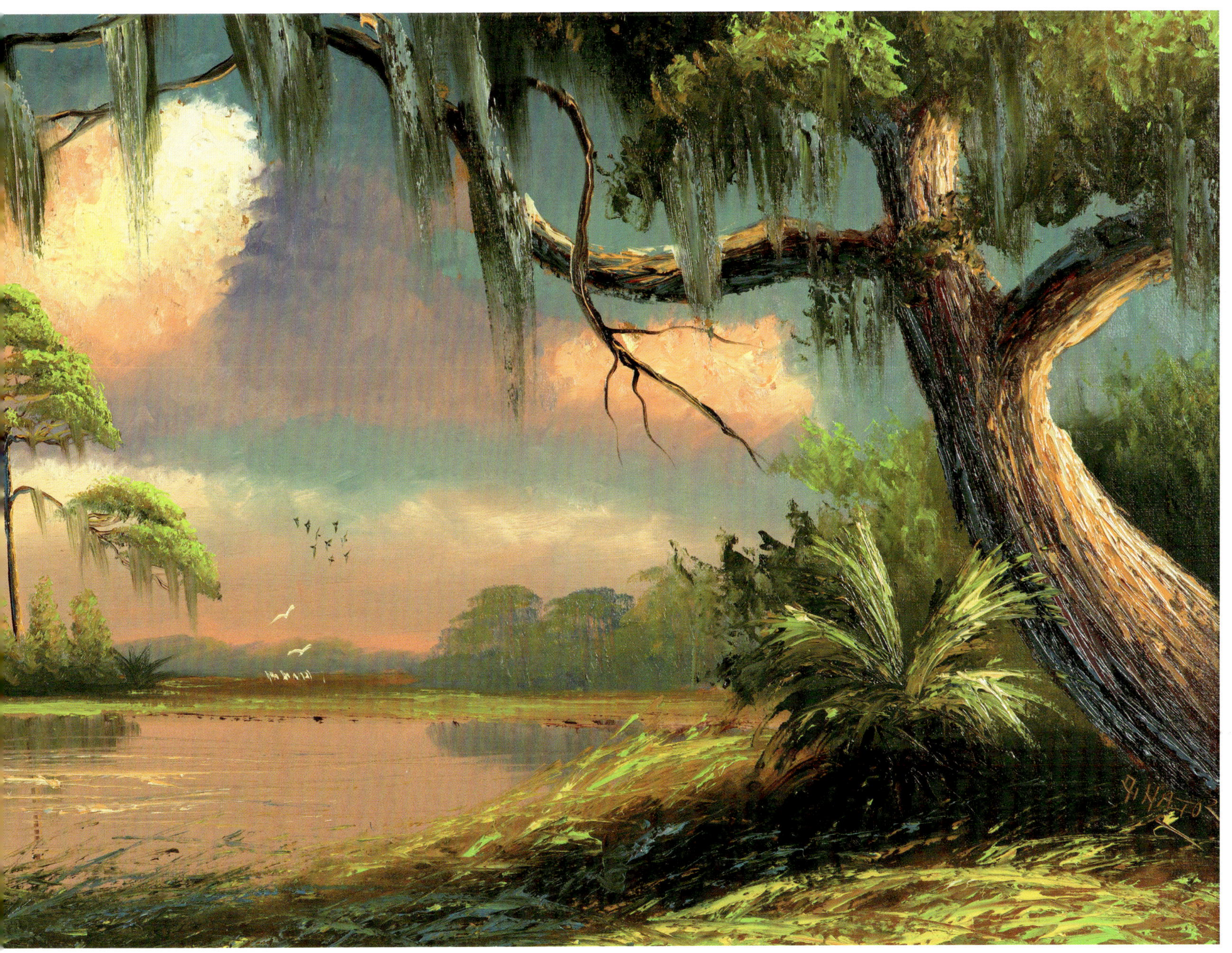

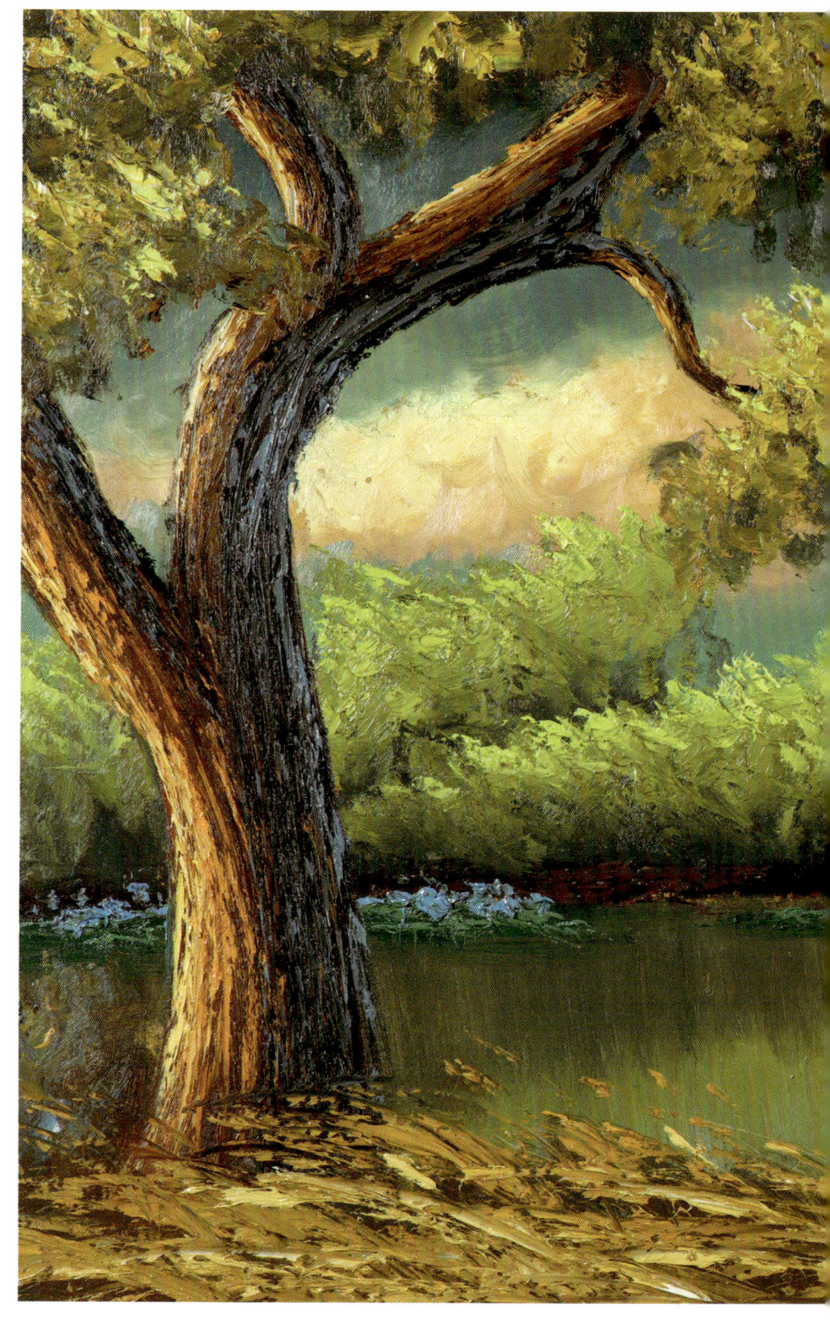

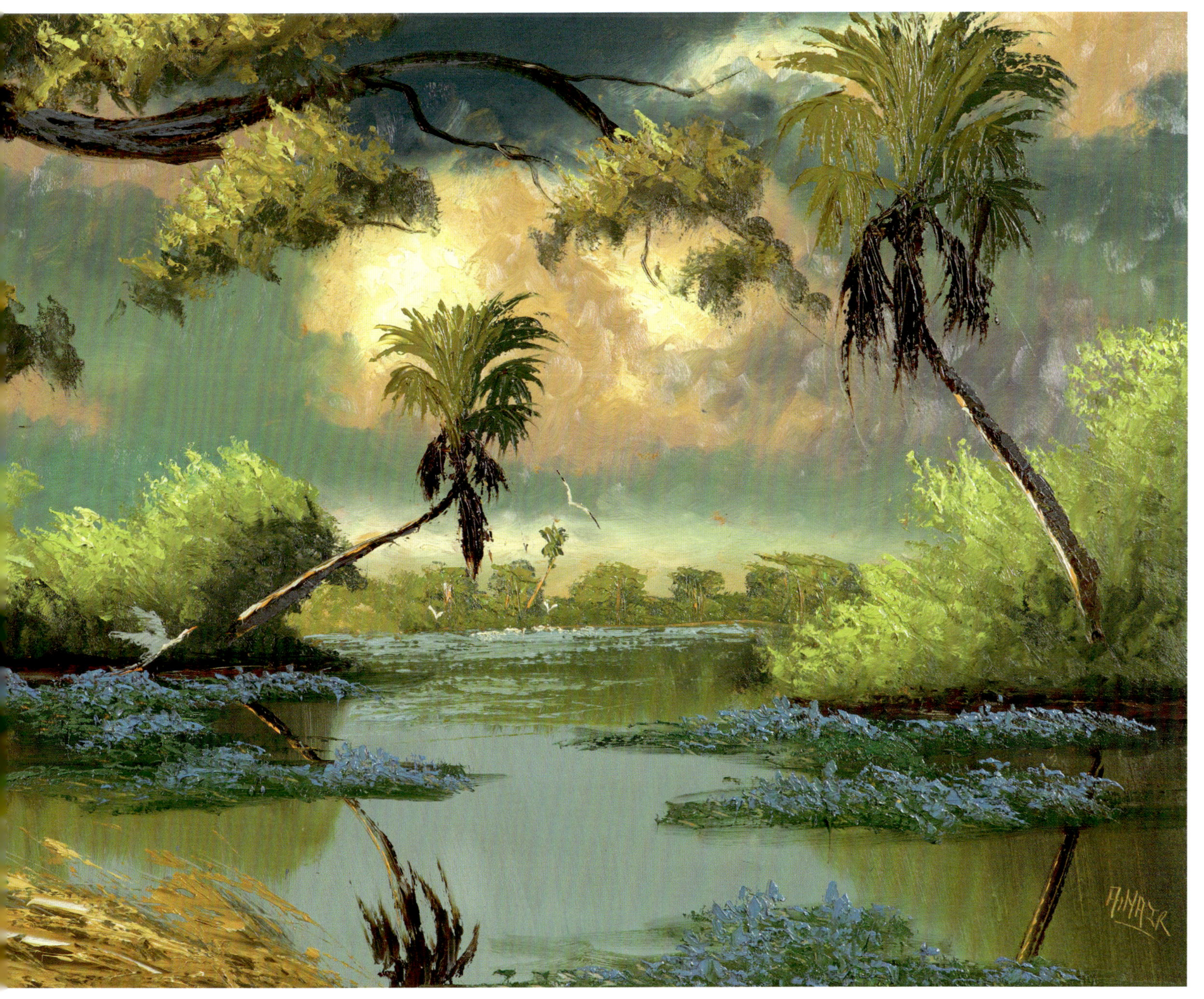

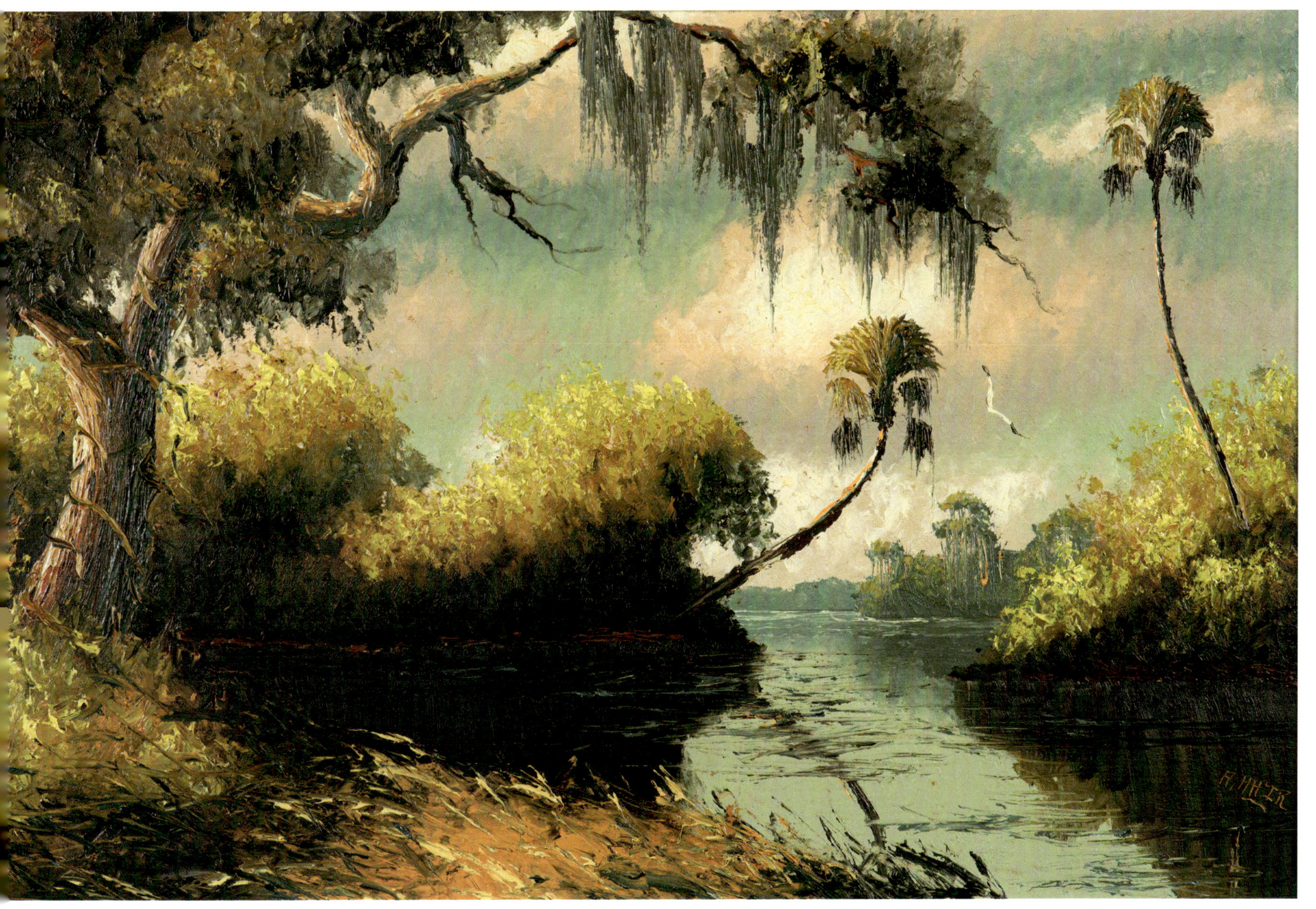

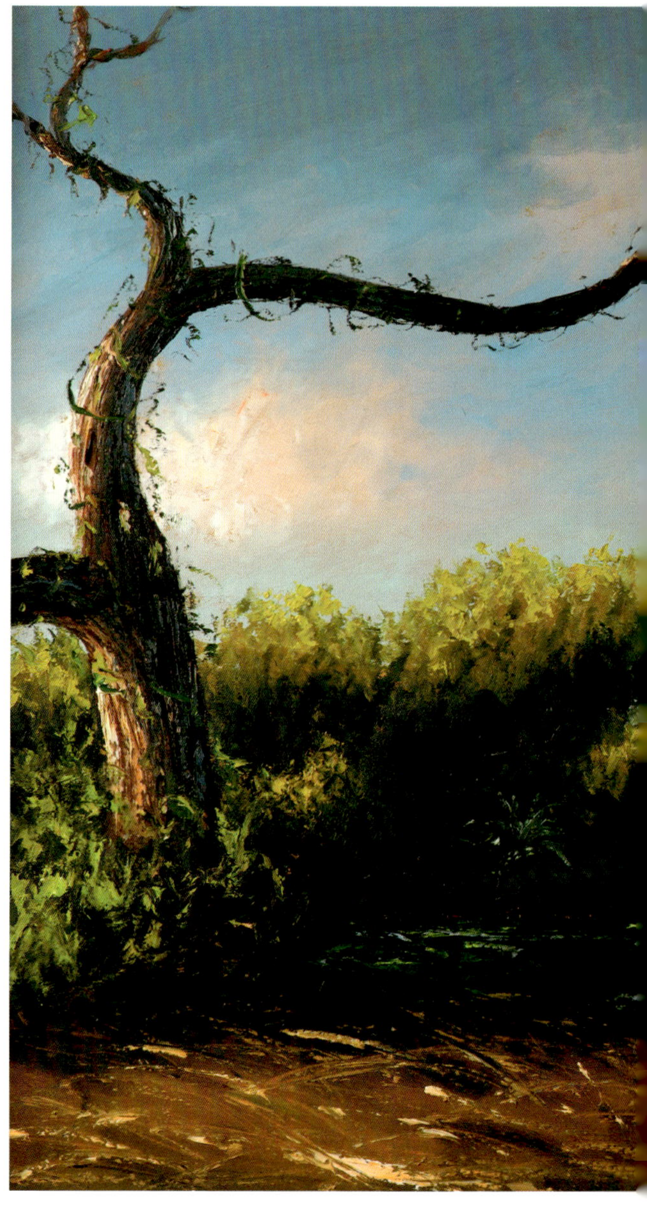

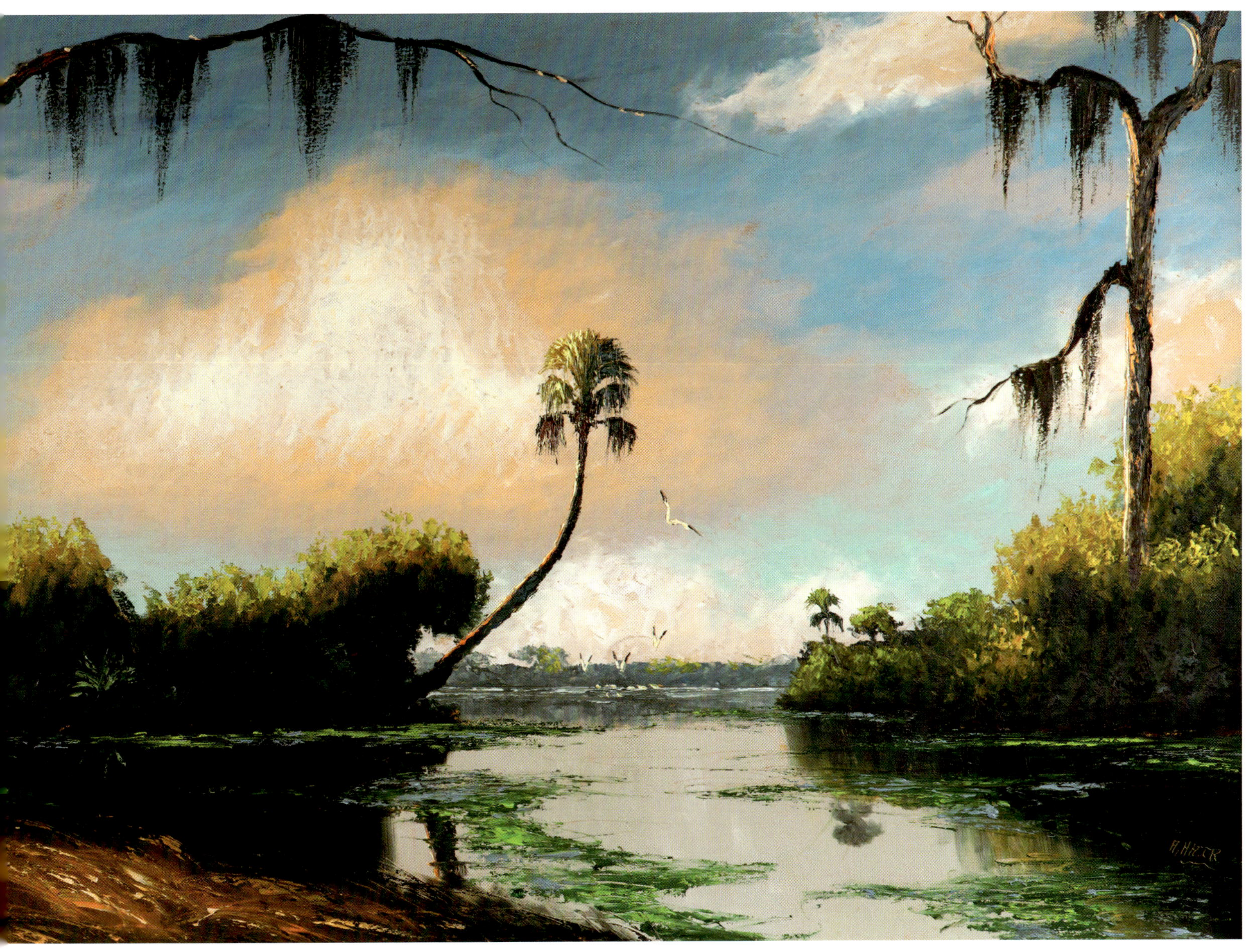
A. HAIR

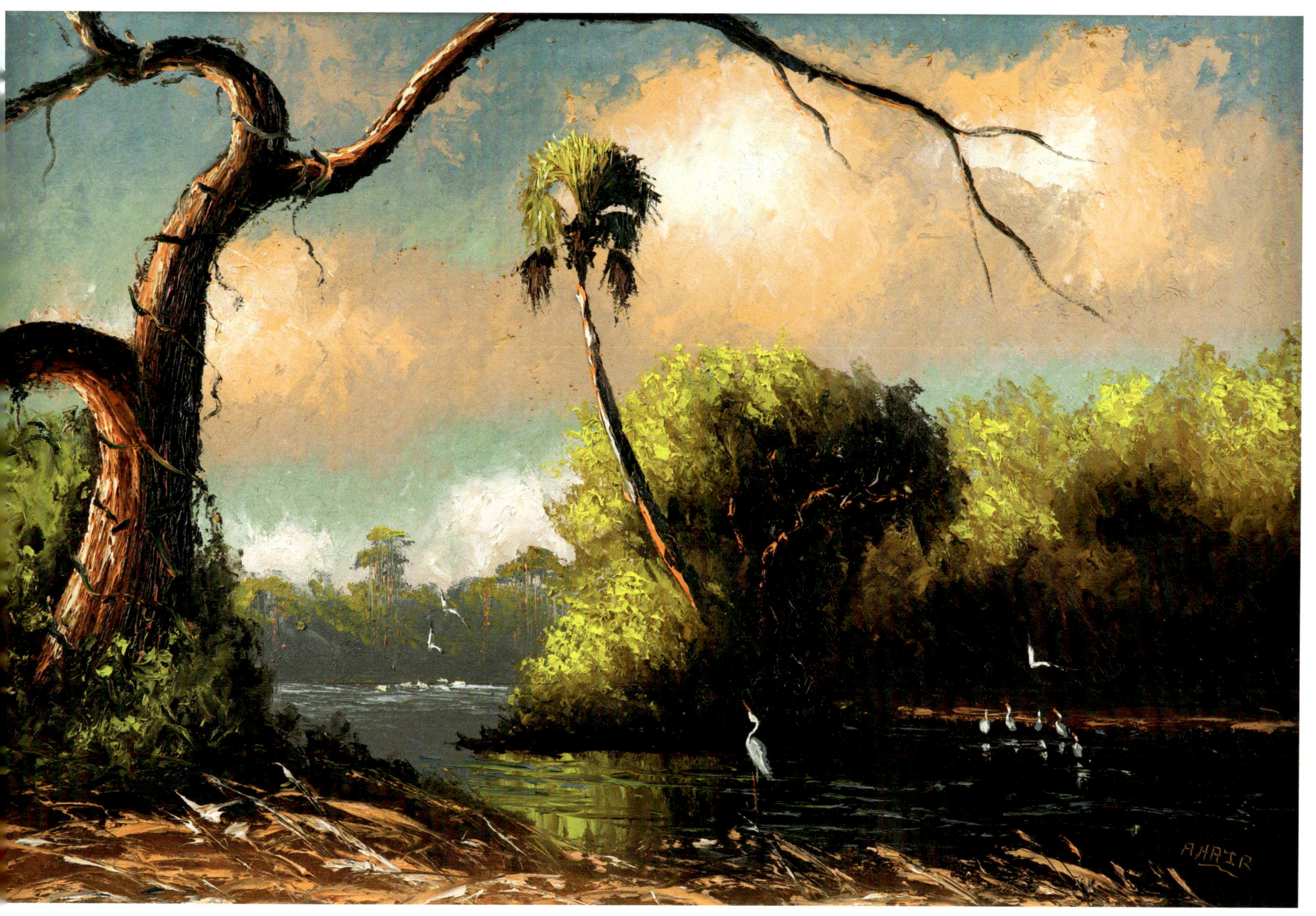
A HAIR

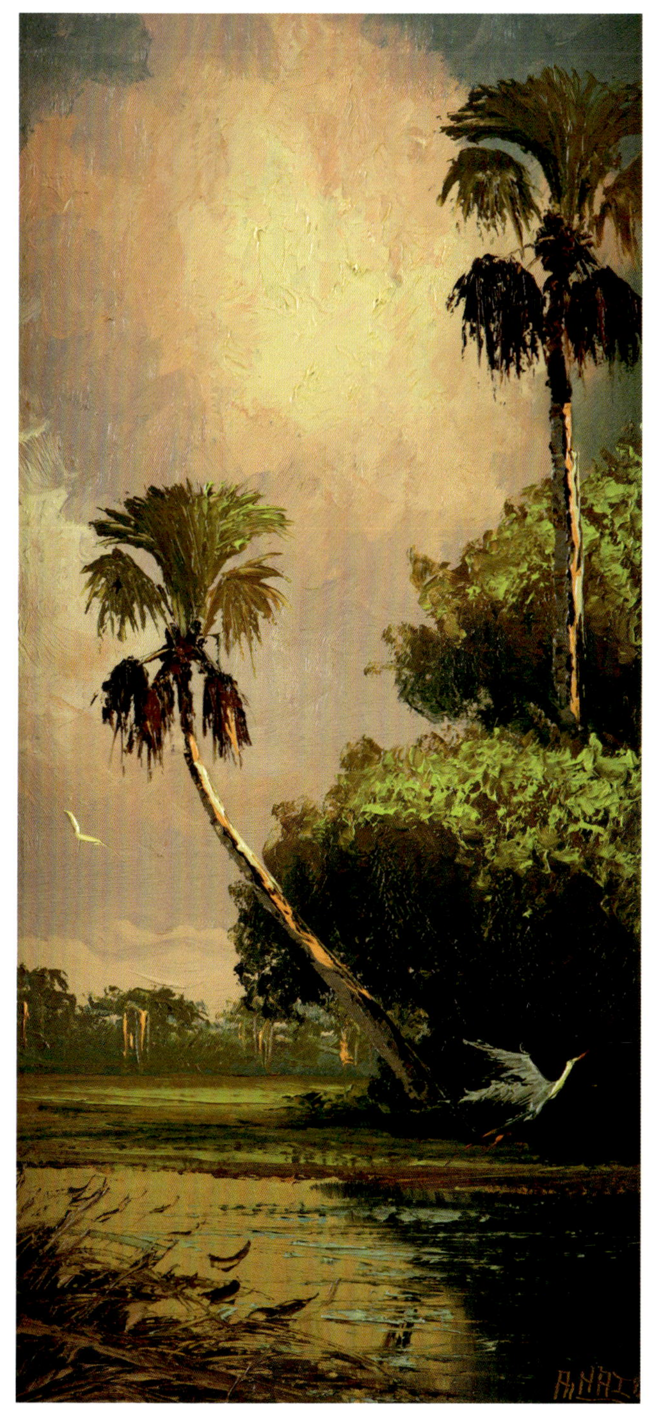

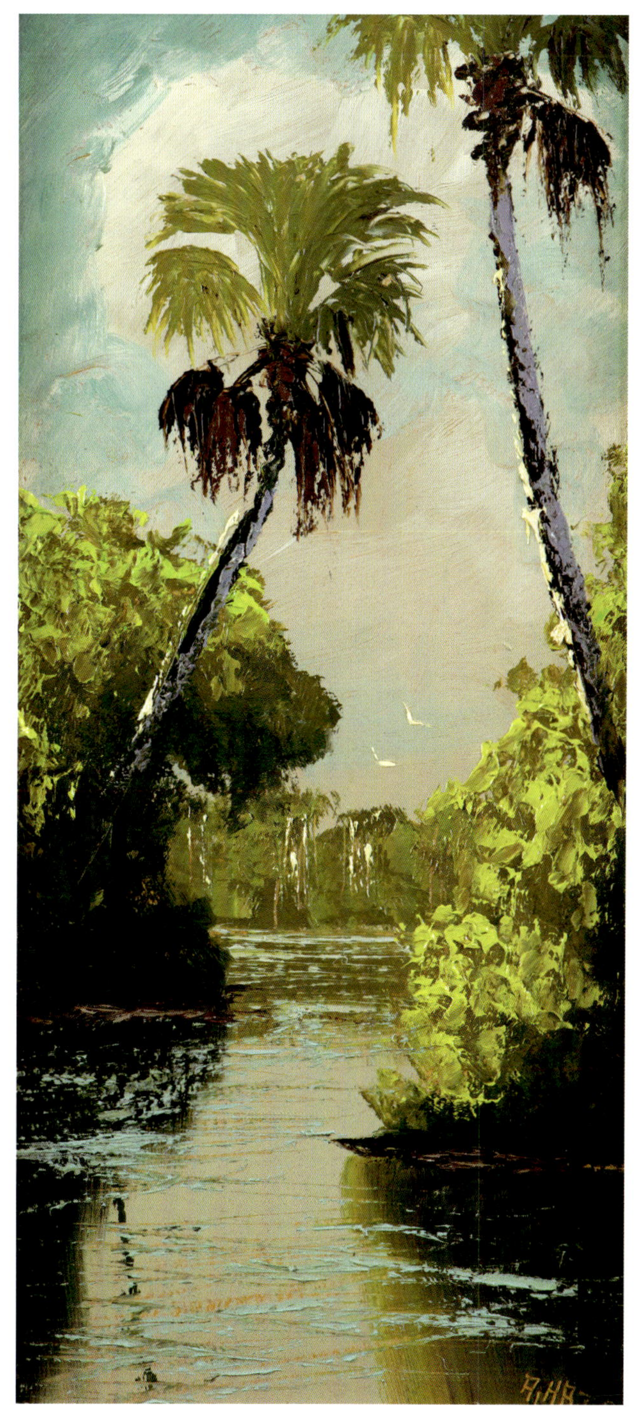

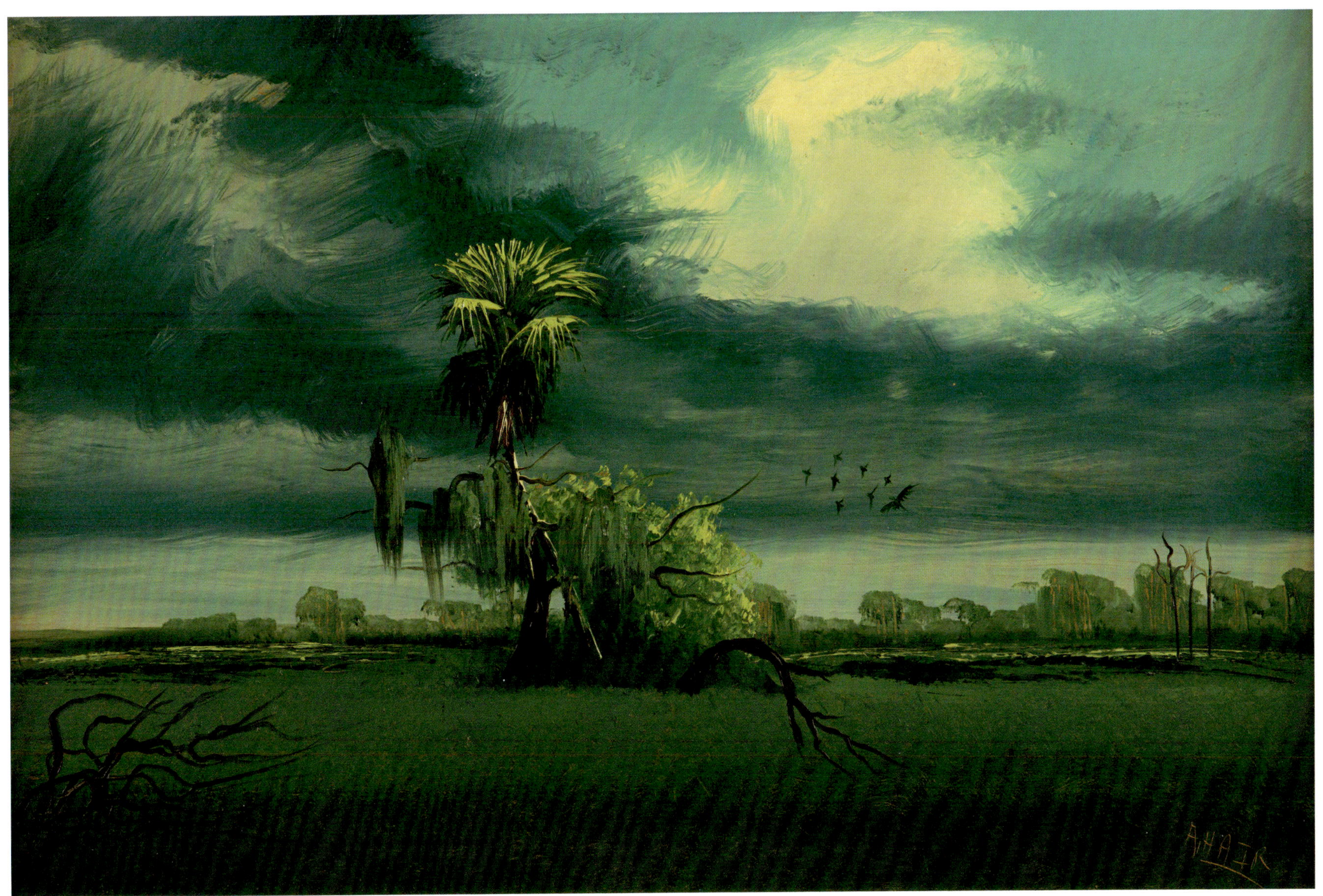
A.HAIR

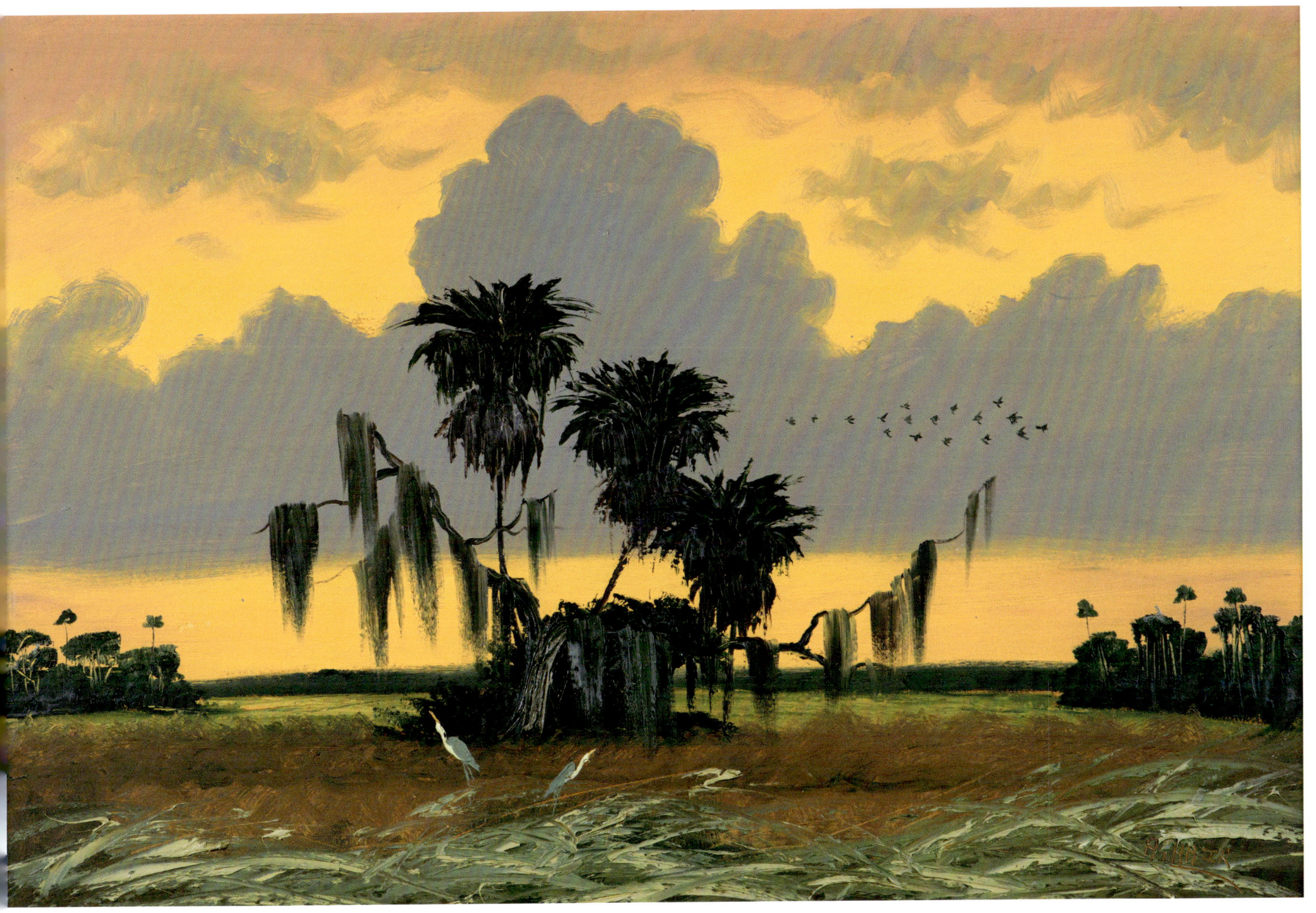

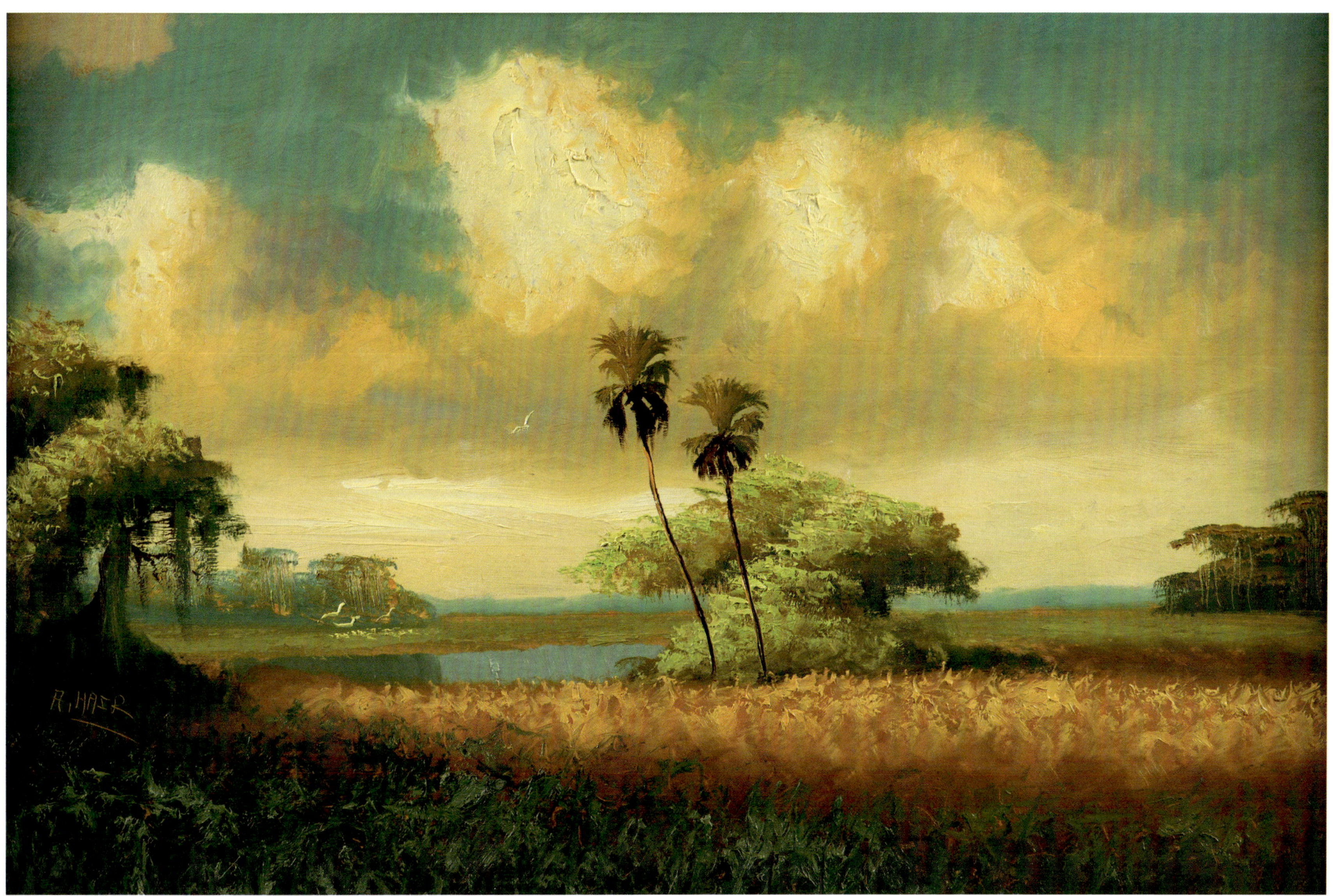
A. HAIR

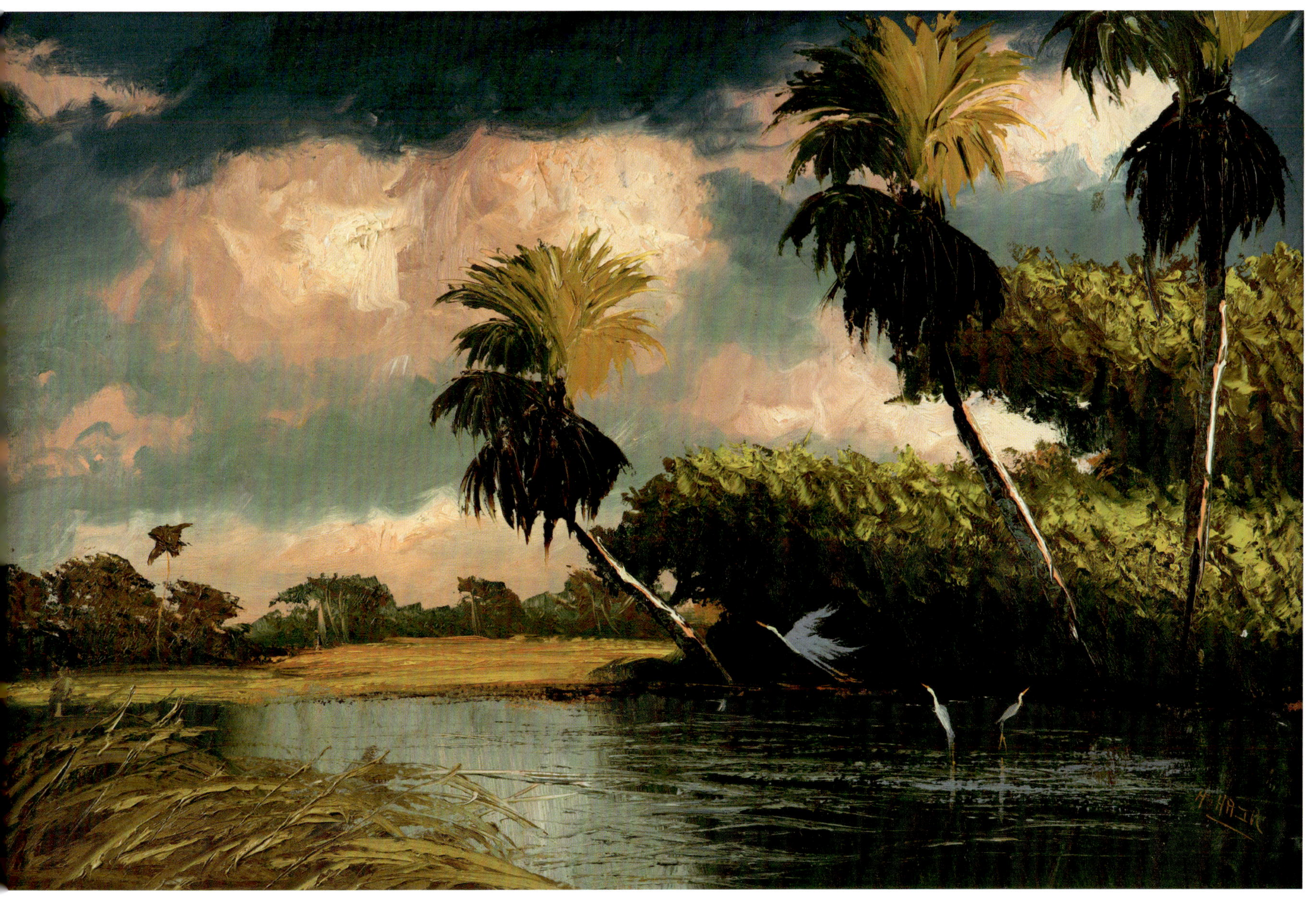

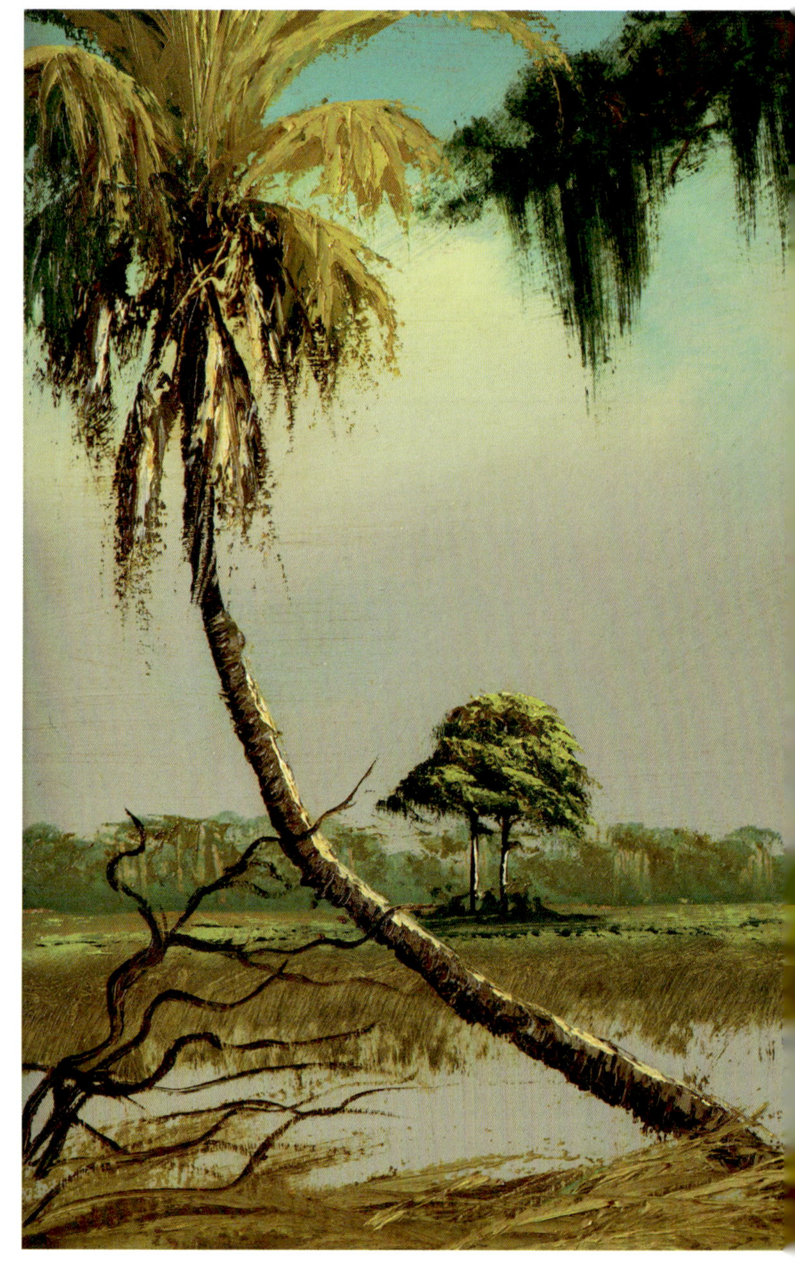

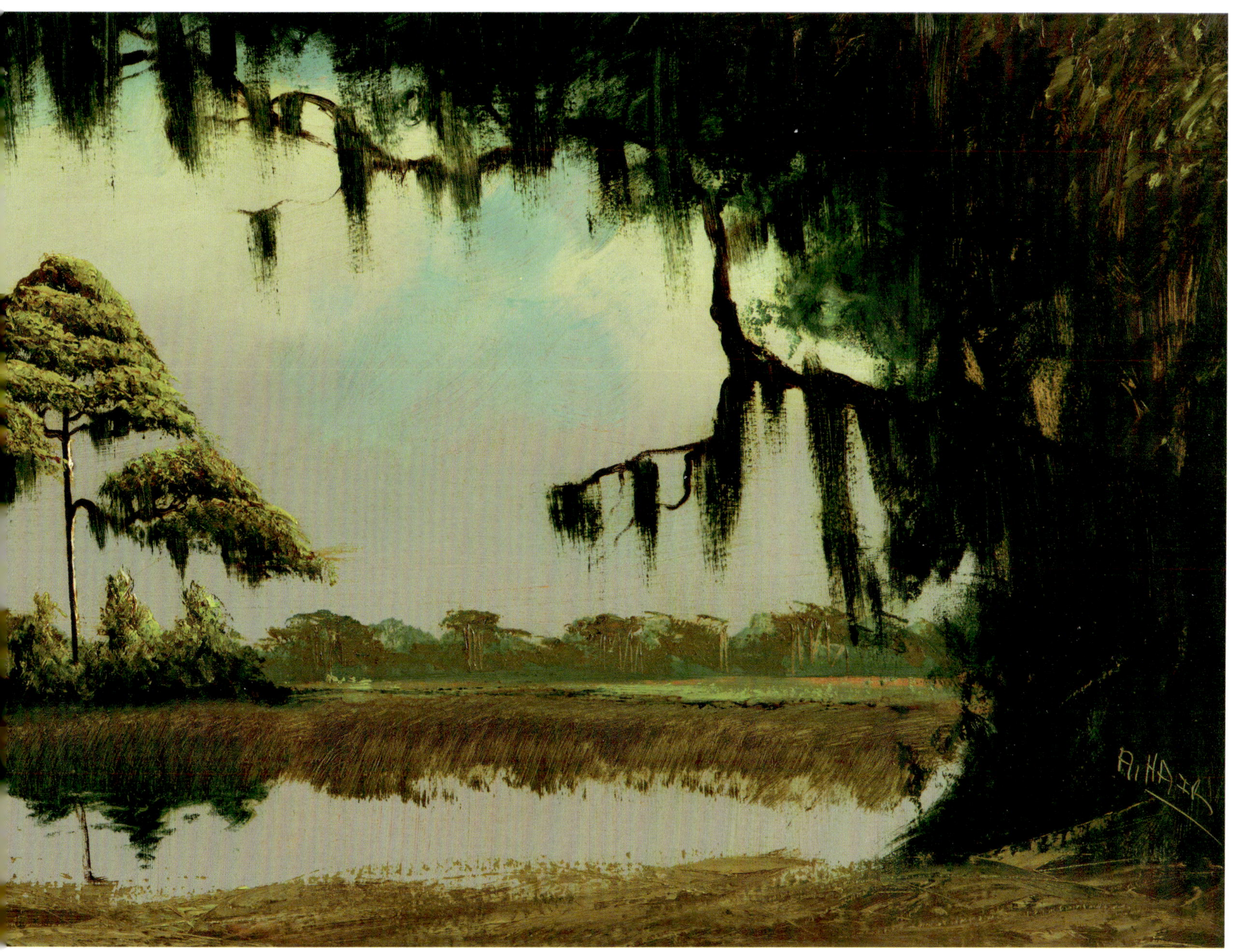
A. HAIR

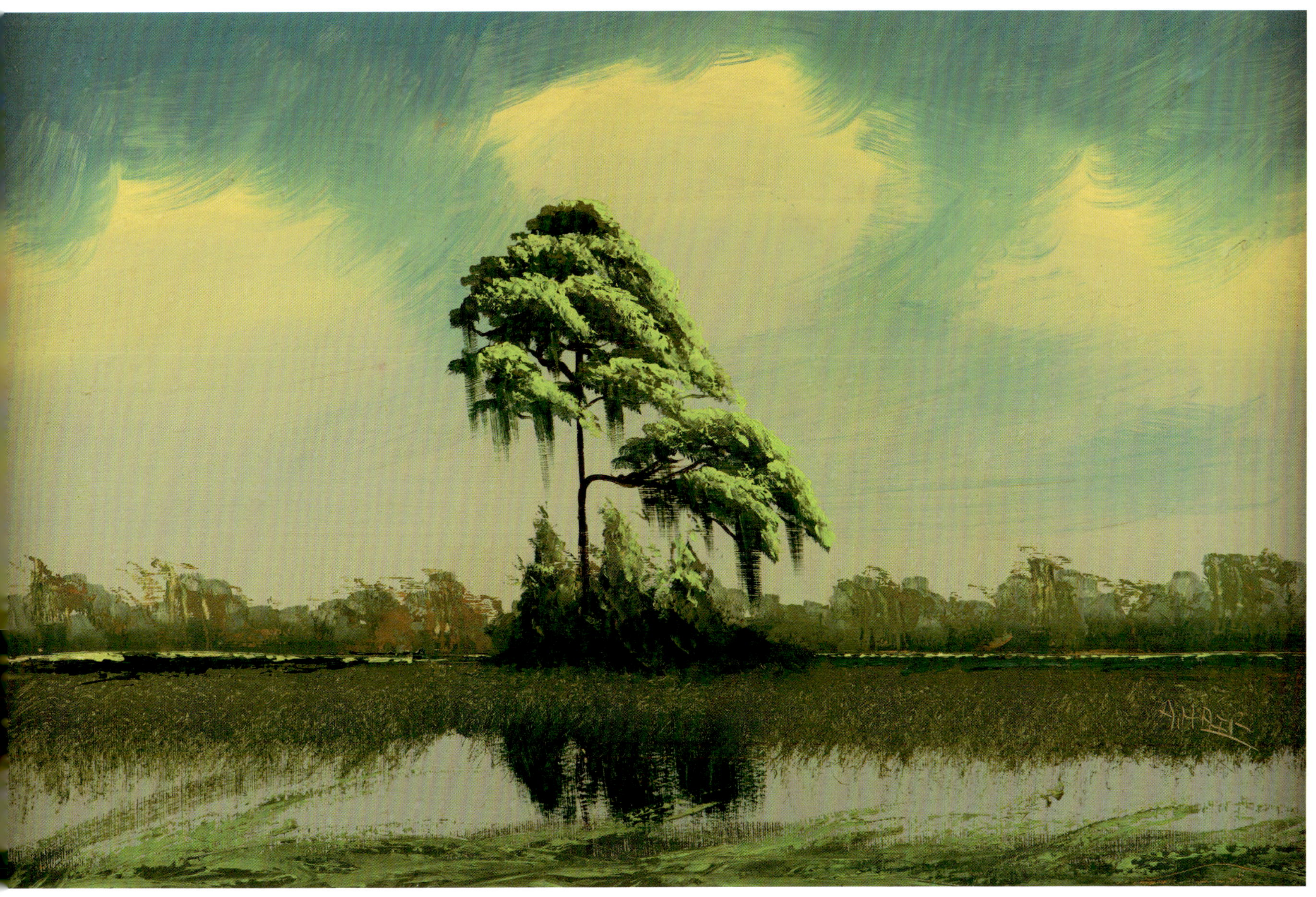

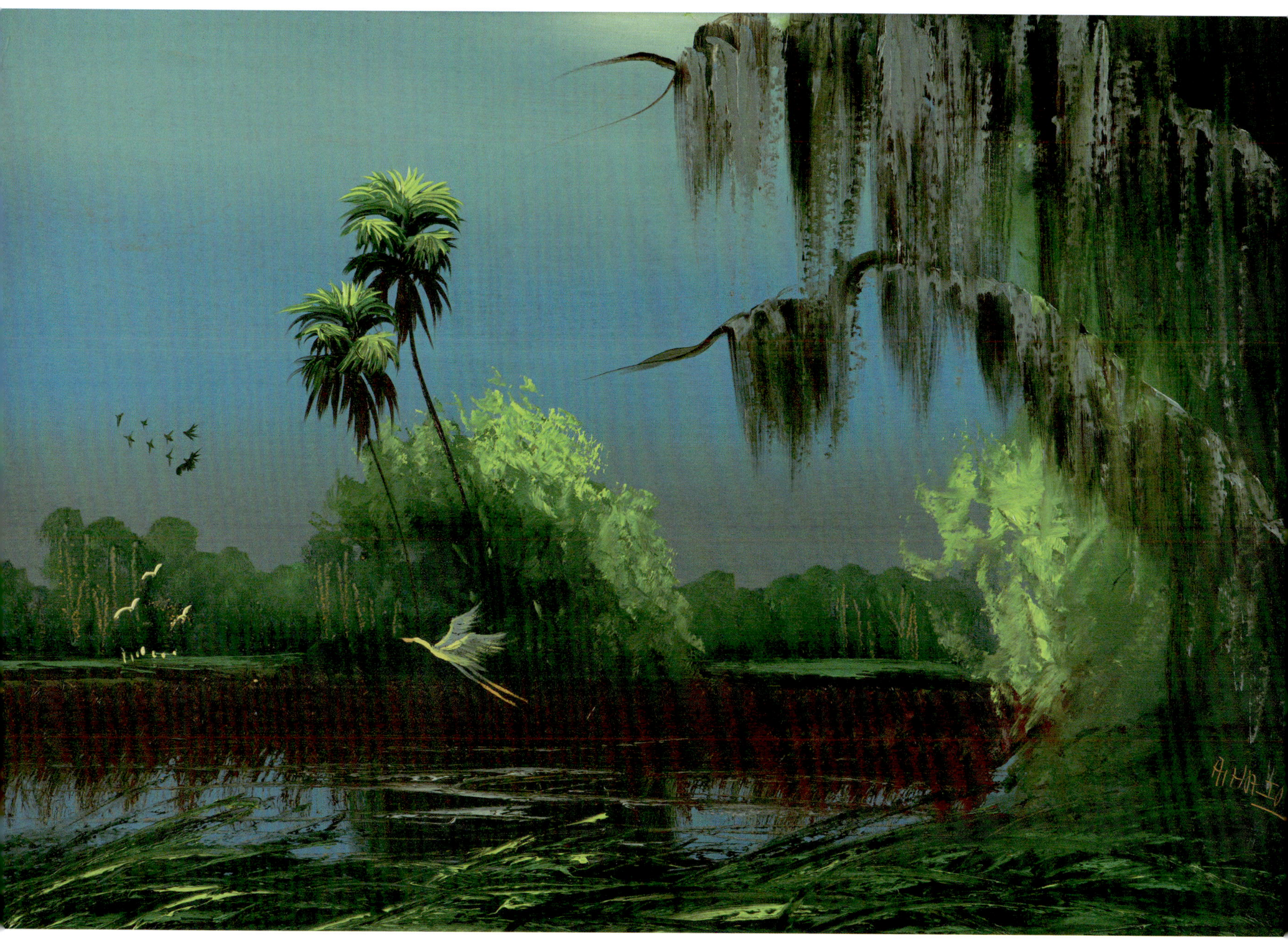

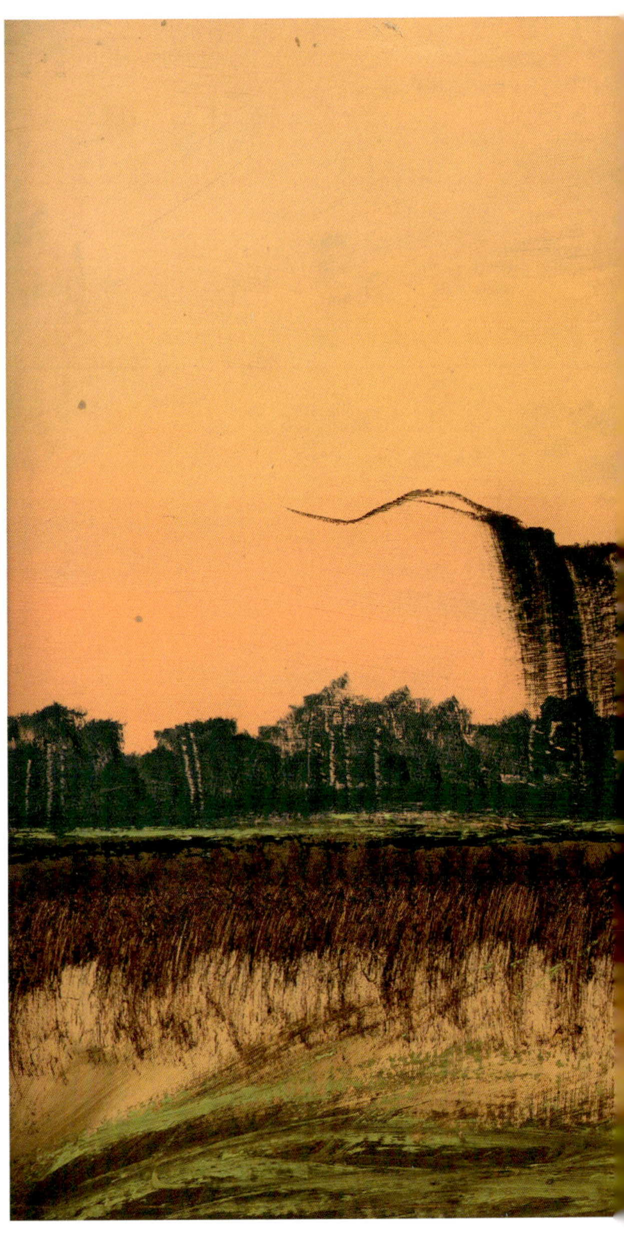

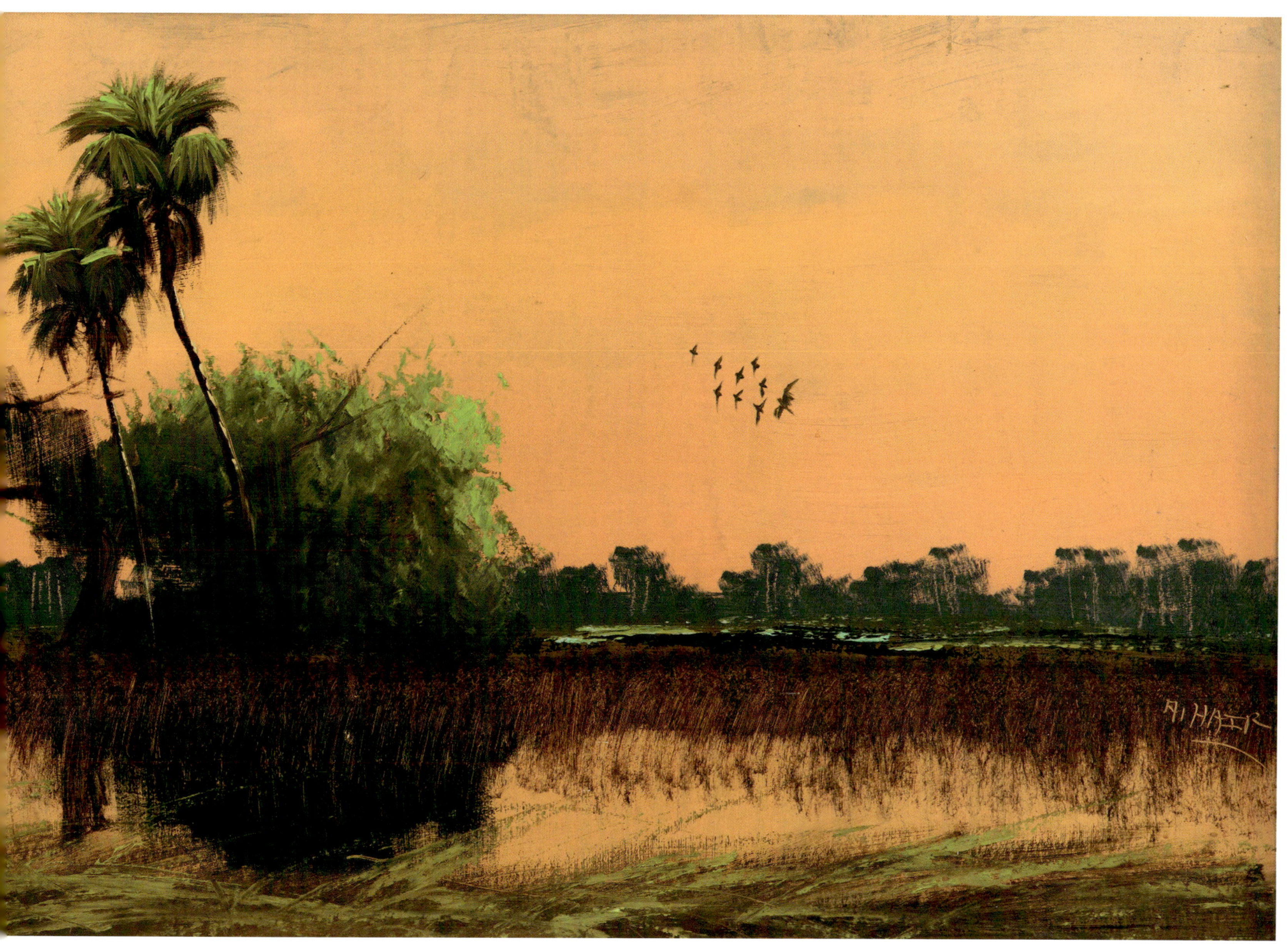

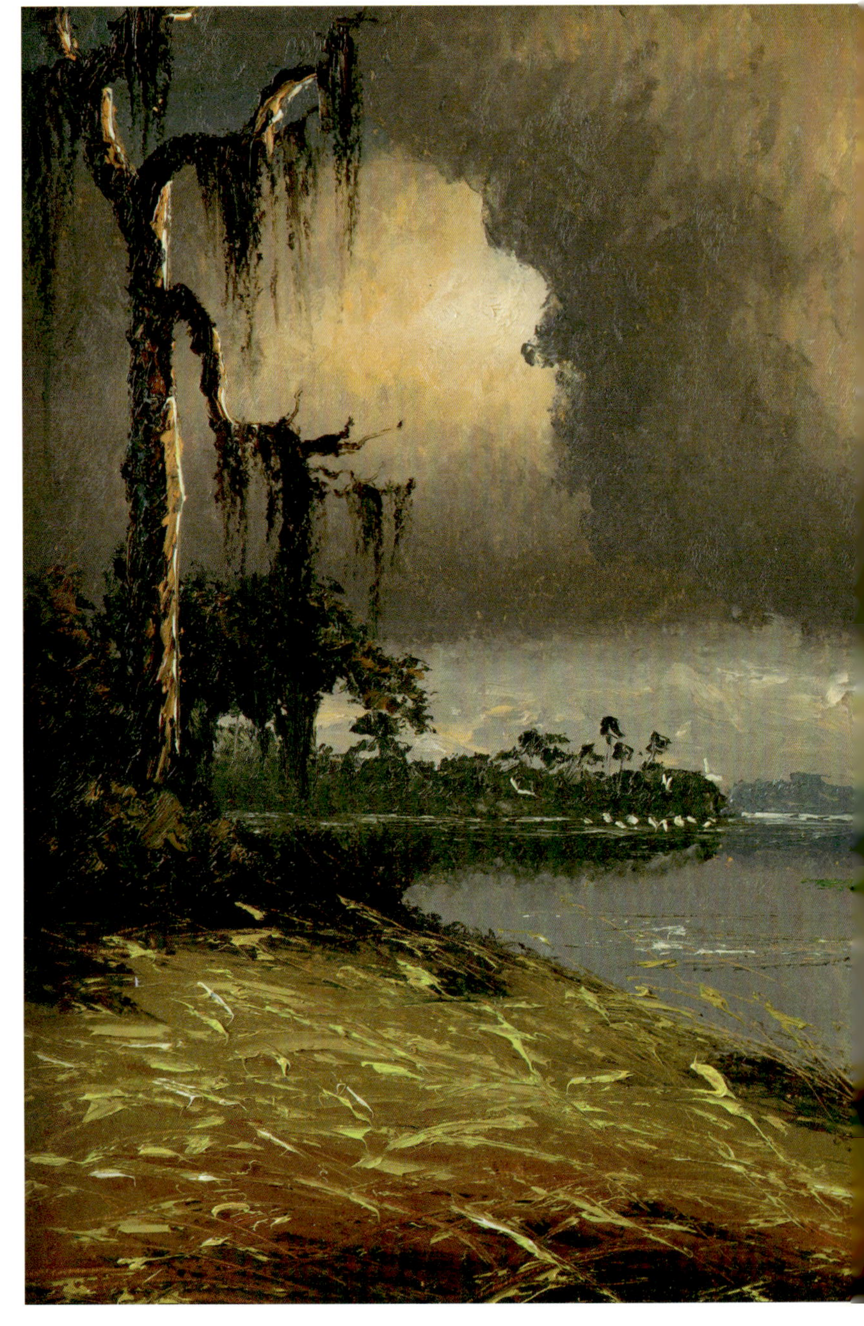

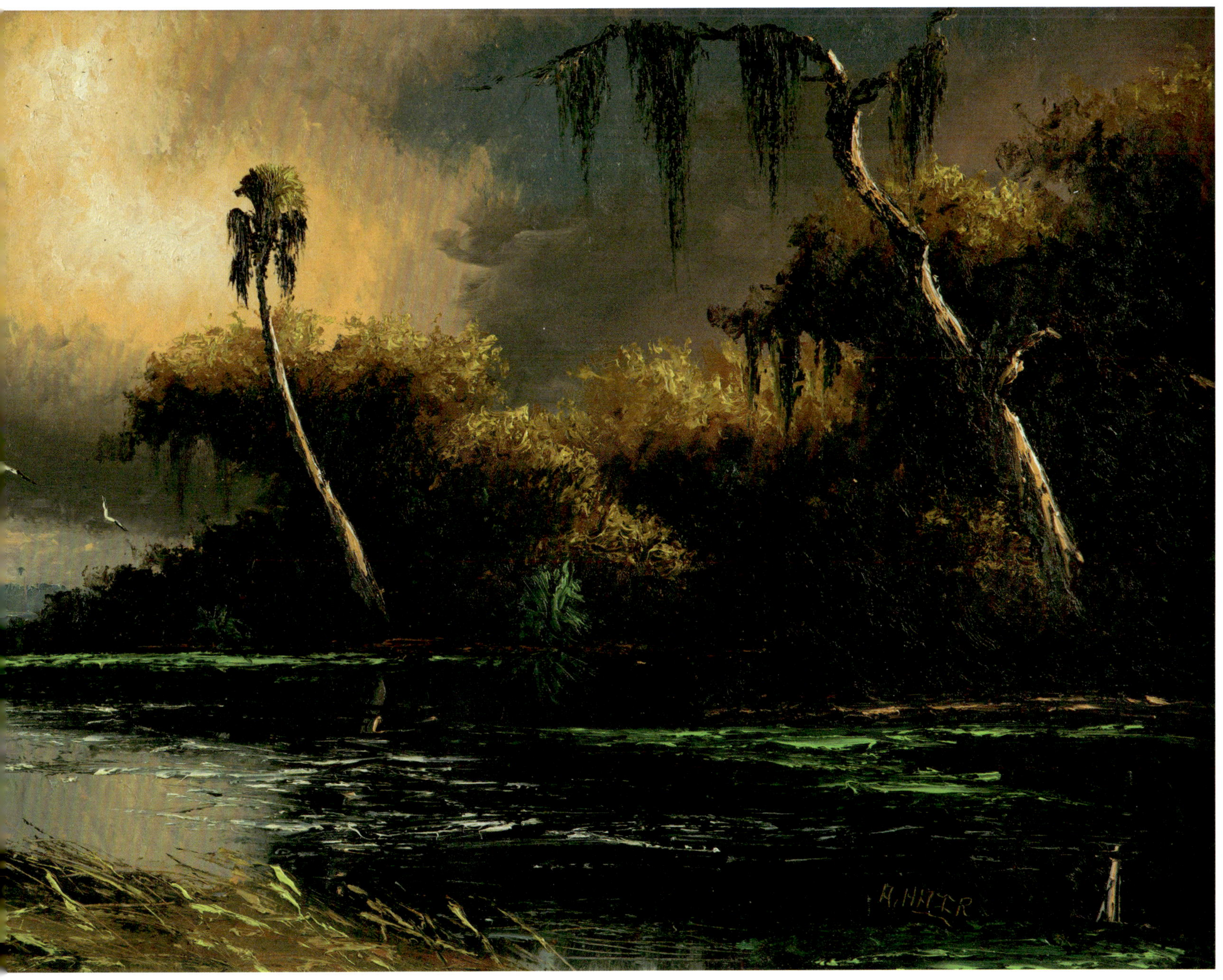

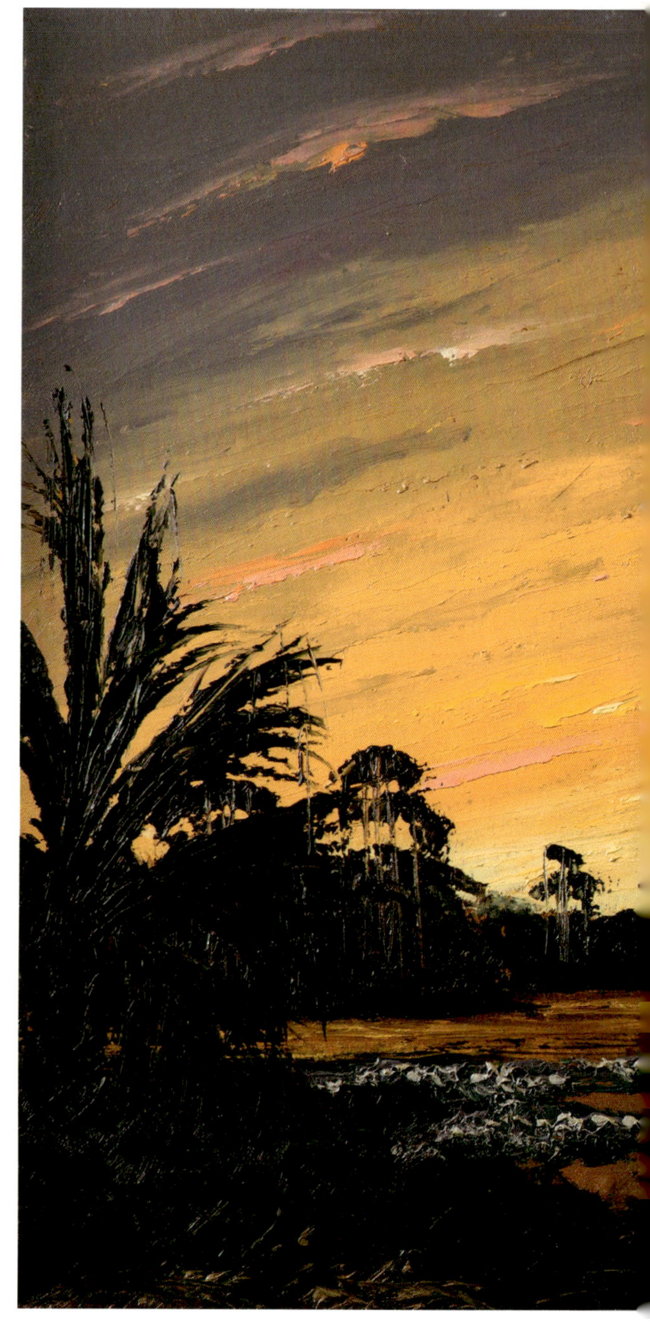

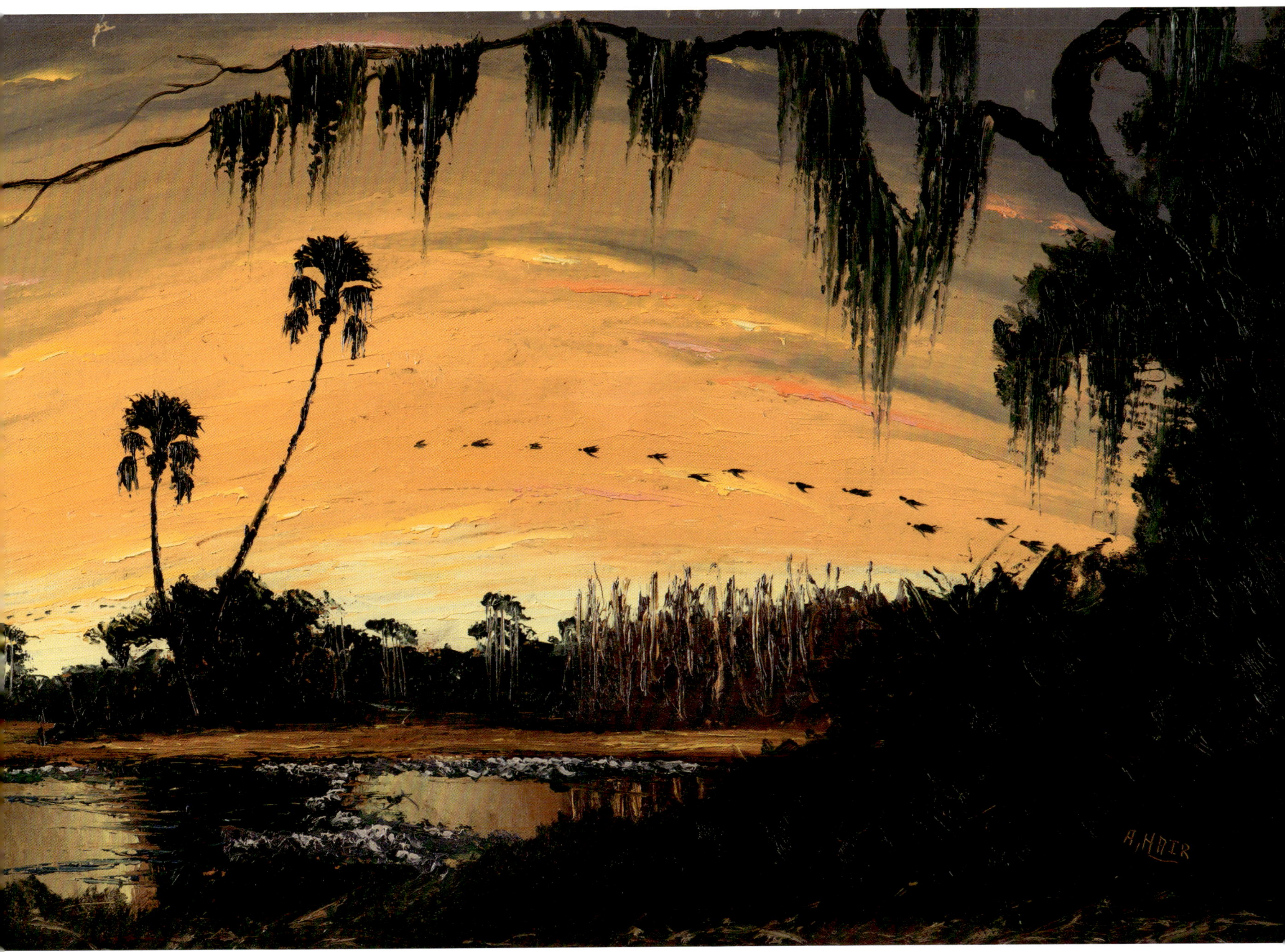
A.HAIR

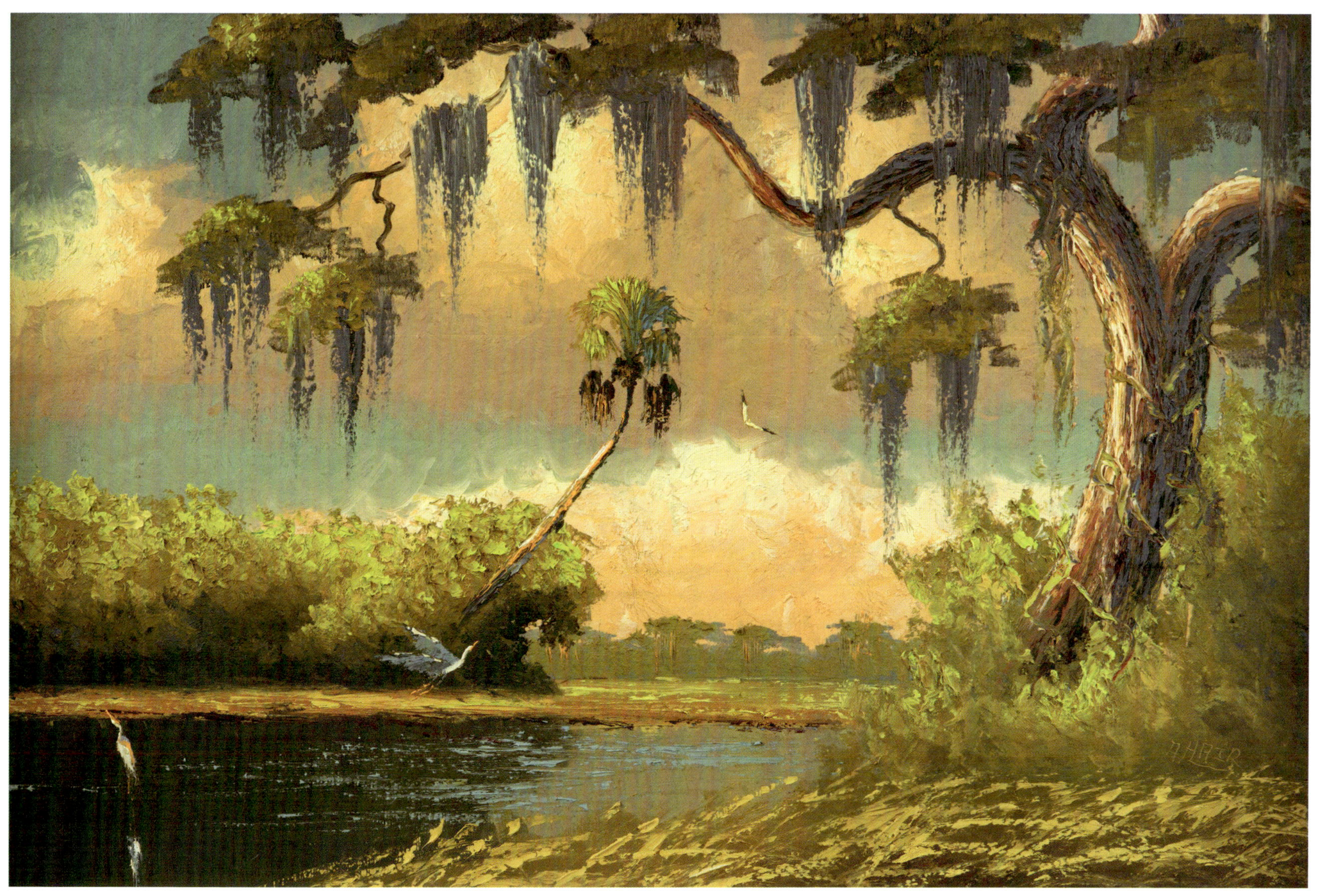

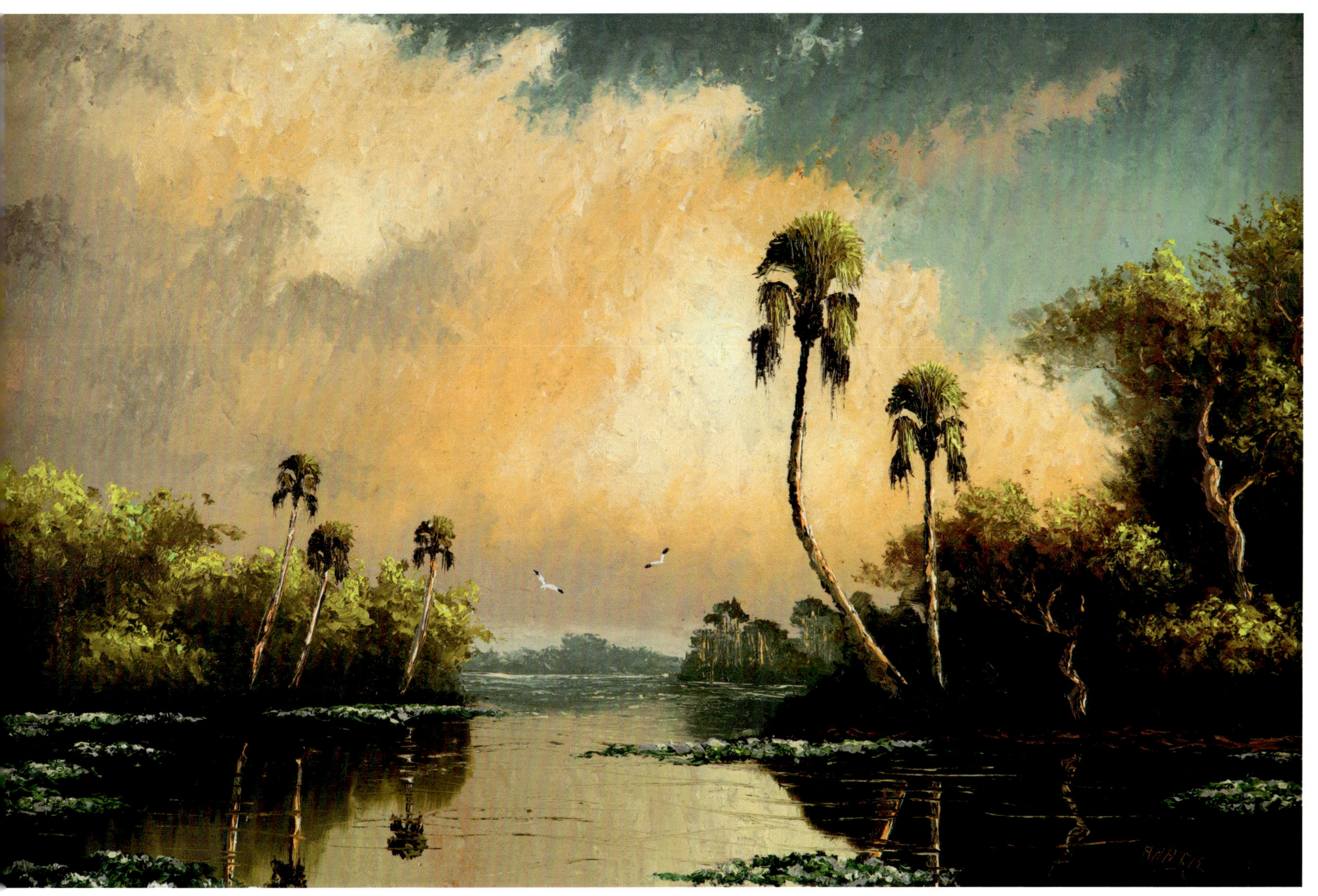

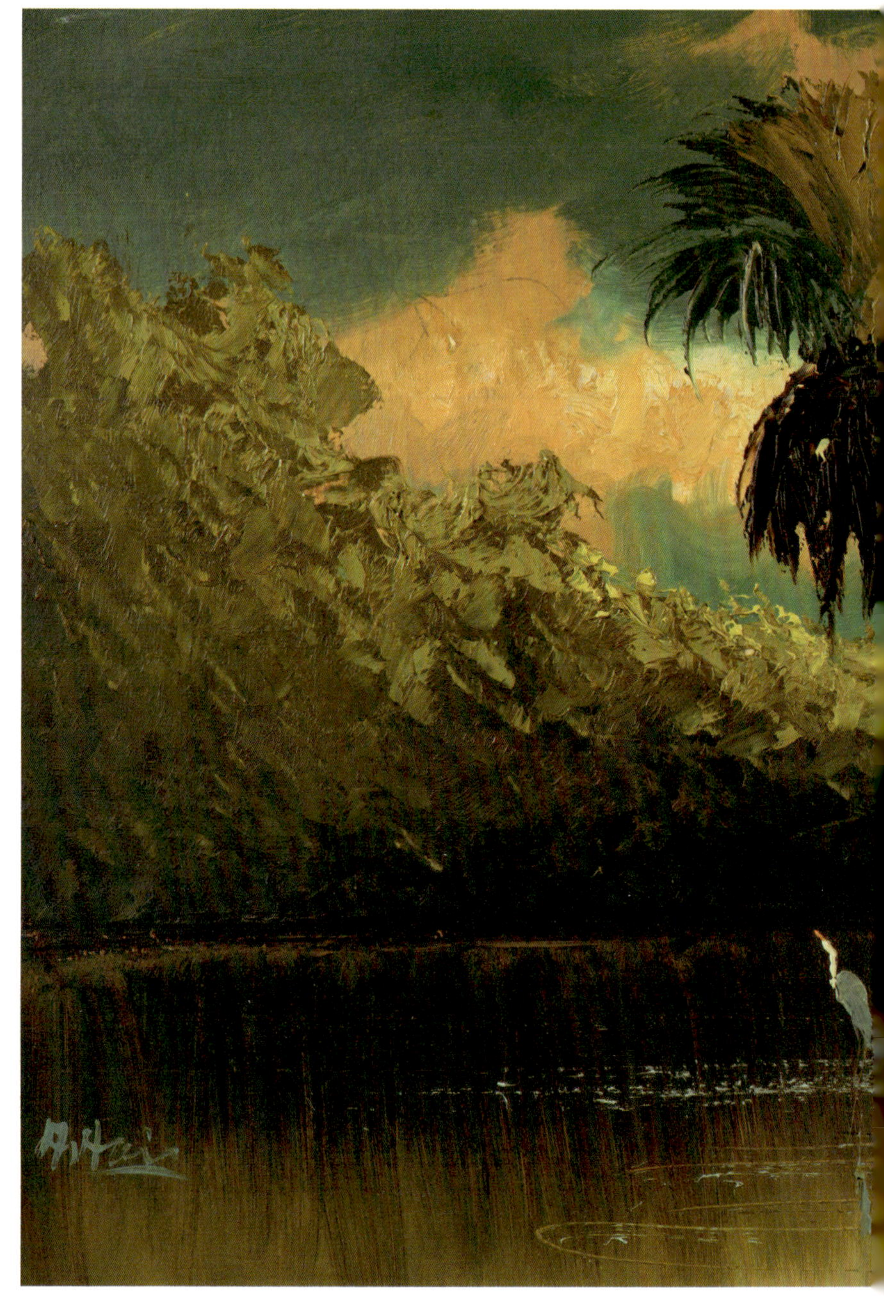

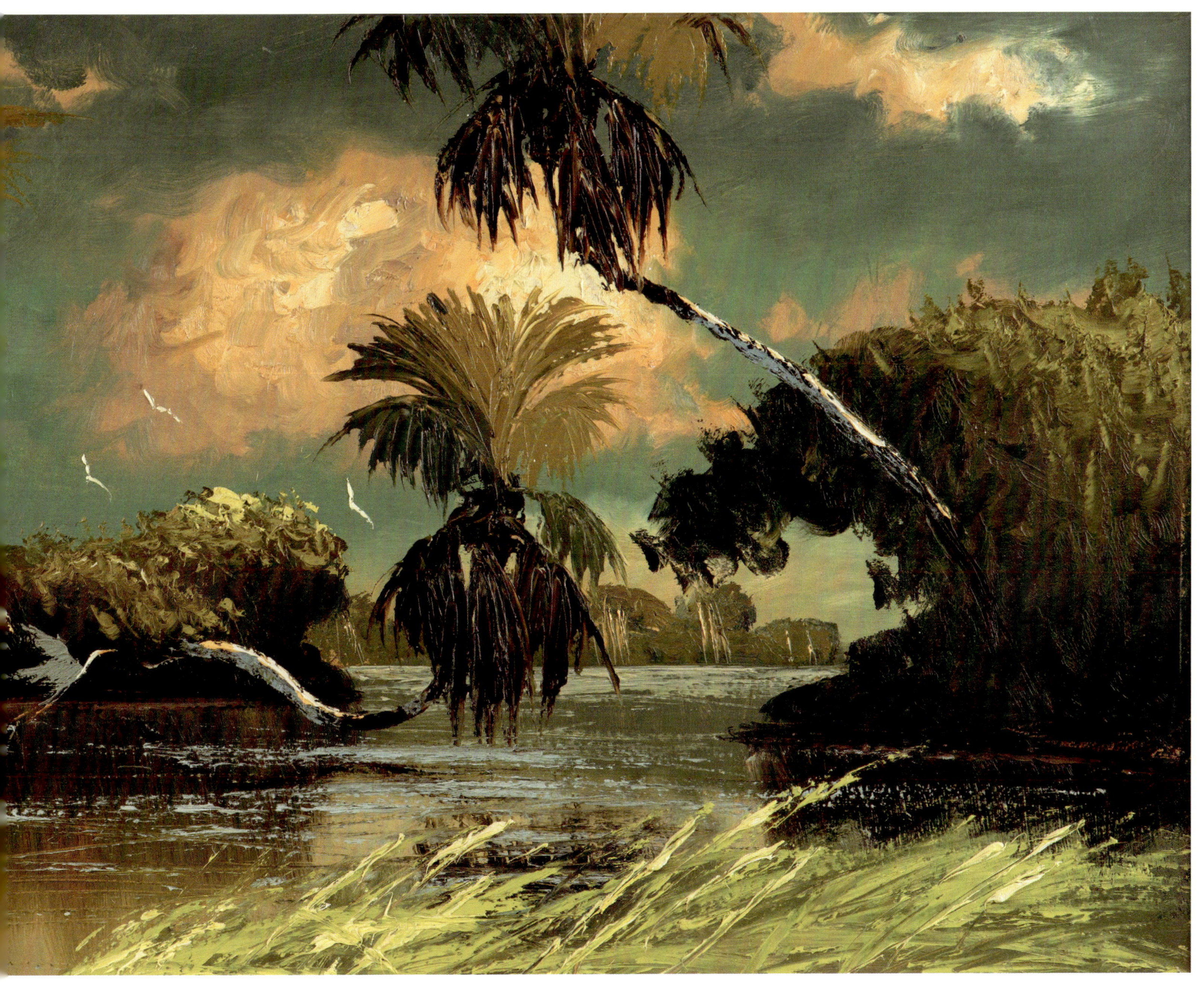

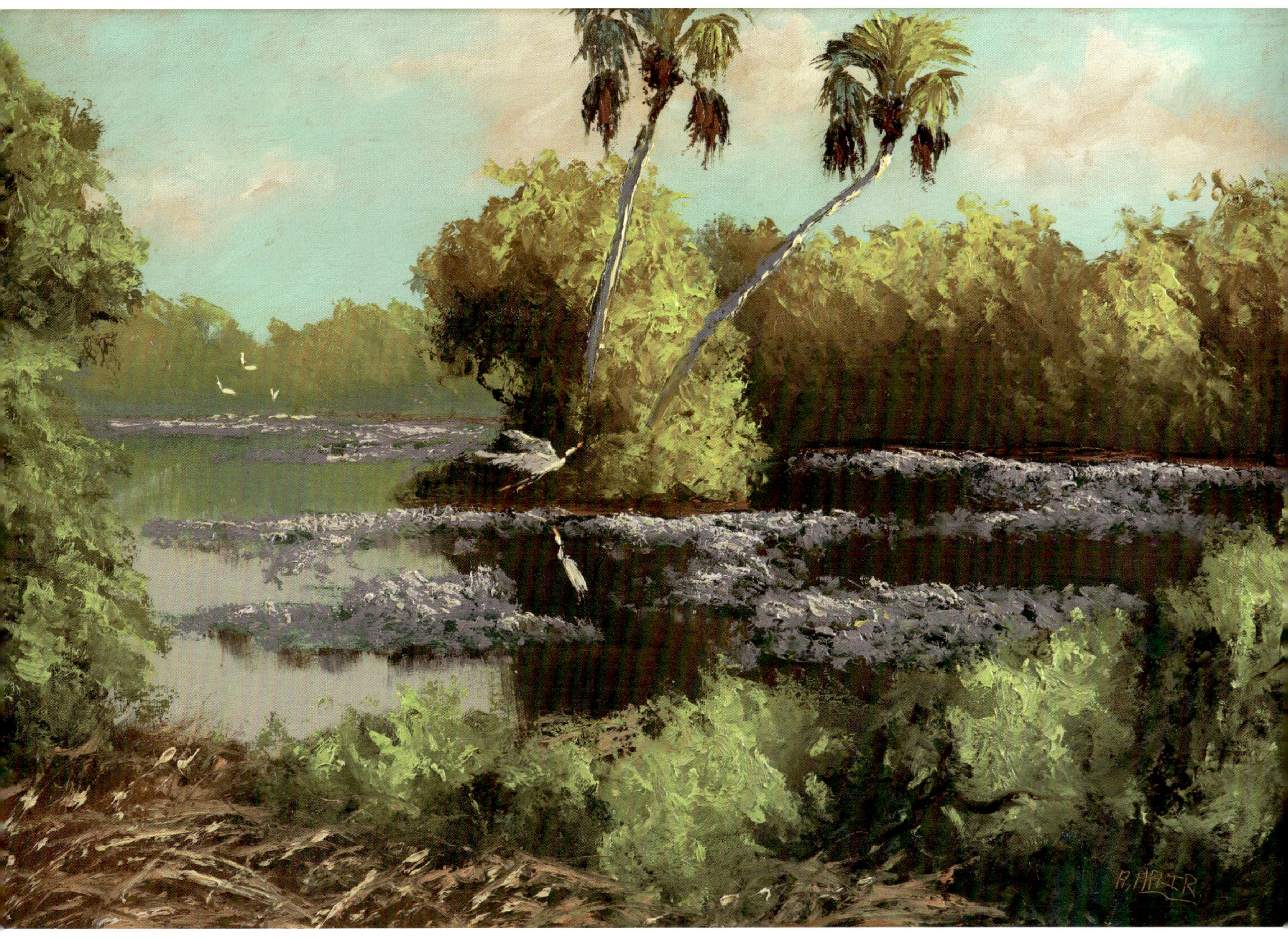

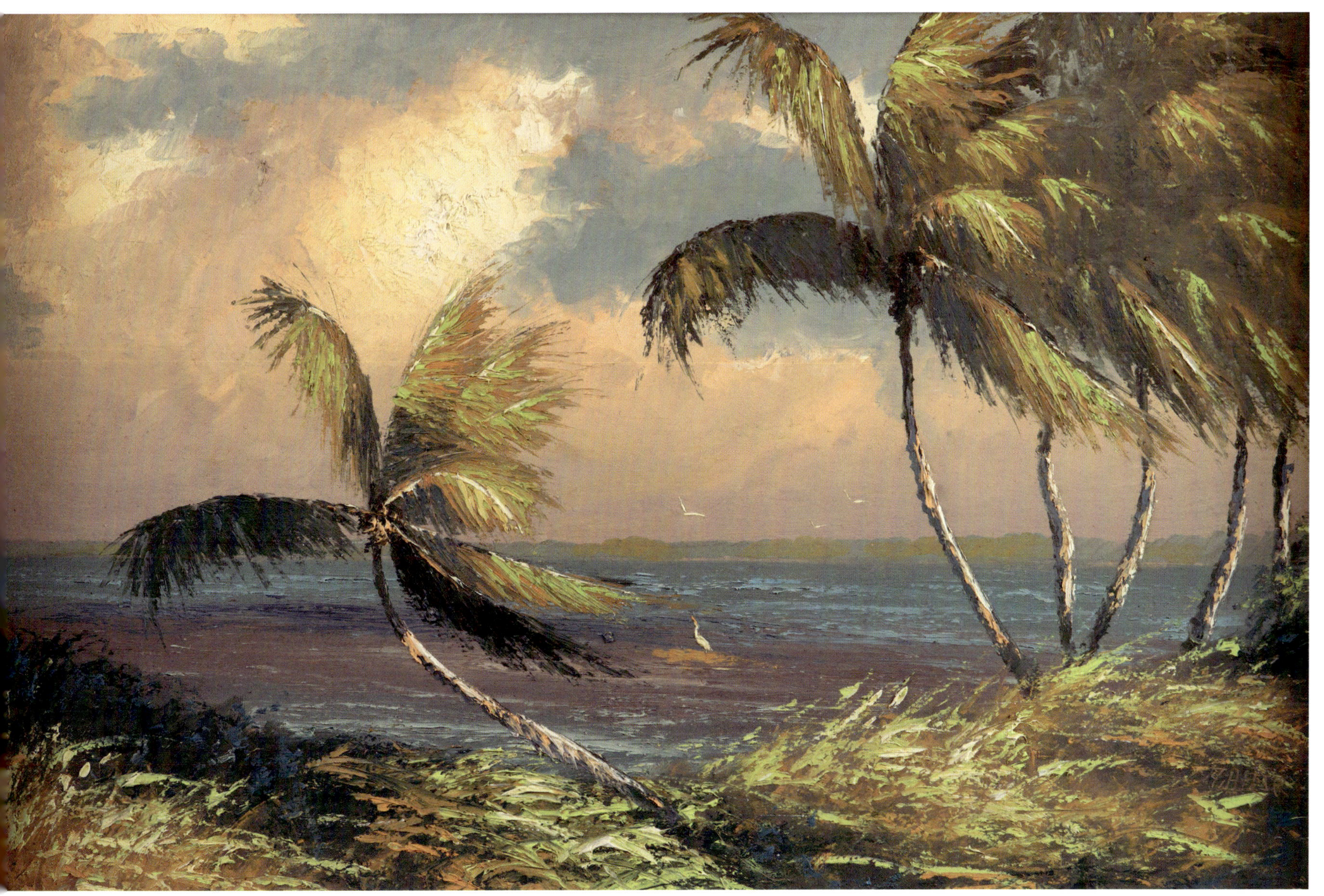

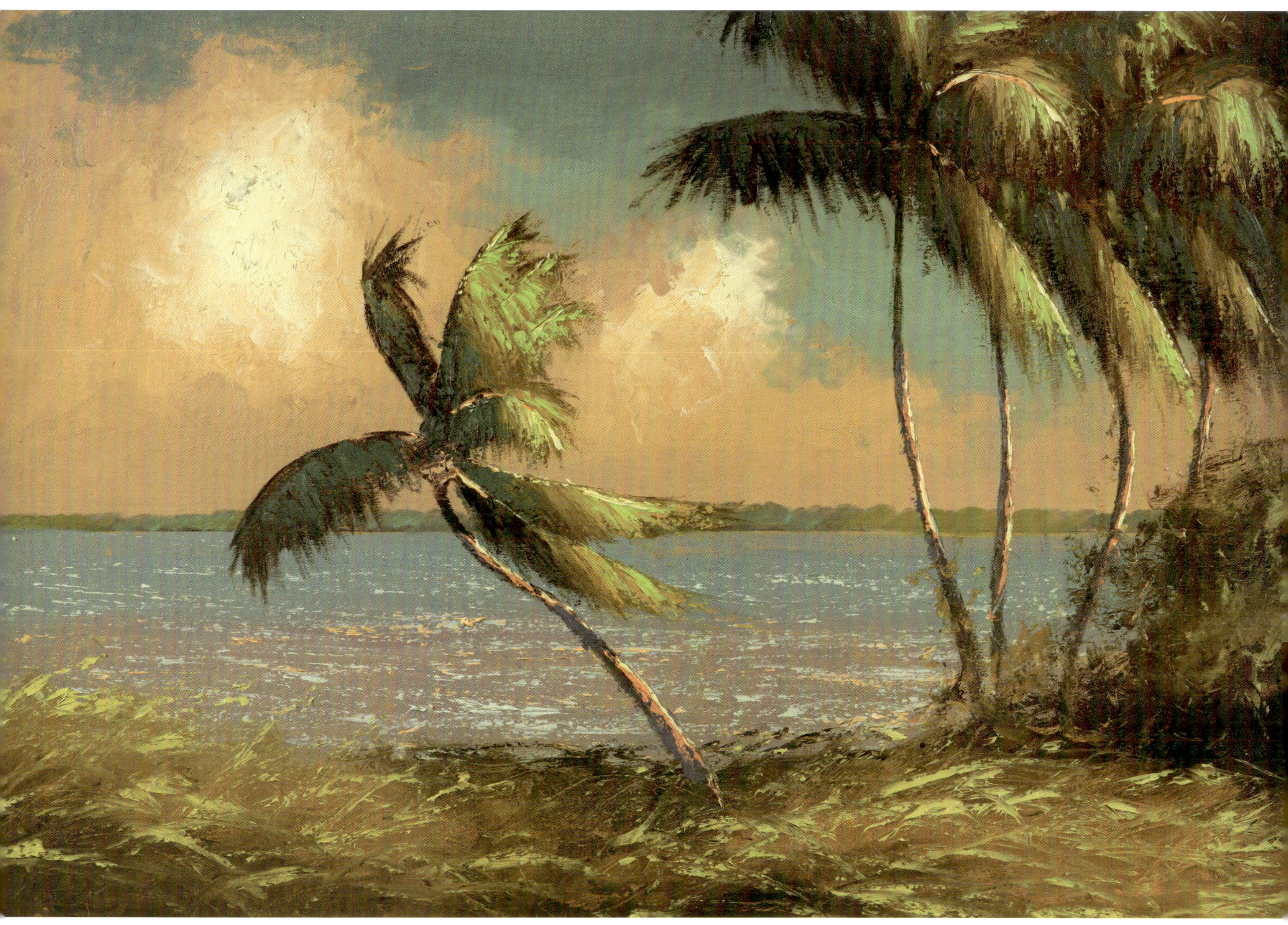

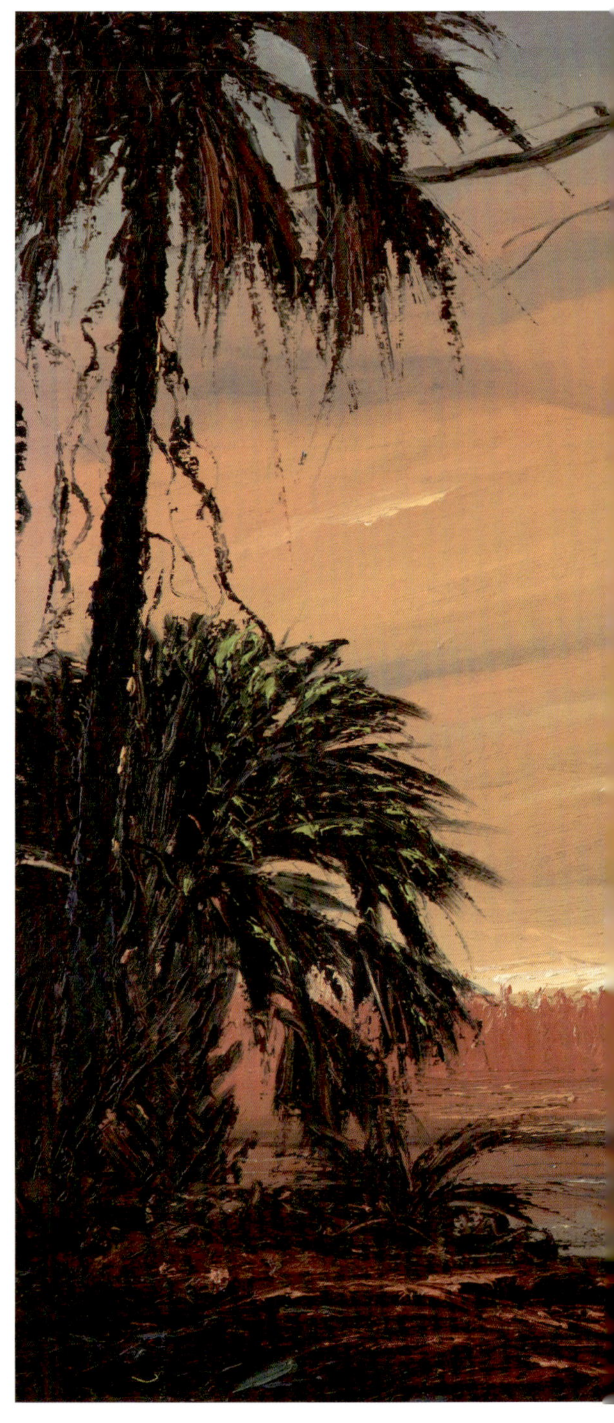

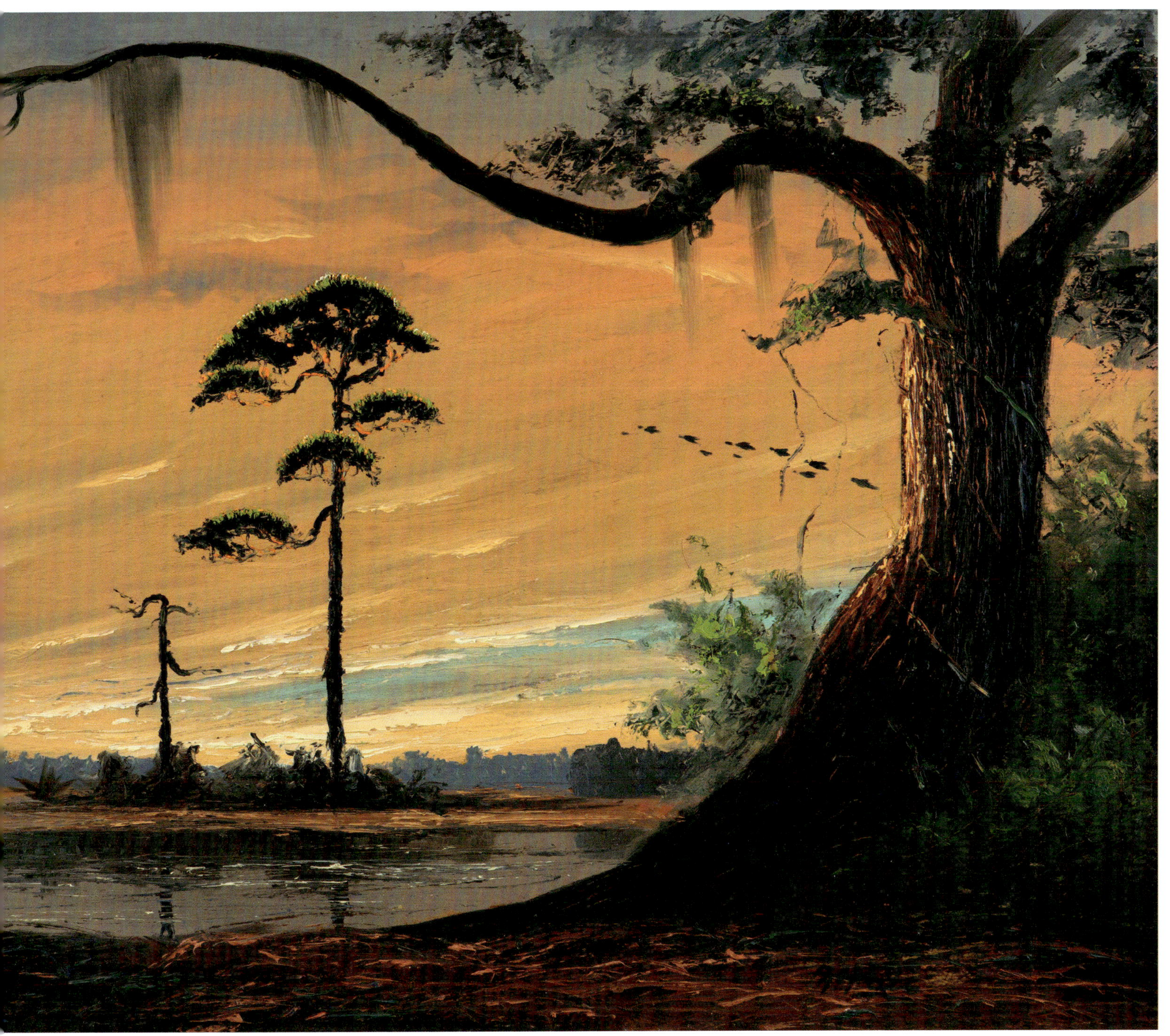

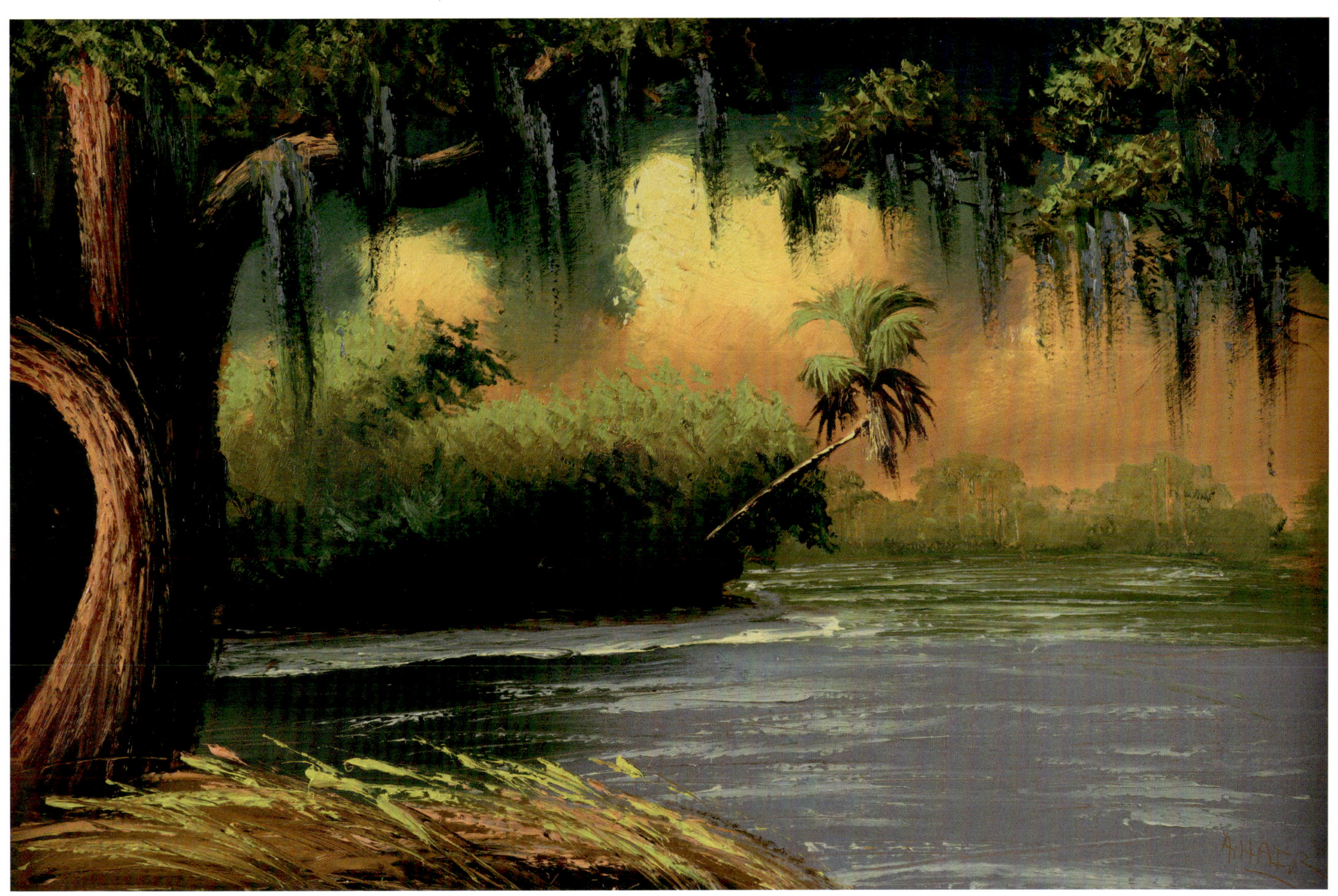

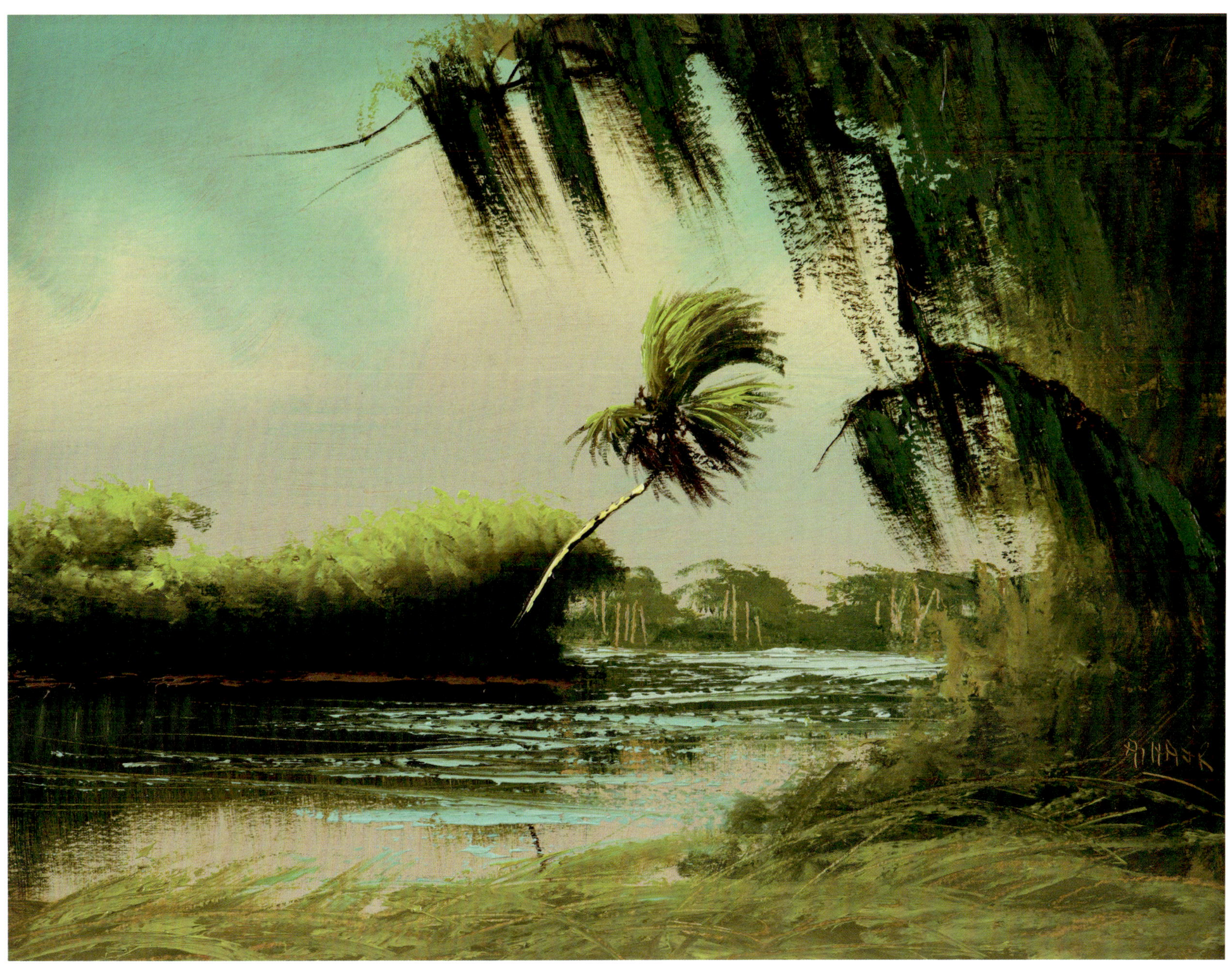

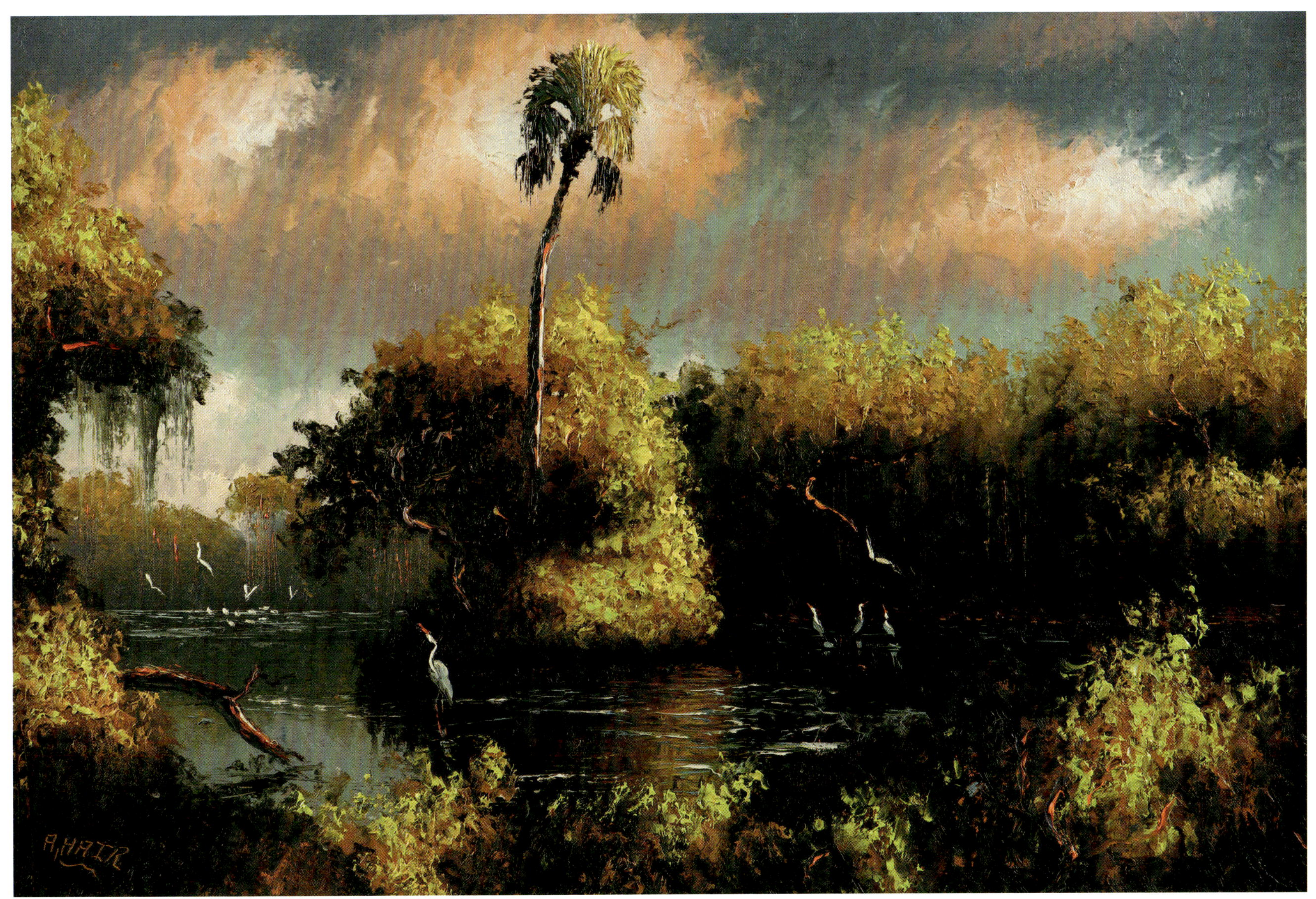
A. HAIR

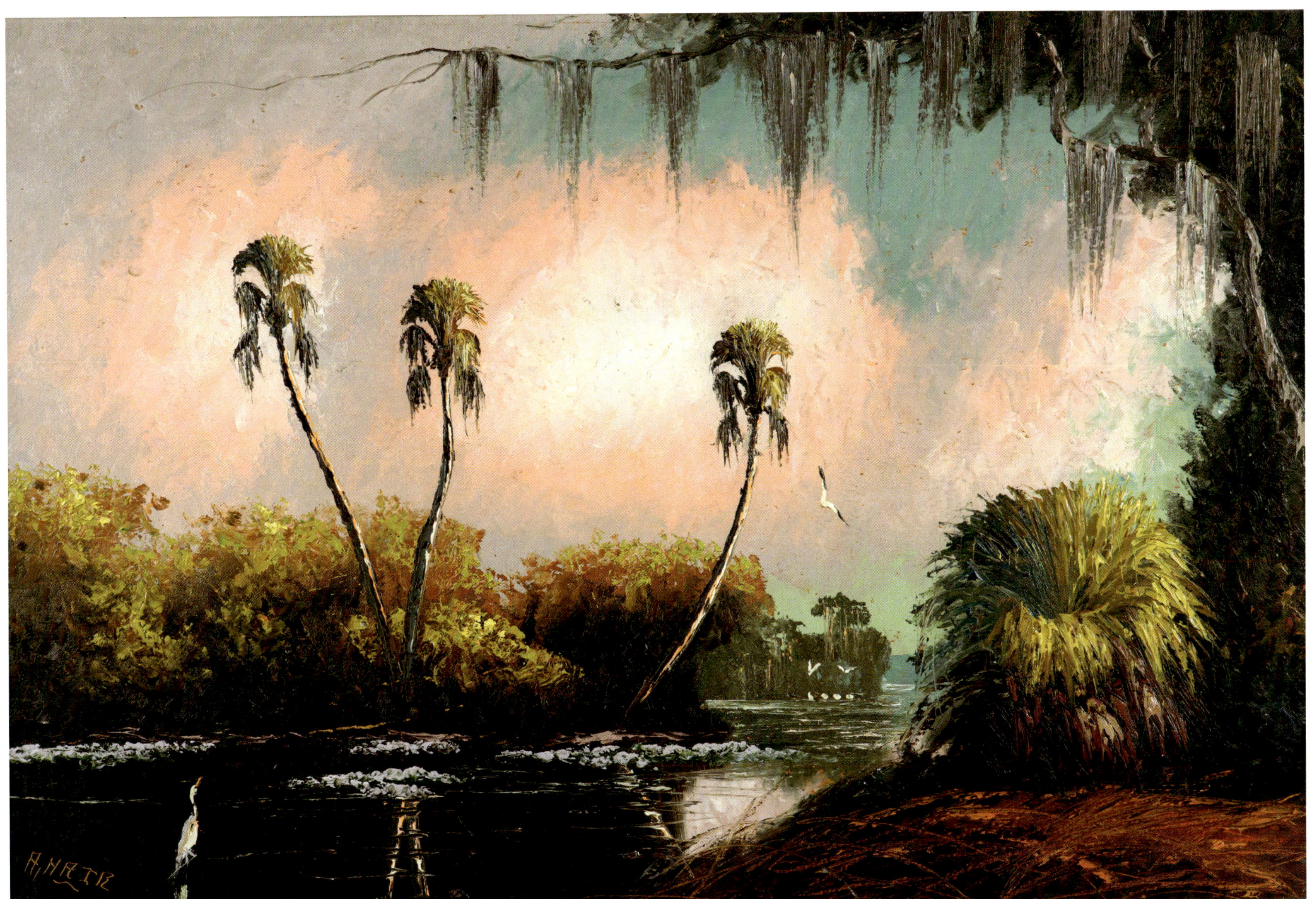
A. HAIR

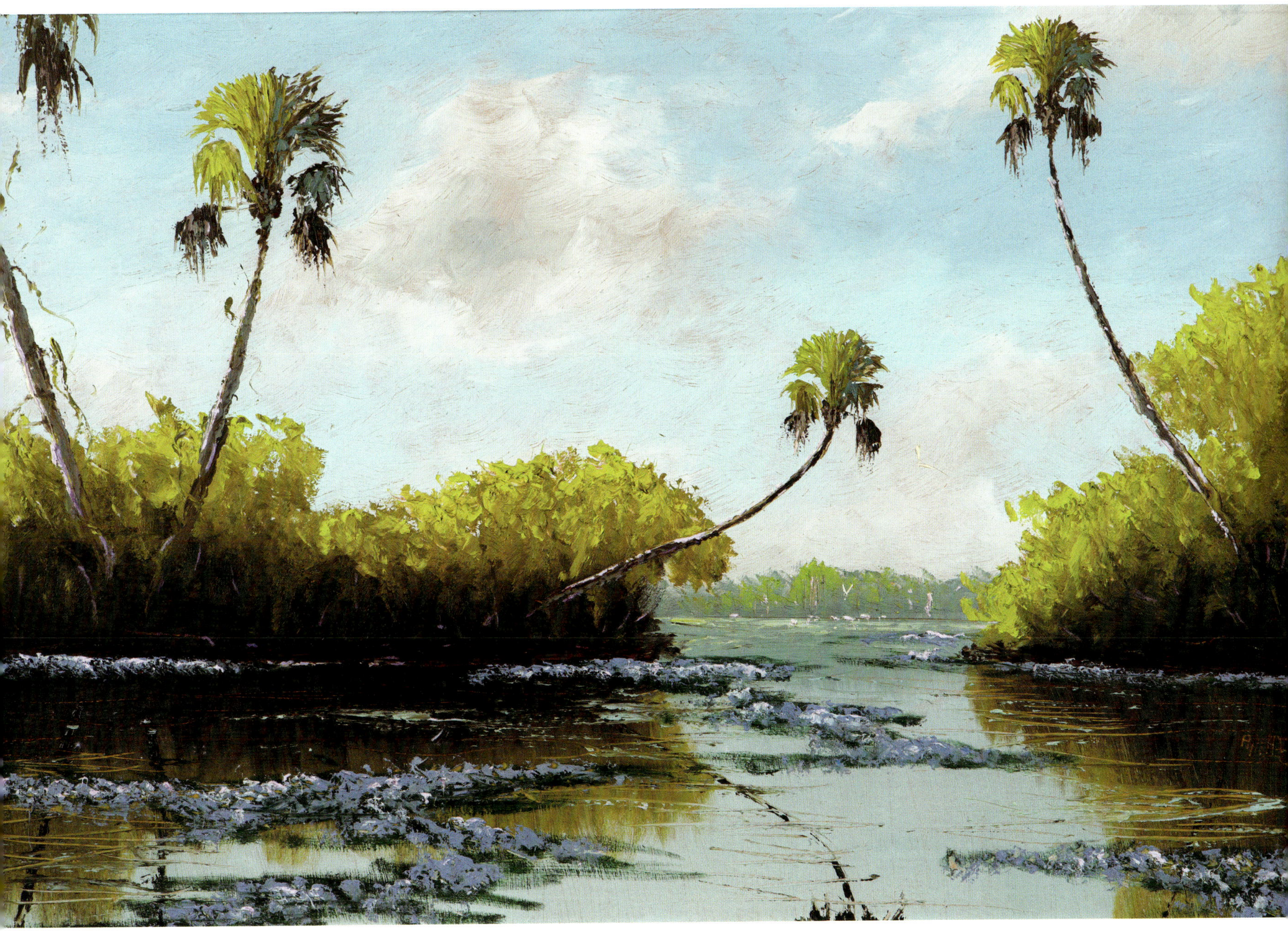

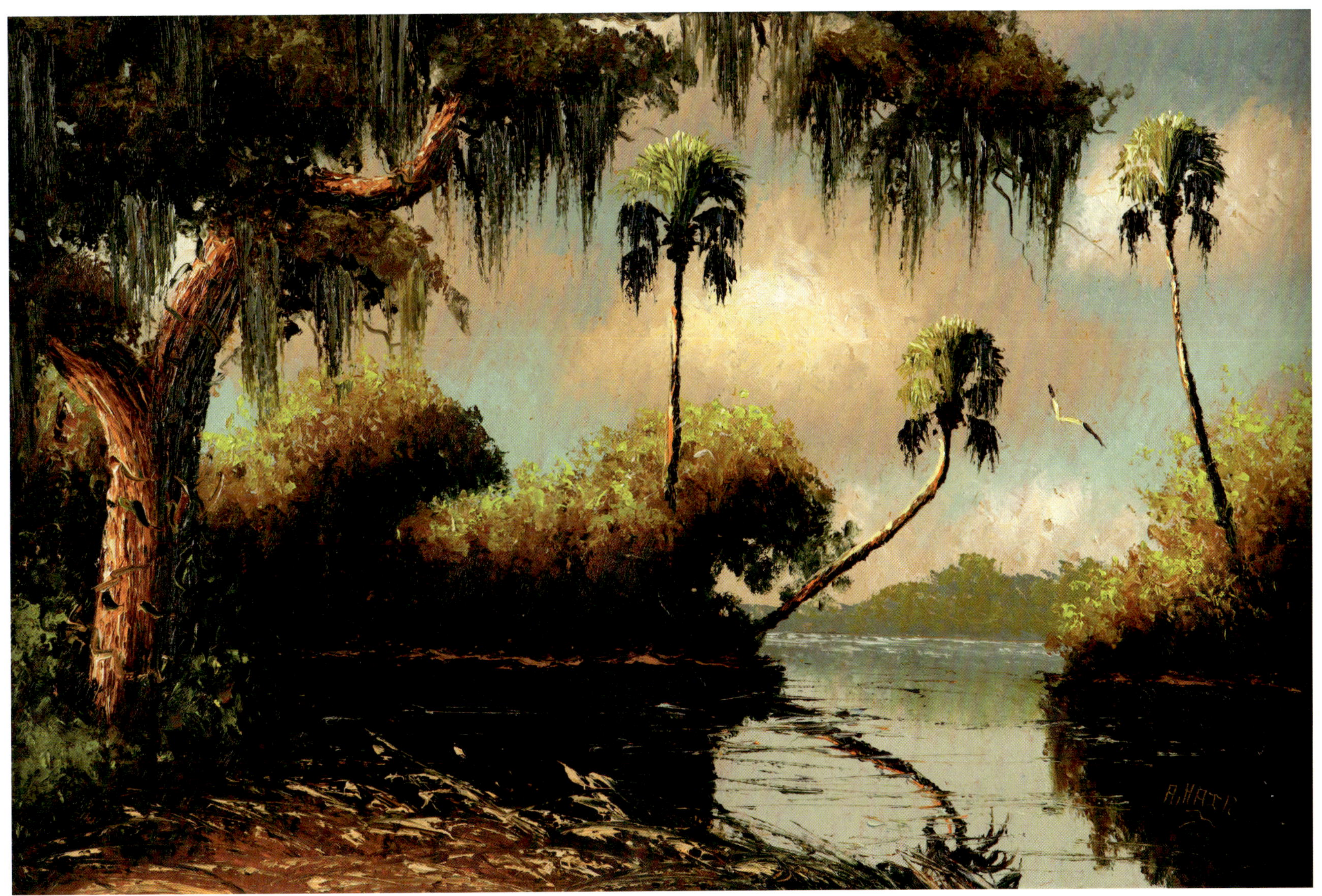
A.HAIR

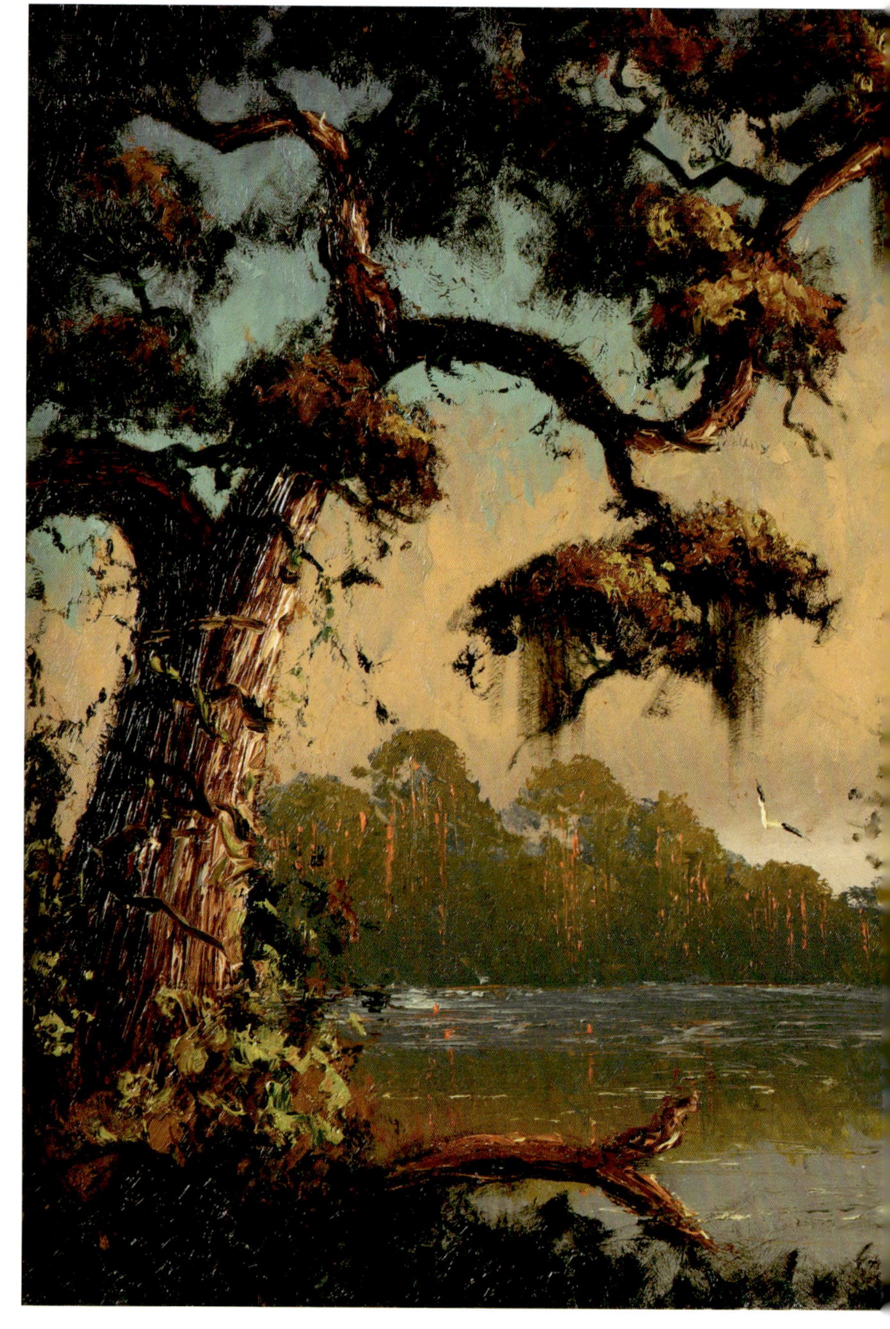

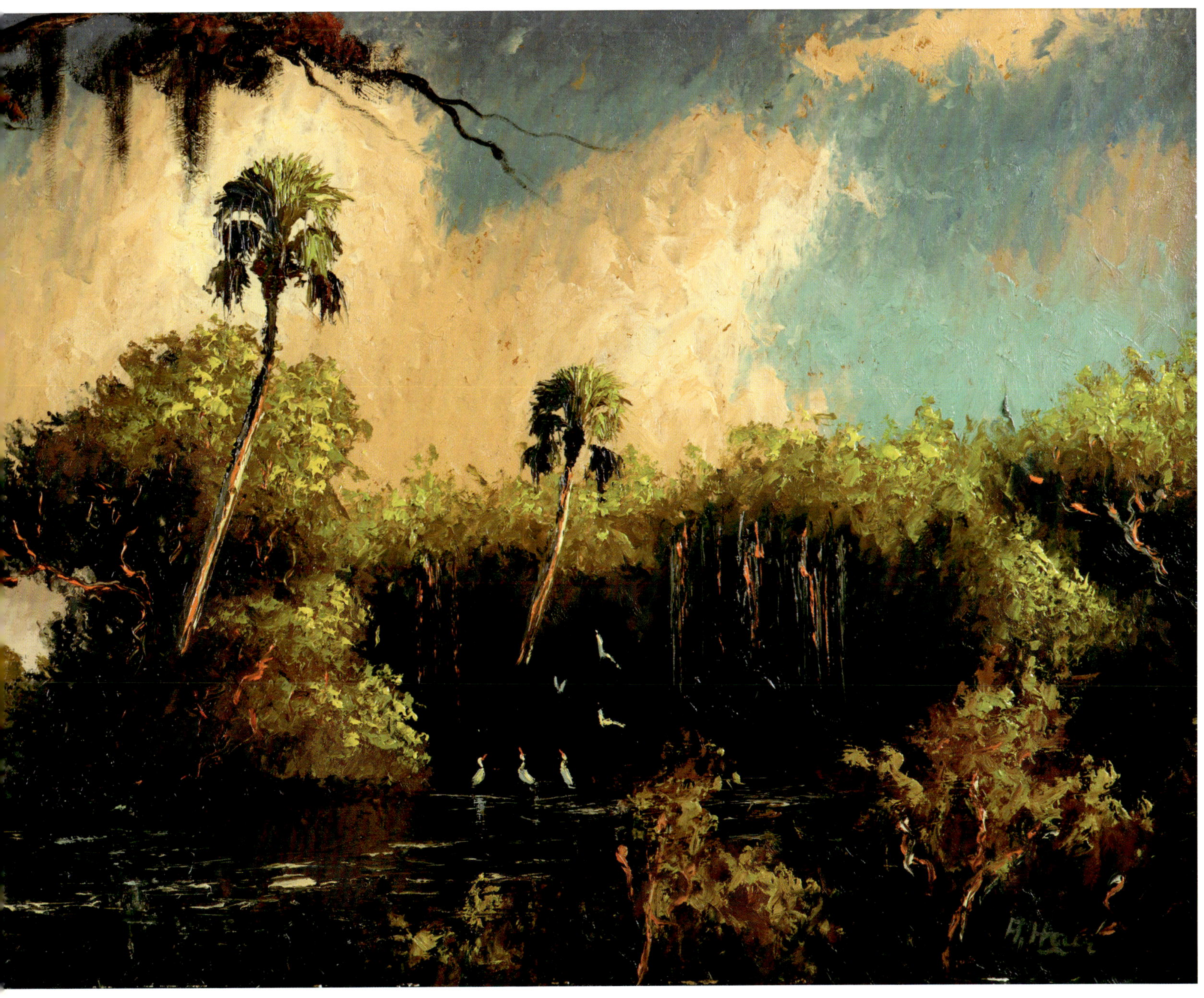

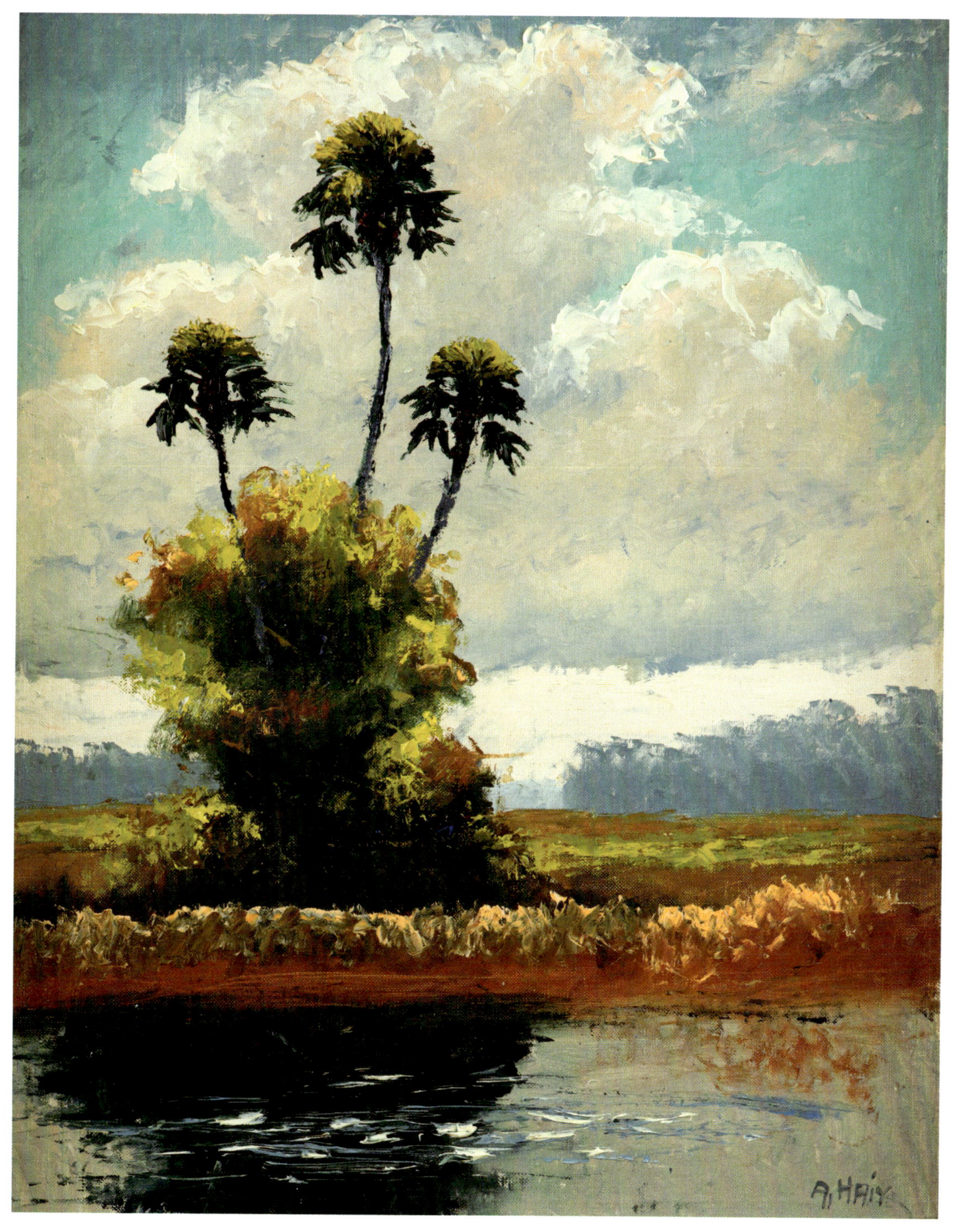
A. Hair

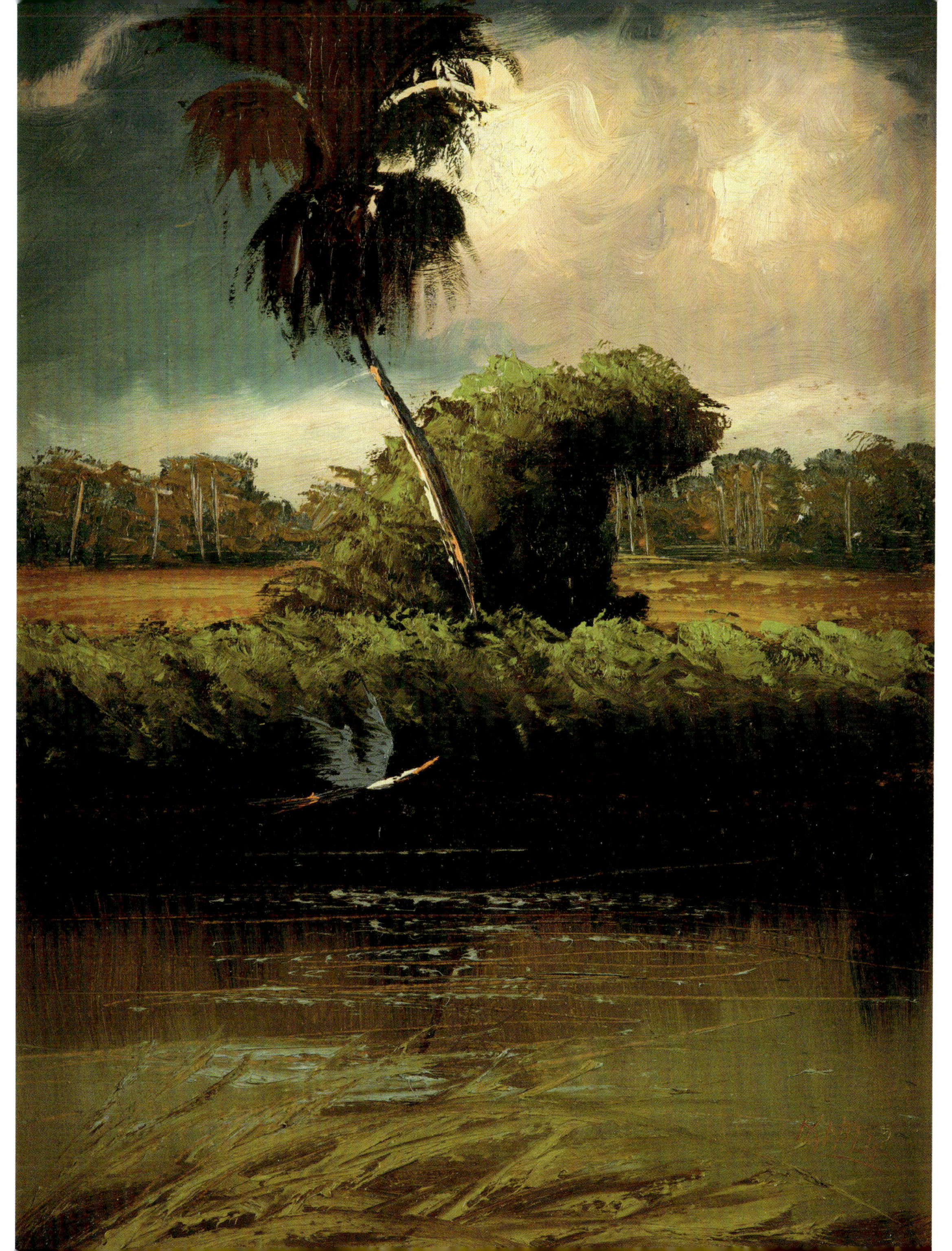

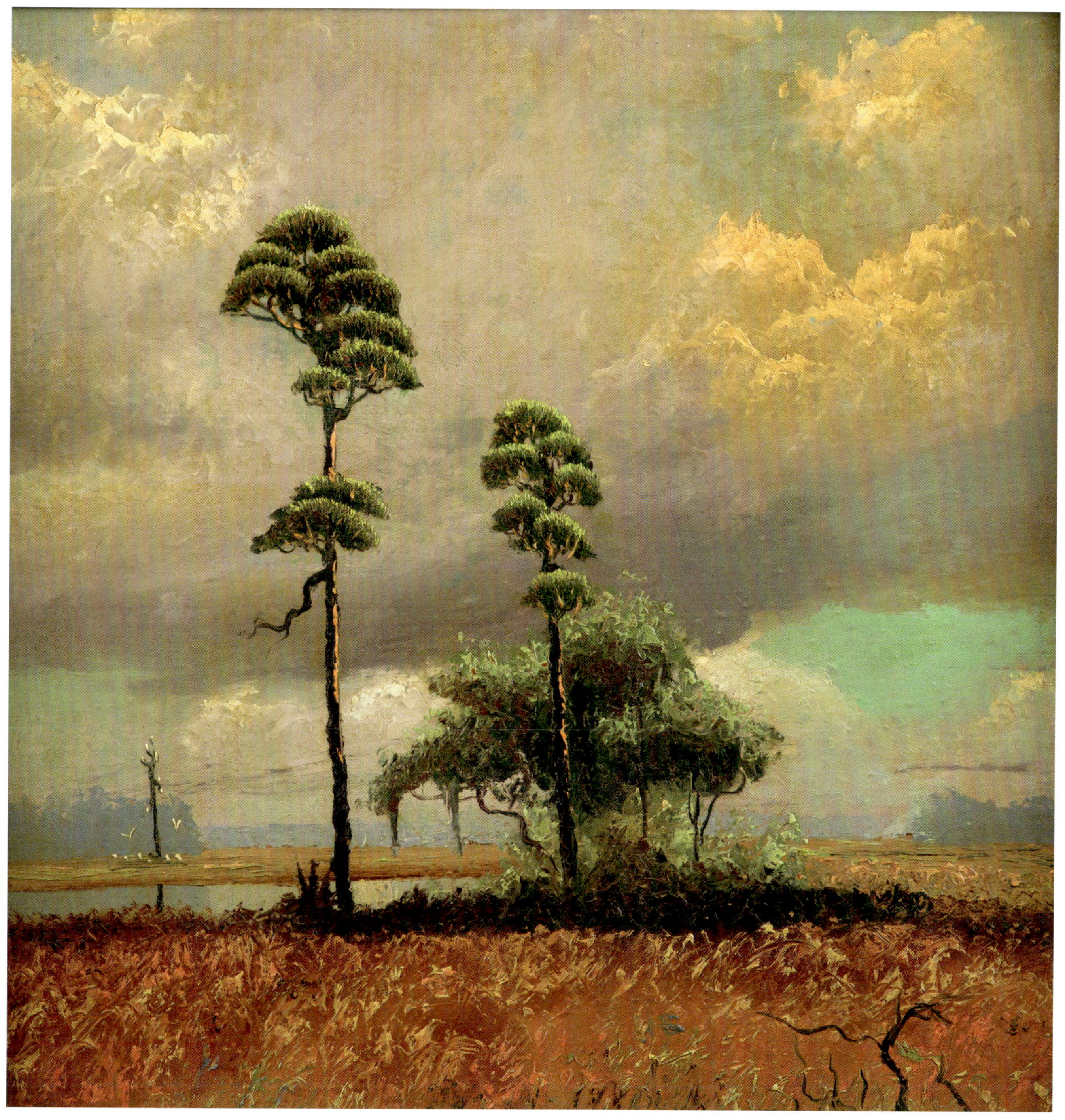

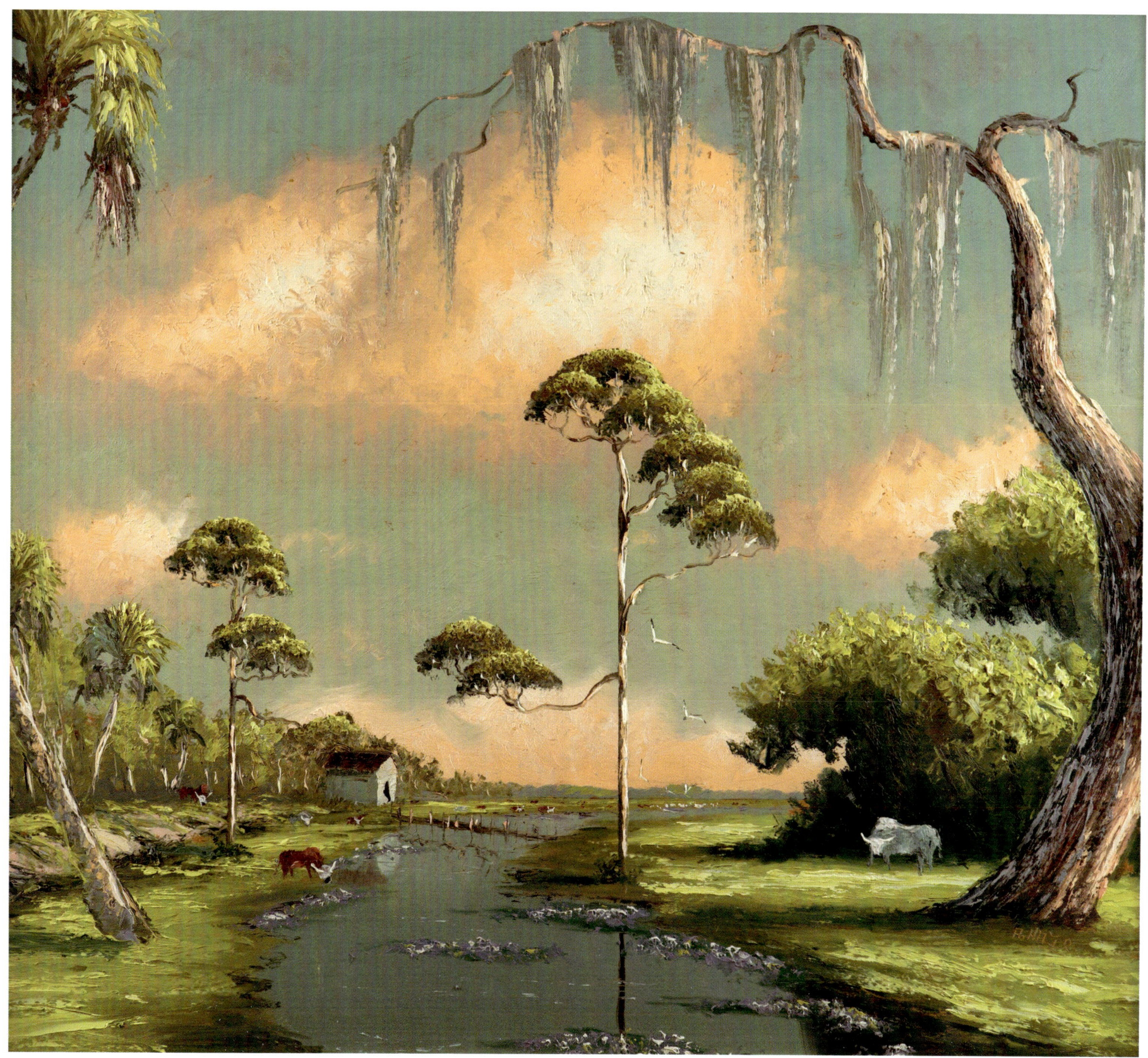

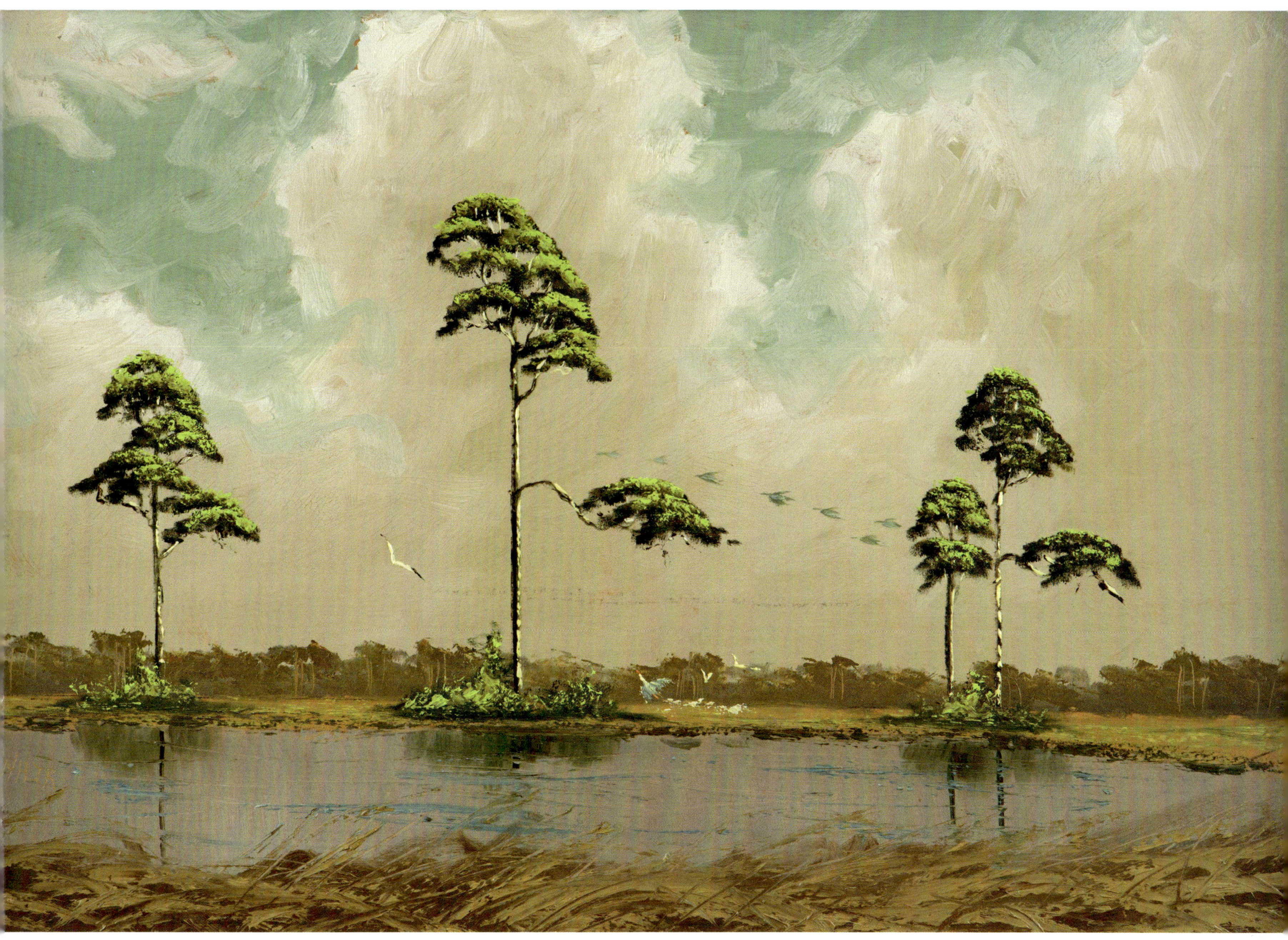

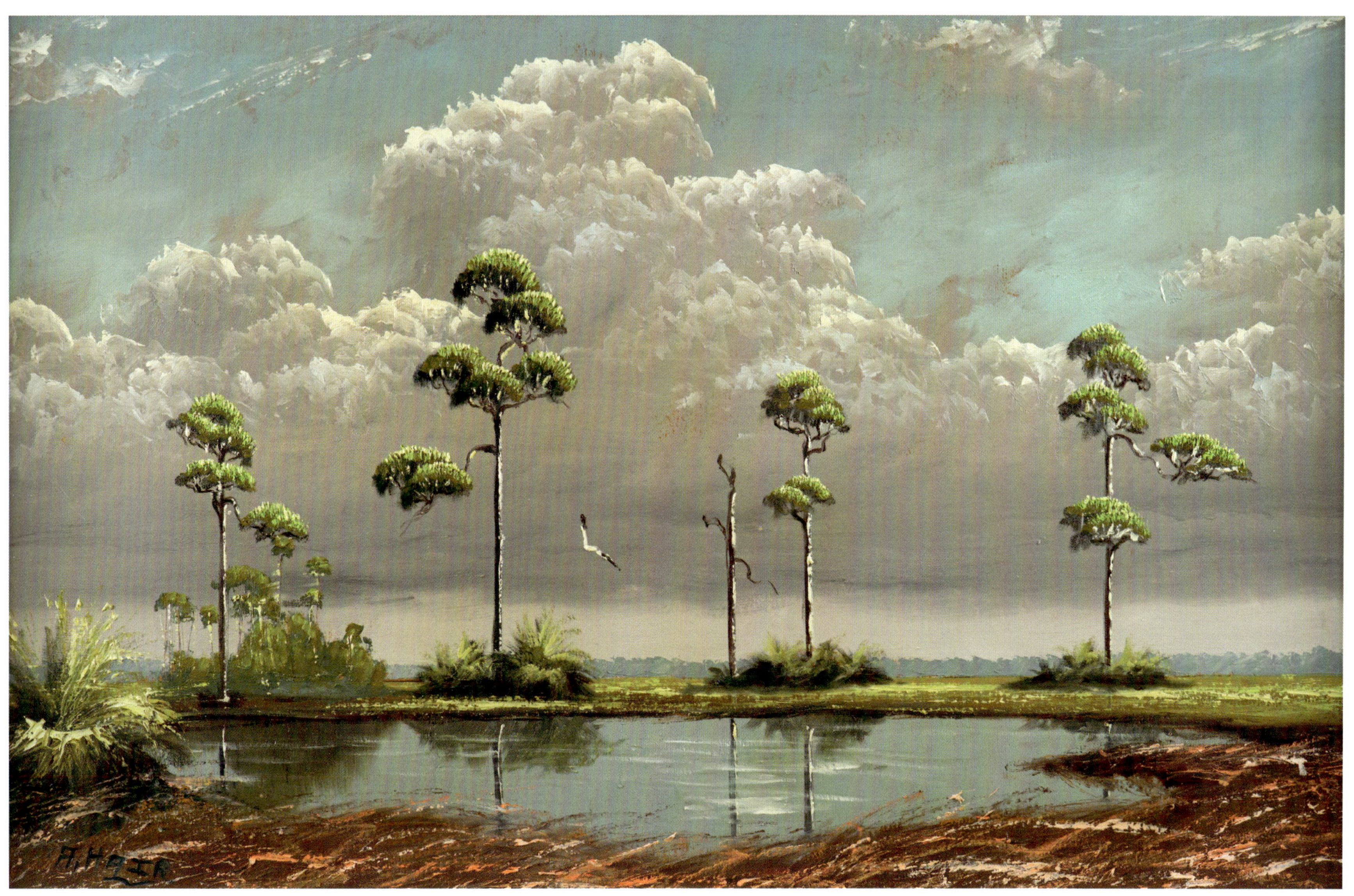
A.HAIR

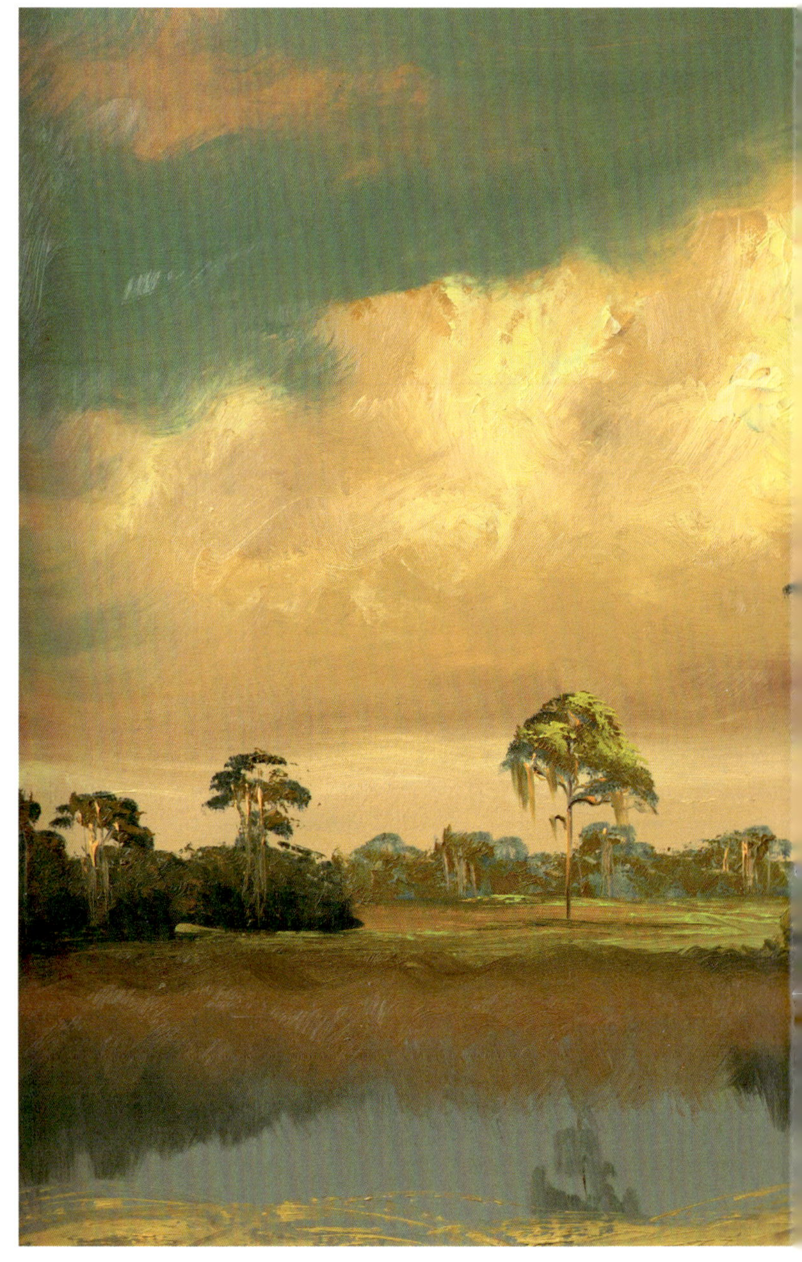

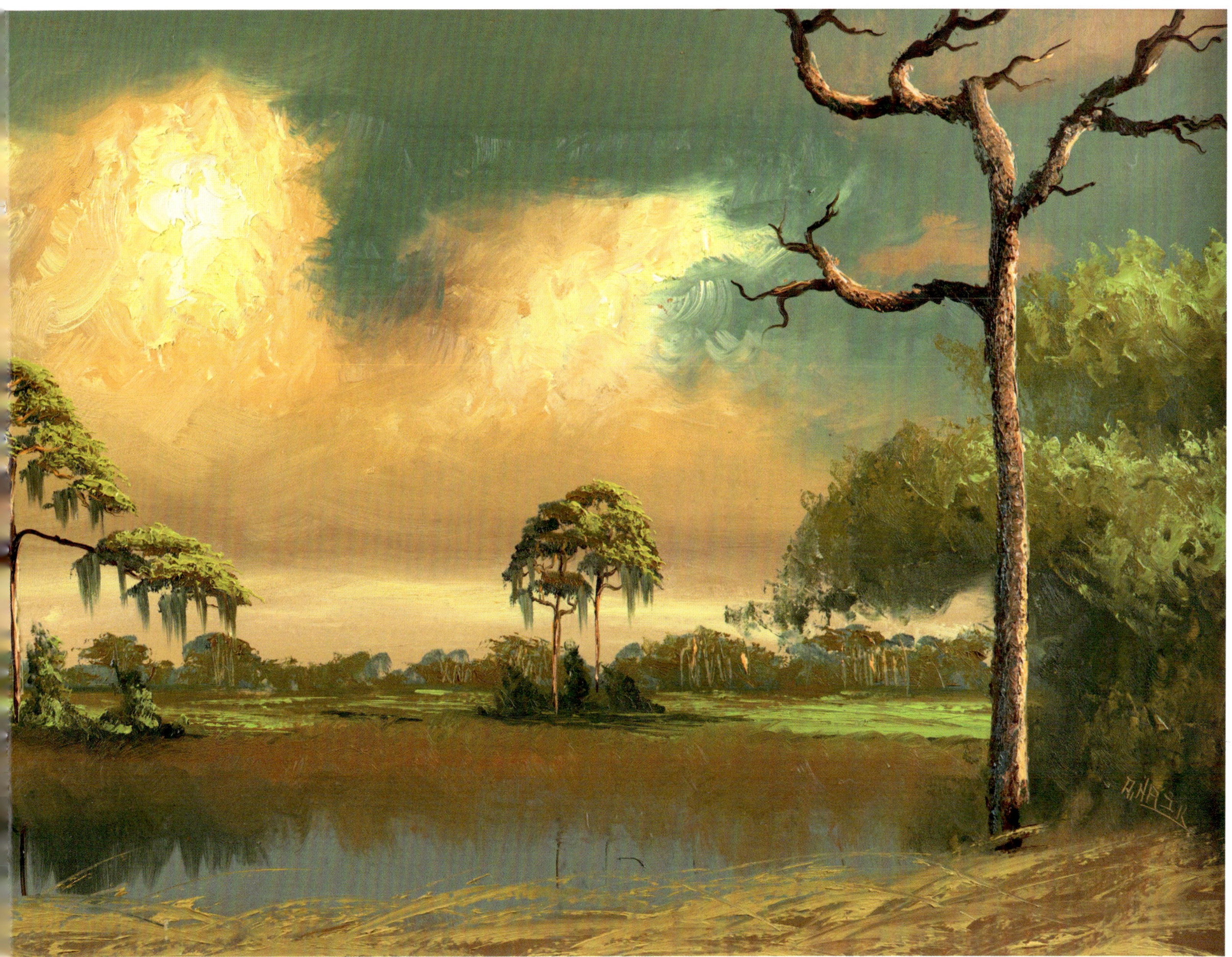

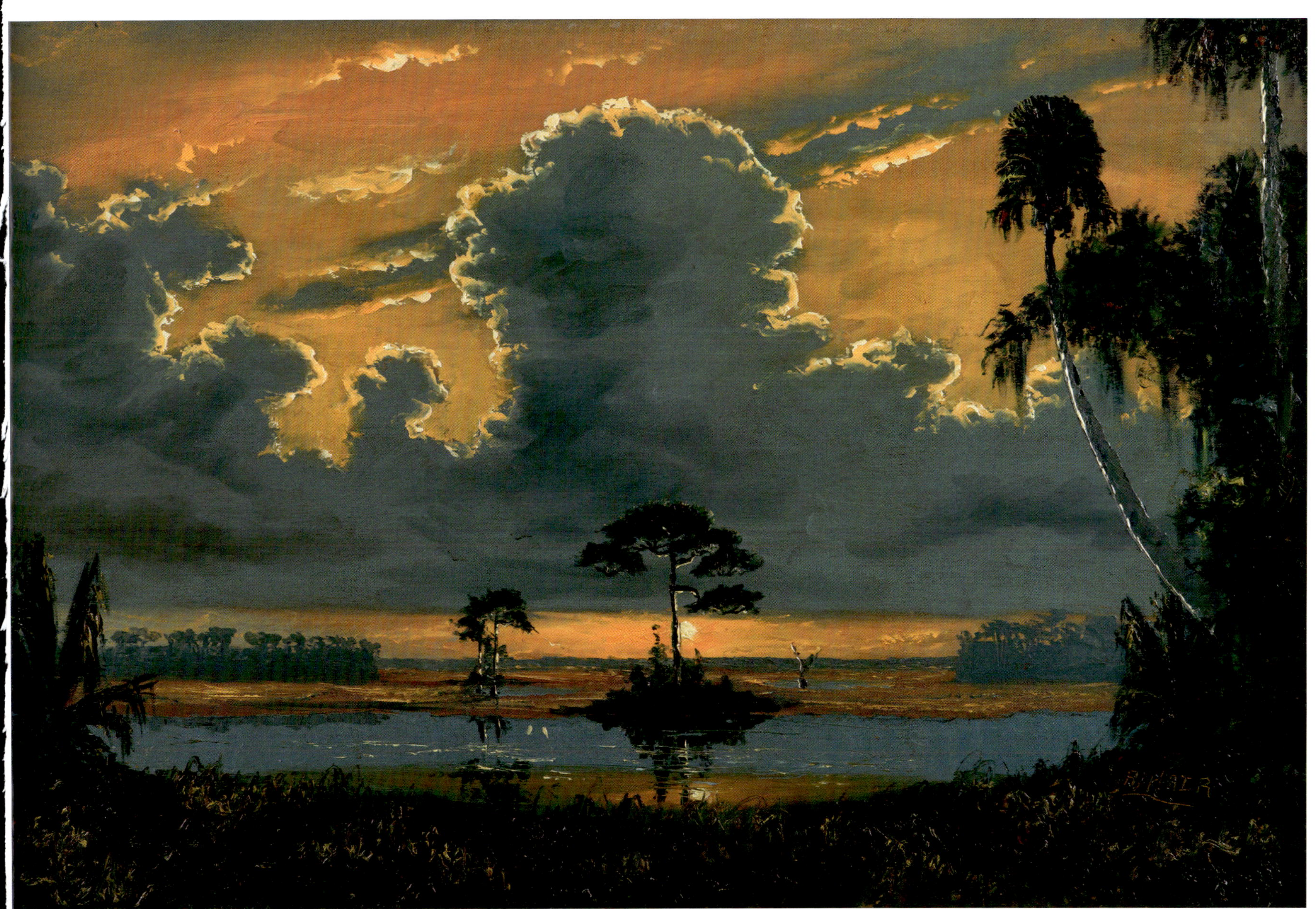

Focusing on self-taught and vernacular art, Gary Monroe began his literary pursuits with *The Highwaymen: Florida's African-American Landscape Painters.* In this seminal book, published in 2001, he tells the story of these painters and offers a fresh interpretation of their art. Consequently, public interest in these compelling but forgotten artists was revived. The *New York Times* published a Lively Arts front-page article about the book, saying, "These colorful landscapes . . . shaped the state's popular image as much as oranges and alligators." In some of his subsequent articles and books, such as *Harold Newton: The Original Highwayman, The Highwaymen Murals: Al Black's Concrete Dreams,* and *Mary Ann Carroll: First Lady of the Highwaymen,* Monroe has told more of the Highwaymen's inspiring stories. Based on his nomination, these painters were inducted into the Florida Artists Hall of Fame in 2004. He has written other books about Florida art, including *Extraordinary Interpretations: Self-Taught Florida Artists, Silver Springs: The Underwater Photographs of Bruce Mozert, Florida's American Heritage River: Images from the St. Johns Region,* and *E. G. Barnhill: Florida Photographer, Adventurer, Entrepreneur.*

Gary Monroe has been awarded grants for his work from the National Endowment for the Arts, Florida Department of State's Division of Cultural Affairs, Florida Humanities Council, and Fulbright Foundation. Through his writing, Monroe has given voice to disenfranchised but fascinating creative people, and in doing so he has enriched readers' lives by introducing new ways of thinking about art and culture.